Electronic Healthcare Information Security

Advances in Information Security

Sushil Jajodia
Consulting Editor
Center for Secure Information Systems
George Mason University
Fairfax, VA 22030-4444
email: jajodia@gmu.edu

The goals of the Springer International Series on ADVANCES IN INFORMATION SECURITY are, one, to establish the state of the art of, and set the course for future research in information security and, two, to serve as a central reference source for advanced and timely topics in information security research and development. The scope of this series includes all aspects of computer and network security and related areas such as fault tolerance and software assurance.

ADVANCES IN INFORMATION SECURITY aims to publish thorough and cohesive overviews of specific topics in information security, as well as works that are larger in scope or that contain more detailed background information than can be accommodated in shorter survey articles. The series also serves as a forum for topics that may not have reached a level of maturity to warrant a comprehensive textbook treatment.

Researchers, as well as developers, are encouraged to contact Professor Sushil Jajodia with ideas for books under this series.

For a complete list of titles published in this series, go to www.springer.com/series/5576

Charles A. Shoniregun • Kudakwashe Dube
Fredrick Mtenzi

Electronic Healthcare Information Security

Professor Charles A. Shoniregun
Infonomics Society
United Kingdom and Ireland
cshoniregun@infonomics-society.org

Dr. Kudakwashe Dube
Massey University
Computer Science and Information Technology
School of Engineering & Advanced Technology (SEAT)
Palmerston North 4442, New Zealand
K_Dube@massey.ac.nz

Dr. Fredrick Mtenzi
Dublin Institute of Technology
Kevin Street
Dublin 8
Ireland
fredr_mtenzi@comp.dit.ie

ISSN 1568-2633
ISBN 978-1-4614-2746-9 ISBN 978-0-387-84919-5 (eBook)
DOI 10.1007/978-0-387-84919-5
Springer New York Dordrecht Heidelberg London

Softcover reprint of the hardcover 1st edition 2010

Printed on acid-free paper

Springer is part of Springer Science+Business Media (www.springer.com)

Dedications

To our families and friends ...

Acknowledgements

It is difficult to acknowledge all the people that have directly or indirectly contributed to this book. But some names cannot be forgotten many thanks to our editors Jennifer Maurer and Susan Lagerstrom-Fife.

A special thank you to the following people and families: Galyna Akmayeva, Tinashe Zakaria, Dr. Bing Wu, Professor Jane Grimson, Professor Brendan O'Shea, Mariam Mussa, Professor Hans Guesgen, Professor Elizabeth Kemp, The Shoniregun's family, The Dube's family, and The Mtenzi's family, for their never-ending contributions.

We are also deeply indebted to the security and privacy research community and our sincere thanks to all the organizations that voluntarily participated in our search for knowledge.

Preface

The adoption of Information and Communication Technologies (ICT) in healthcare is driven by the need to contain costs while maximizing quality and efficiency. However, ICT adoption for healthcare information management has brought far-reaching effects and implications on the spirit of the Hippocratic Oath, patient privacy and confidentiality. A wave of security breaches have led to pressing calls for opt-in and opt-out provisions where patients are free to choose to or not have their healthcare information collected and recorded within healthcare information systems. Such provisions have negative impact on cost, efficiency and quality of patient care. Thus determined efforts to gain patient trust is increasingly under consideration for enforcement through legislation, standards, national policy frameworks and implementation systems geared towards closing gaps in ICT security frameworks.

The ever-increasing healthcare expenditure and pressing demand for improved quality and efficiency in patient care services are driving innovation in healthcare information management. Key among the main innovations is the introduction of new healthcare practice concepts such as shared care, evidence-based medicine, clinical practice guidelines and protocols, the cradle-to-grave health record and clinical workflow or careflow. Central to these organizational re-engineering innovations is the widespread adoption of Information and Communication Technologies (ICT) at national and regional levels, which has ushered in computer-based healthcare information management that is centred on the electronic healthcare record (EHR). A critical and determinant factor in this scenario is the heightened awareness and concern about ensuring patient privacy and confidentiality, which are under threat within the distributed networked environment of ICTs and EHRs. The domain of healthcare information management offers a significant, complex and challenging testing ground to Information Security due to the complex nature of healthcare information. The security of healthcare information in the context of a networked, sensor-enabled, pervasive and mobile computing infrastructure is at the core of both the main challenges and potential risks of Healthcare ICT adoption.

The domain of healthcare has become a challenging testing ground for information security due to the complex nature of healthcare information and individual privacy. This is the first comprehensive book that explores the challenges of Electronic Healthcare Information Security, Policies and Legislation. We proposed a framework and an evaluation approach for the e-Healthcare Information Systems Security. This book also reflects our knowledge and experience in the field of security and privacy.

London – UK, New Zealand and Dublin - Ireland
May 2010

Charles Shoniregun
Kudakwashe Dube
Fredrick Mtenzi

Contents

1 Introduction to e-Healthcare Information Security 1
1.1 Introduction 1
1.2 The e-Healthcare Information: Nature and Trends 1
1.3 Security Impact of Trends in e-Healthcare Information Management 3
1.4 Trends in e-Healthcare Environment 4
1.4.1 Case Study: Canada 5
1.4.2 Case Study: IZIP and General Health Insurance Company of the Czech Republic 8
1.4.3 Case Study: Danish Health Data Network (DHDN) 9
1.4.4 Case Study: The Norwegian Healthcare System 13
1.4.5 Case Study: Sweden 15
1.4.6 Case Study: UK - NHS Direct Online (NHSDO) Information Service 17
1.5 Securing e-Healthcare Information: Significance and Challenges . . . 19
1.6 Concepts of e-Healthcare Information Security 20
1.7 Frameworks and Approaches 21
1.8 Issues in e-Healthcare Information Security 23
1.9 Summary 25
References 25

2 Securing e-Healthcare Information 29
2.1 Introduction 29
2.2 Breaches of Privacy and Confidentiality in e-Healthcare 30
2.2.1 Accidental Privacy and Confidentiality Breaches 30
2.2.2 Ethically Questionable Conduct 31
2.2.3 Breaches Due to Illegal Actions 32
2.2.4 Laxity in Security for Sensitive e-Healthcare Information . . . 32
2.3 The IT Security Challenge for Securing e-Healthcare Information . . 32
2.4 The Privacy and Confidentiality Challenge 33
2.5 Utilisation Challenges 35
2.6 Legal Protection Challenges 36

2.7 The Nature of Secure e-Healthcare Information 36
2.8 The Principles for Securing e-Healthcare Information 38
2.9 Combining Security with Privacy and Confidentiality 40
2.10 Identifiability in Securing e-Healthcare Information 42
2.11 Anonymisation and Pseudonymisation 43
2.12 Technological Frameworks in Securing e-Healthcare Information .. 45
2.13 Engineering of Secure e-Healthcare Information.................. 47
2.13.1 Methodologies for Engineering Secure e-Healthcare Information Systems 47
2.13.2 Measures and Security Metrics for Securing e-Healthcare Information 49
2.13.3 Evaluation of Secure e-Healthcare Information 50
2.14 Discussion and Summary of Issues in Securing e-Healthcare Information 50
References 51

3 Laws and Standards for Secure e-Healthcare Information 59
3.1 Introduction 59
3.2 The Rationale for Laws and Standards in Securing e-Healthcare Information 60
3.3 Laws and Standards: Relationships, Roles and Interactions 61
3.4 Legal Protection of Privacy in e-Healthcare Information Management 62
3.4.1 International and EU Law on Protection of e-Healthcare Information 62
3.4.2 Irish Law on Protection of e-Healthcare Information 64
3.4.3 UK Law on Protection of e-Healthcare Information........ 66
3.4.4 Australian Law on Protection of e-Healthcare Information .. 66
3.4.5 New Zealand Law on Protection of e-Healthcare Information 66
3.4.6 Japanese Law on Protection of e-Healthcare Information ... 67
3.4.7 US Law on Protection of e-Healthcare Information 67
3.4.8 Canadian Law on Protection of e-Healthcare Information... 71
3.5 Standards for Secure e-Healthcare Information 72
3.5.1 Health Level 7 (HL7) Standardisation 72
3.5.2 Committee for European Normalisation (CEN) Technical Committee (TC) 251 Standardisation.................... 74
3.5.3 The openEHR Specification Standard 75
3.5.4 International Standards Organisation Technical Committee (ISO/TC) 215 Healthcare Informatics Standardisation...... 78
3.5.5 ASTM Committee E31 on Healthcare Informatics Standardisation 79
3.5.6 Generic IT Security within e-Healthcare Information Management 84
3.6 Discussion and Summary of the Legal and Standardisation Challenges 93

3.7 Summary ... 95
References ... 96

4 Secure e-Healthcare Information Systems ... 101
4.1 Introduction ... 101
4.2 The elements of Security and Privacy in e-Healthcare Information Systems ... 102
4.3 Security and Privacy Provisions in EHR Systems ... 104
4.3.1 The Canadian Health Infoway ... 105
4.3.2 Security and Privacy Provisions in the UK NHS Care Records ... 106
4.3.3 Security and Privacy Provisions in the WorldVistA EHR System ... 108
4.4 Security and Privacy Provisions in Electronic Personal Healthcare Records ... 109
4.4.1 Google Health e-PHR ... 110
4.4.2 The Microsoft e-PHR service: The HealthVault ... 111
4.4.3 The Indivo Open Source e-PHR system ... 112
4.4.4 Summary of Concerns and Issues with e-PHR systems and Services ... 112
4.5 Security and Privacy in Clinical Decision Support Systems ... 114
4.6 The Challenges from Security and Privacy for e-Healthcare Information Security ... 117
4.7 Future e-Healthcare Information Management: Towards the EHR/PEHR Hybridisation ... 118
4.8 Summary ... 120
References ... 121

5 Towards a Comprehensive Framework for Secure e-Healthcare Information ... 123
5.1 Introduction ... 123
5.2 The Problem of Securing e-Healthcare Information ... 124
5.3 The Context and Concepts for Securing e-Healthcare Information ... 125
5.4 Towards Future-Enabled Requirements for Securing e-Healthcare Information ... 128
5.4.1 The Security and Privacy Impact of the Evolution of the Control of e-Healthcare Information in Context of the Patient-Centred Paradigm ... 129
5.4.2 The nature, security and privacy implications of the EHR/PEHR hybrid ... 132
5.4.3 The Role of Security Metrics ... 134
5.4.4 Summary of Security and Privacy Requirements for Future-Enabled e-Healthcare Information ... 135
5.5 The Approach to Securing e-Healthcare Information ... 135

5.6 The Framework for Securing e-Healthcare Information Security and Privacy 137
5.6.1 The Key Drivers to the Security and Privacy of e-Healthcare Information Security 138
5.6.2 The Model for the e-Healthcare Information Control and Security and Privacy Risk Level Over Time 140
5.6.3 The Conceptual Framework for Secure e-Health Information 144
5.7 The Conceptual Architecture 146
5.8 Discussion and Summary 148
References 150

6 Towards a Unified Security Evaluation Framework for e-Healthcare Information Systems 151
6.1 Introduction 151
6.2 Evaluating Privacy and Security in e-Healthcare 151
6.3 Approaches to Evaluation of e-Healthcare Information Security and Privacy 153
6.3.1 Standards-Based Security and Privacy Evaluation 153
6.3.2 Privacy Policy Evaluation 153
6.3.3 Ontology-Based Privacy Evaluation 154
6.3.4 Security and Privacy Metrics 154
6.3.5 Model-Based Approach to Security and Privacy Evaluation . 160
6.4 Frameworks for e-Healthcare Information Privacy and Security Evaluation 160
6.4.1 Information Security Management Model-Based Evaluation Frameworks 160
6.4.2 Security Metric-Based Evaluation Frameworks 161
6.4.3 Security and Privacy Policy-Based Evaluation Frameworks . 161
6.5 Towards a Unified Privacy and Security Evaluation Framework for e-Healthcare Information 162
6.5.1 The Security and Privacy Evaluation Challenges for e-Healthcare Information 162
6.5.2 Towards a Unified Framework for Evaluating Privacy and Security of e-Healthcare Information 163
6.6 Human Factors in Evaluating e-Healthcare Information Security and Privacy 167
6.6.1 Impact of Technological Human Factors 167
6.7 Summary 168
References 169

7 Discussions 173
7.1 Introduction 173
7.2 Securing Personal e-Healthcare 174
7.3 Proliferation of New Technologies 176
7.4 Health Identifier 178

7.5 Problem of Securing e-Healthcare Information 179
7.6 Contribution to Knowledge 181
7.7 Conclusion 182
7.8 Future Work and Research Directions........................ 182
References 183

A International Standards Organisational Technical Committee (ISO/TX) 215 Healthcare Informatics Standardisation 185

List of Figures

1.1 The Healthcare Process Supported by the DHDN 11
1.2 No Direct Connection between Individual Pharmacies and the NIA .. 14
1.3 The Role of NHSDO 18
1.4 Major issues in e-Healthcare security 24

2.1 Major issues in Securing e-Healthcare Information 30

3.1 Major issues in Laws and Standards for Secure e-Healthcare Information 60

4.1 Current and future e-Healthcare Information Systems 102
4.2 The evolution of e-healthcare information systems 103
4.3 Security Issues in CPG Management 116
4.4 The move towards hybrid e-Healthcare information systems and away from pure EHR and PEHR systems 119

5.1 The Contextual Framework for e-Healthcare Information Security and Privacy 126
5.2 The Evolution of e-Healthcare Information Management and Future of EHR/PEHR 130
5.3 Characteristics of the PEHR/EHR Hybrid 133
5.4 The Pyramid of Security and Privacy for e-Healthcare Information .. 137
5.5 The drivers to e-Healthcare information security and privacy 138
5.6 The Graph of "e-Healthcare Information control" or "Security and Privacy Risk Level" over time 140
5.7 Security and Privacy Characterisation Framework 144
5.8 The process of establishing a secure e-Healthcare information infrastructure 146
5.9 The e-Healthcare Information Privacy and Security Conceptual Architecture 148

6.1 The ACIO Framework for the evaluation of security and privacy for e-Healthcare Information 165
6.2 The spinning discs illustrating the dynamics of the ACIO framework 166

List of Tables

3.1 Published CEN TR XXXXX Standards of CEN/TC 251 74
3.2 Published CEN TS XXXXX standards of CEN/TC 251 75
3.3 Published CR XXXXX Standards of CEN/TC 251 75
3.4 Published EN XXXXX standards of CEN/TC 251 76
3.5 Published ISO-Related Standards of CEN/TC 251 77
3.6 Published ENV XXXX standards of CEN/TC 251 77
3.7 ASTM Committee E31 Standards for Security and Privacy in Healthcare Informatics 79
3.8 ASTM Committee E31 Standards for Healthcare Vocabularies 80
3.9 ASTM Committee E31 Standards for Documentation in Healthcare . 80
3.10 ASTM Committee E31 Standards for Modelling and E-Healthcare Records.. 80

4.1 Elements of Privacy and Security in e-HIS based on ISO/TS 18308 .. 104
4.2 Services within the Canadian Health Infoway Privacy and Security Conceptual Architecture (PSCA) 107
4.3 Comparison of e-PHR systems 114
4.4 Summary of Security Challenges facing modern e-HIS 117

5.1 Characteristics of the EHR/PEHR Hybrid 134

A.1 Security and Privacy Standards of the ISO/TC 215 - Health informatics 185
A.2 ISO/IEEE Standards of the TC 215 - Health informatics 186
A.3 ISO Standards of the TC 215 - Health informatics 186
A.4 ISO/TS Standards of the TC 215 - Health informatics 187
A.5 ISO/TR Standards of the TC 215 - Health informatics 187

LIST OF CONTRIBUTORS AND ORGANISATIONS

Deloitte LLP, United Kingdom
Environmental Policy Research Centre, Germany
Empirica Gesellschaft fuer Kommunikations und Technologieforschung mbH, Germany
ESYS Consultancy, United Kingdom
IBM, USA
Information and Communications Technology Council, Canada
Infonomics Society, United Kingdom and Ireland
Dublin Institute of technology, Ireland
InternetSecurity.com
Jagiellonian University, Poland
KADRIS Consultants, France
Massey University, Palmerston North and Auckland, New Zealand
Microsoft Corp, USA
TanJent Consultancy, United Kingdom
University of KwaZulu-Natal, South Africa
University of Potsdam, Sweden
University of Zimbabwe, Harare, Zimbabwqe
National University of Science and Technology, Bulawayo, Zimbabwe
University of Dar es Salaam, Dar es Salaam, Tanzania
Data Management Solutions Technologies Limited, Dar es Salaam, Tanzania

Chapter 1
Introduction to e-Healthcare Information Security

1.1 Introduction

The e-Healthcare information offers unique security, privacy and confidentiality challenges that require a fresh examination of the mainstream concepts and approaches to information security. The significance of security and privacy in e-Healthcare information raised the issues of individual consent, confidentiality and privacy, which are the main determinants in adopting and successful utilising the e-Healthcare information. Current trends in the domain of e-Healthcare information management point to the need for comprehensive incorporation of security, privacy and confidentiality safeguards within the review of e-Healthcare information management frameworks and approaches. This raises major challenges that demands holistic approaches spanning a wide variety of legal, ethical, psychological, information and security engineering. This introductory chapter explores information security and challenges facing e-Healthcare information management.

1.2 The e-Healthcare Information: Nature and Trends

The adoption of ICTs has created the electronic-healthcare (e-Healthcare) environment. At the core of e-Healthcare is e-Healthcare information, which is healthcare information that is managed and delivered through ICTs. The major promises from e-Healthcare include the lowering of costs, improvement of quality of patient care and enabling of better planning and decision-making. The delivery of these promises are hinged on e-Healthcare's focus on the challenging goal of meeting the clinician's information requirements and enabling the integration of e-Healthcare information with decision support systems and their delivery as on-line resources (Albert, 2007). However, the success of e-Healthcare will depend on whether it can ensure patient privacy, confidentiality and trust in managing e-healthcare information.

The e-healthcare information is varied and complex in nature. It is collected, maintained and utilised by a variety of players within the healthcare profession as well as in other sectors, where it is required for purposes such as insurance, employment and research. The structure of healthcare is multi-dimensional as it can be viewed in time-oriented, source-oriented and clinical problem-oriented terms (Grimson, 2001) with further dimensions being possible. In practice, health information is scattered across and within organisations and countries. The period for utilising health information spans over a lifetime of an individual, i.e., from cradle-to-grave, and even beyond. There may be a statutory time period from the death of a person after whose expiry the deceased's healthcare information may be destroyed (Lennon, 2005). The destruction of health information by a controller of such information is a legally regulated process (Roach et al., 2006).

A key aspect of the nature of healthcare information is that it is personal. This perception has been recognised since the 4th Century BC at the inception of the medical profession through the Hippocratic Oath (Baker and Masys, 1999). It is recognised that health information belongs to the individual who is the subject of such information. The assertion that the health service provider owns health information while the law merely grants some interest and rights over the information to the patient is true for the USA (Roach et al., 2006). It appears that this approach is increasingly being discarded in Europe, where it seems legal ownership of health information is bestowed on the patient while the healthcare unit is designated as a controller with legal rights, interests and obligations over the information. Thus, use of health information always requires the consent of the individual owner. In practice, there is a separation between ownership and control of health information, the owner of healthcare information may not be the one who controls its collection, storage and processing. Therefore, this necessitates distinction between owners, the controllers, processors and users of healthcare information (Lennon, 2005). The later are governed by the laws on the protection of information to ensure the consent and preserve the owners' privacy and confidentiality.

In 2001, Grimson envisaged the next generation Electronic Healthcare or Medical Records (EHR) as *"a longitudinal cradle-to-the-grave active record readily accessible and available via the Internet to drive the delivery of healthcare to the individual citizen"* (Grimson, 2001). The attainment of such an EHR remains a future goal up to now. In present practices, the EHRs are healthcare information that is controlled and managed through ICTs. Thus, largely inaccessible to the individual control and use. While, Electronic Personal Healthcare Records (EPHRs) (Lafky and Horan, 2008) are primarily healthcare information that is directly controlled and managed through ICTs by the owner of the information, i.e., the individual who is the subject of the healthcare information. The individual is responsible for creating, maintaining and controlling access to the information.

The content and nature of both the EHRs and EPHRs would reflect the complexity of healthcare information and need not necessarily differ. In fact, the need for interoperability and information sharing and exchange between the EHRs and EPHRs is widely recognised. The concept behind the EHRs has been in existence since start of the medical practice profession in the form of paper-based medical records. However, the EPHRs are emergent concepts, that are not widely used. The universal adoption of EPHRs could be difficult, if not almost impossible, due to privacy and confidentiality concerns. Other negative factors for EPHR adoption include computer literacy, affordability, computing resources, time constraints on the individual and internet connectivity. These factors also vary with geographic location with Third World regions offering the most challenges.

1.3 Security Impact of Trends in e-Healthcare Information Management

The current drive towards patient-centred approaches and paradigms in healthcare practice places patient consent, security, privacy and confidentiality concerns at the core of e-Healthcare information management challenges. At the local, national and international levels, information protection laws are acting as catalysts for privacy and confidentiality.

Generally speaking, healthcare information is scattered and distributed into disparate domain-specific islands of information that exist within and between healthcare service providers. The EHRs promise to manage, to deliver and distribute computing environment based on Internet Technologies. The introduction of wireless devices, sensor, network-enabled devices integration, interoperability, security and trust among and between the EHR systems are emerging as the key ingredients for successful management of e-Healthcare information in this complex environment. The efforts directed to guarantee the information quality, privacy, confidentiality and easing complexity of e-Healthcare information are focusing on standardisation. A number of standards covering a wide variety of e-Healthcare information are already in existence with more evolving challenges:

- The American Society for Testing and Materials (ASTM) International Continuity of Care Record (CCR) is a standard for patient health summary standard based upon XML. The CCR can be created, read and interpreted by various EHR or EMR systems. This standardisation effort allows easy interoperability between otherwise disparate entities.
- The American National Standards Institute (ANSI) X12 Electronic Data Interchange (EDI) is a standard that defines set of transaction protocols used for transmitting virtually any aspect of patient data. This standard has become popular in the United States for transmitting billing information.
- The standard, CEN-CONTSYS (EN 13940), sets up a system of concepts to support continuity of care.
- The Comit Europen de Normalisation (CEN) Electronic Health Record Communication (EHRcom) (EN 13606) is the the European standard for the communication of information from EHR systems. The CEN Healthcare Information Systems Architecture (HISA) (EN 12967) is a European services standard for inter-system communication in a clinical information environment.

- The Digital Imaging and Communications in Medicine (DICOM) is a standard for representing and communicating radiology images and reporting.
- In the Health Level 7 (HL7) standard, standardised messages are used for interchange between hospital and physician record systems, and between EMR systems and practice management systems. A component of this standard called HL7 Clinical Document Architecture (CDA) allows physician notes and other material to be communicated between healthcare services.
- The International Standards Organisation (ISO) Technical Committee (TC) 215 has defined the EHR, and produced a technical specification, ISO 18308, describing the requirements for EHR Architectures.
- The openEHR open source community standardisation provides the next generation public specifications and implementations for the EHR systems and communication. The main emphasis in the openEHR standard is on an software and data engineering approach that focuses on the complete separation of software and clinical models. It is notable that there is a continued lack of substantial convergence of standardisation among and within the key domains of law, organisational policy, daily practice, individual stakeholder profiles, advances in medical science and technological implementations within the resulting standards (Scott et al., 2004).

However, the past decade has seen the computerisation of patient records, which has increased at a moderate rate not like the phenomenal growth, which has been observed within other areas of life.

1.4 Trends in e-Healthcare Environment

The pressing demands for care quality from patients are clashing with the cost of health service delivery. The compromise is a search for solutions that improve care quality while, at the same time, lowering cost of health service delivery. Healthcare Informatics researchers have focused on integration of EHRs with decision-support systems (DSS), work-flow or care-flow and evidence-based best practice in the form of clinical practice guidelines (CPGs).

The phenomenon of globalisation has given birth to the trend of offshore outsourcing or off-shoring business activities. The effect of offshore outsourcing in healthcare includes the storage and processing of e-Healthcare information in foreign jurisdictions as well as the movement of personnel. In the US, the Secure Authentication Feature and Enhanced Identification Defense Act (SAFE-ID) Act 2005, was enacted to regulate the transmission of personally identifiable information to foreign affiliates and subcontractors in response to privacy and confidentiality concerns arising from off-shoring. Furthermore, in Canada, privacy legislation the Personal Information Protection and Electronic Documents Act (PIPEDA) 2000 was triggered by EU information privacy requirements imposed on information recipient countries in international trade and off-shoring arrangements, the EU requirements are currently a subject of dispute between the EU and Australia. Another healthcare environmental trend is brought about by regional grouping (social, economic, political and cultural integration) and cooperation among states. The migration of people between states necessitates the need for health information exchange and sharing within regional groupings. The later is more common within the European Union (EU), where the healthcare service interoperability between states is in demand to support the free movement of persons.

The emergence of free, universal and well-maintained on-line infrastructures, i.e. the recently introduced Google Health [1] service help to empower every individual to create their own EPHRs and the formal acceptance by healthcare practitioners. The security, privacy and confidentiality concerns may even be compounded in the case EPHRs services provided by private companies who operate outside both the health professional and legal frameworks. For instance, the Google Health service admits that Google system administrators can access and transfer an individual's EPHRs and that, in the US, HIPAA 1996 does not apply to Google's handling and transfer of health information from Google Health. Therefore, the prevention of EPHRs interference by governments in the case of Google Health service is not guaranteed. This has already proved to be difficult with less personally sensitive services like the Google search service in China (Zittrain and Edelman, 2003).

Moreover, EPHRs have proved to be useful in cases where there is lack of trusts in the collection and storage of genomic data. The increasing use of genomic data in healthcare and in legal evidence poses major personal security, privacy and confidentiality risks, although the support for EPHRs is increasingly receiving acceptance within healthcare practice and national health programmes. The integration of the EPHRs with hospital-maintained EHRs (Mandl et al, 2007), on-line health information databases and on-line health information (Doupi and van der Lei, 2005) has contributed to information requirements in chronic disease management informative and of didactic value individual EPHRs. The following e-Healthcare case studies were selected from six countries that have implemented e-Health. The case studies observation were used to identify any useful data and information that impacts the e-Healthcare environment.

1.4.1 Case Study: Canada

Canadas international leadership in modern health promotion began in 1974, with the publication of A New Perspective on the Health of Canadians, under the leadership of Marc Lalonde, the Minister of Health and Welfare Canada at the time

[1] Google introduces its Personal e-Healthcare Record service application as: "*Google Health puts you in charge of your health information. It's safe, secure, and free. Organize your health information all in one place. Gather your medical records from doctors, hospitals, and pharmacies. Keep your doctors up-to-date about your health. Be more informed about important health issues. Google stores your information securely and privately. We will never sell your data. You are in control. You choose what you want to share and what you want to keep private.*"(http://www.google.com/health, accessed: 16 August 2010)

(Lalonde, 1974). The past twenty years have seen a significant move forward in the area of health informatics in Canada and abroad. In Canada, during this period, academic institutions have developed, implemented and graduated trained health informatics professionals who have gone on to become CIOs at large hospitals. Canada has an internationally recognized national Electronic Health Record (EHR) strategy under the leadership of Canada Health Infoway and has made a significant investment in funding ICT projects to advance the implementation of an interoperable EHR. The adoption and utilization of technology across the continuum of care continues to advance, and the field of health informatics will continue to play a significant role in transforming our health system and in using information for improved clinical decisions and health system planning.

Since its inception in 2000, Canada Health Infoway (Infoway) has had the mandate to invest in and support the development of a pan-Canadian EHR infrastructure to accelerate the use of electronic health records in Canada. The internationally recognized EHR blueprint architecture establishes the framework for the development and deployment of ICT to support an EHR system. Infoway works with various industry stakeholders technology vendors, provincial e-Health agencies, industry associations and health care organizations to provide leadership and investment in e-Health projects that support its objective. In 2005, Branham Group Inc. asked leading e-Health thought leaders and key decision makers to dust off their "crystal ball" and offer their perspective on how e-Health would be used to deliver health care services in 2015. By combining these various predictions, a composite picture emerges in which:

- The existing "silos" of information and expertise no longer exist.
- "Patients" have become "consumers" of health care services and are taking a more active role in their care. "Patient self-service" emerges as a viable option for routine tasks such as booking appointments or monitoring certain aspects of a chronic condition.
- eHealth technologies are in use across the continuum of care and are an integral, largely "invisible" component in the delivery of nearly all health care services.
- Health care providers make extensive use of mobile devices to access the information they need, when they need it, wherever they might be located.
- Clinicians are shifting from a mindset of having to remember everything to routinely consulting handheld devices and on-line applications to order tests, review test results, refine a diagnosis, select the most appropriate care plan, schedule therapy and prescribe medication.
- Health care providers no longer need to be in the same room as the person they are treating in order to make a diagnosis or even deliver many aspects of care.

The year, in which these predictions were made, held obvious challenges, such as funding shortages, slow adoption of e-Health applications by clinicians, and a lack of skilled human resources. With these challenges still present in the Canadian health care environment today, it has been difficult to achieve the promise of health system reform. To realize true cost savings and improved clinical outcomes, clinicians must be able to leverage these tools independently, with the knowledge, training, and resources to be effective. A major contribution from the health informatics discipline is the work that has been done on clinical decision support systems (CDSS). Progress into the utilization of technology to develop information systems in health care came in 1966 with the development of MUMPS, a programming system created by Nell Pappalardo and Curt Marble. The system supported the development of medical information systems and was heralded as an easy to use and powerful programming language. The success of MUMPS has been attributed to the collaboration throughout its development by end users and system designers. The Health information management professionals provide leadership in all aspects of clinical information management at both the micro and macro levels. At the micro (or individual record level) HIM professionals support the collection, use, access and disclosure, to the retention and destruction of health information regardless of format. At the macro (or aggregate data level), HIM professionals deal with the information through the health system, analyze statistics, manage complex information systems including registries and work with public, private and key stakeholders in understanding and using health data to improve the health of Canadians.

The Health care provider organizations play a dual role in the advancement of e-Health. They are a source of information on the types of competencies required, as they implement more advanced clinical systems to realize the potential of an interoperable Electronic Health Record (HER). While most hospitals in Canada have implemented core clinical applications (e.g. ADT, RIS, LIS, etc), the advanced clinical applications like CPOE and eMAR systems are in the early stages of implementation. Some of the competencies required include data definitions, data integration, and interoperability between the various components of an EHR. In 2003 CIHR report on the future of a public health system noted that "Public health" is the science and art of promoting health, preventing disease, and prolonging life through the organized efforts of society. The report specified that the functions of this system should include:

- Population health assessment
- Health surveillance
- Health promotion
- Disease and injury prevention
- Health protection

Experts in public health systems can contribute to the overall understanding of our health system and how it is changing. In order to carry out this mandate, they need a large amount of aggregate data on the health system. The competencies required to supply this data include, but are not limited to, statistical analysis, data modelling and aggregation, biomedical sciences, and health information sciences (Canada-Health-Research, 2003). The health consumers are more knowledgeable about their health, and many use the Internet as a research tool. Pew Internet, in its 2009 report noted that 75% of all adults use the Internet to obtain health information (Pew-Internet-Project, 2009). The questions that arise are: how trustworthy are these health information sites to provide accurate health information, and how well organized and easy to use are the search engines? Health informatics and health information management professionals have the competencies to support and develop robust search tools to support the health consumer. They can also act as consumer advocates with respect to Personal Health Records (PHRs) by ensuring the privacy and confidentiality of health information ((eHealth-in Canada, 2009), see sub-section 4.3.1 for further details).

1.4.2 Case Study: IZIP and General Health Insurance Company of the Czech Republic

IZIP is an electronic health record (EHR) system with Internet access. The EHR includes all relevant information about all contacts of the citizen with healthcare services, compiled from regular GP visits, dental treatments, laboratory and imaging tests and healthcare, such as complicated surgery, provided by hospital services. The IZIP system allows doctors to access the EHR at the time and point of care, so that each doctor can resume treatment where the previous doctors have stopped.

The principal role of IZIP is to shift the medical database from individual healthcare professionals and healthcare provider organisations (HPOs) to the insured citizen. It is achieved by replacing paper-based records with secure electronic files on the public information network, the Internet. Citizens have the right to access and read their own EHR, but they cannot change them. They can authorise healthcare professionals to view their data, converting citizens to an active element of the healthcare system. The citizens are active partners and well-informed. They are then better placed to make responsible decisions, cooperate better and gain a picture of the technical, resource and financial limitations of the proposed or available services and procedures. This is an extensive change to the conventional system of health record administration, where the HPO, not the citizen, had the power to disclose information.

Internet health files comprise selected parts of the medical documentation. Only healthcare professionals are authorised to insert data and records into the IZIP system. Healthcare professionals write into the IZIP system through an interface, which allows for data transmission from emergency rooms, laboratories, complementary services, and pharmacies. Records in the IZIP system contain:

- Anamnesis
- Results of examinations performed by a GP or specialist, in chronological order
- Results of laboratory tests and examinations
- A list of prescribed and issued medicines and drugs
- X-rays, scans and other images
- Reports on hospitalisations
- Vaccination history
- Information on other treatment, including type and location.

Modules to be introduced in the near future include e-Prescribing, emergency service support and messaging. Plans for further development beyond these include smart cards and digital signatures and improved structuring of the data in the health records, enabling expanded statistical and clinical analyses. Data security is currently guaranteed by a password and PIN system. Healthcare professionals have to register with the system and can log in using their own password and PIN, identifying them as professionals. The system was developed by a private company, IZIP Ltd., in cooperation with the General Health Insurance Company of the Czech Republic (GHIC CR). It has spread over the whole of the Czech Republic since the beginning of 2003. IZIP includes registrations not only from doctors, but other healthcare organisations: laboratories, pharmacies, rehabilitation clinics, and hospitals.

1.4.3 Case Study: Danish Health Data Network (DHDN)

The Danish Health Data Network (DHDN) developed by MedCom is a long-term project that enables effective data transfer between several parts of the health service. It begins at the point of care for patients and General Practitioners (GPs). From there, services that citizens may need access to include pharmacists, diagnostic services at hospitals, specialist consultation at hospitals, referral to a hospital, if admitted, discharge from a hospital, and transfer to home care and care home services. Effective access to these by citizens depends on efficient and effective communication between healthcare providers.

The setting of data standards for effective communication, information and data transfer between healthcare providers is essential. In the DHDN, these are achieved within the dynamic of the connected MedCom phases. From this, the DHDN aims to achieve consistent data definitions that achieve almost 100% data reliability, and so enable EDI and e-Health to be used effectively, and, in turn, create a net benefit for the investment. These are delivered by the application of the data standards and protocols by suppliers and users that, from 1994, have operated within the DHDN. The e-Health applications can then enable benefits for citizens from faster and more reliable and efficient communication between healthcare and social care professionals. GPs benefits include costs savings on secretarial and clerical services in preparing and sending information to other healthcare services. Pharmacists can receive prescriptions directly and electronically from GPs, a faster reliable process than paper prescriptions transferred by hand. By receiving prompt notification of transfers to their services, social services benefit from earlier preparation and information about patients discharged from hospital, and so earlier, and more effective, care provision. Hospitals and diagnostic services receive and send information that is more consistent, and so can be more efficient and responsive.

The Danish Centre for Health Telematics has a core role in achieving and improving this communication within a process completed as a set of projects that improves national data standards and takes advantage of networks and new technology in healthcare. This is the MedCom process. It started in 1994 and has four main phases:

- MedCom I pioneer spirit and professionalism 1995 - 1996
- MedCom II dissemination and consolidation 1997 - 1999
- MedCom III quality, dissemination development 2000 2001
- MedCom IV adopt Internet and web based technologies current phase.

Electronic data interchange (EDI) is used for the process, including:

- GP referrals to hospitals
- GP prescriptions
- GP requests for diagnostic tests
- Test reports
- Discharge letters to GPs
- Notifications of discharges to community and home care services
- Reimbursements.

A critical strategic goal for the DHDN is to achieve consistent data definitions that achieve almost 100% data reliability, and so enable EDI and e-Health to be used effectively, and, in turn, create a net benefit for the investment. During the MedCom years, National IT strategies laid foundations for e-Health. In 1999, the Health Ministry published a national strategy for IT in the healthcare sector. Its focus was communication between the various partners in the healthcare sector. The e-Health offered better support and effective exchange of information and communication of data about citizens to ensure more cohesive and coherent treatment and care. Furthermore, electronic communication was to support healthcare professionals in accessing relevant information across several different systems. MedCom was included in the strategy because the project had reached a high degree of consent and showed proven results. In May 2003 a new strategy was published. It proposed that proven local initiatives should be implemented nationally, and that the co-ordination of e-Health deployment should be strengthened to be a prerequisite for effective e-Health. This would enable e-Health to contribute to the goals of the healthcare system, such as high levels of quality and patient satisfaction, shorter waiting lists and times, improved efficiency, improved effectiveness, and expanded choice. The DHDN extends across almost all the healthcare provider organisations in Denmark, and the home care sector of social services. Healthcare that relies on communication between GPs, pharmacies, diagnostic services, hospitals, counties, private clinics and social services care homes and home care services are all within the boundary of the DHDN (see Figure 1.1).

Developing the DHDN encountered both victories and defeats. It demonstrated that persistent and consistent project management was critical to success. So, if local pilot projects did not live up to the expectations and goals, they were phased out. Similarly, when system providers did not live up to demands and obligations, it was revealed clearly to the others. In the same way, results from each region were revealed each month on the EDI-topix. This exchange of experience was very significant for the development work as more and more players were connected to the DHDN. After about five years in 1999, the DHDN had proven its worth and shown its weaknesses. One challenge was that the standards were not precise enough. Quality assurance was needed for further expansion of the DHDN, and a new system for

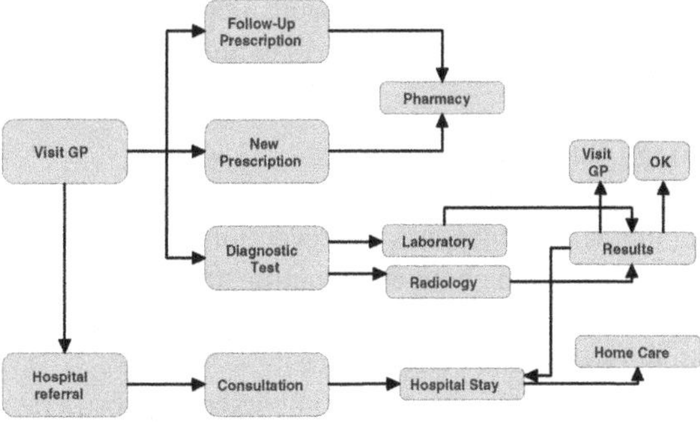

Figure 1.1 The Healthcare Process Supported by the DHDN

hospital communication which became some of the focus areas behind the third MedCom project between 2000 and 2001. Collaboration services are now available in the DHDN. The MedCom installed a server that is free of charge for all health service partners. To secure the right to use the service, several pilot projects have been launched, that focus on four areas:

- Communication between hospitals for a second opinion, or where patients are treated at more than one hospital.
- Communication between hospitals and home-care units, especially about elderly people.
- Communication between psychiatric departments and social workers about children.
- Making the collaboration server available from different mobile devices.

The DHDN plays an important role as the technical back-bone for the integration of electronic healthcare records based on the national Basic Electronic Healthcare Record (BEHR). In this work, the National Board of Health has decided to base the semantic integration on SNOWMED terminology, replacing the ICD terminology as a National terminology database. This work started at the end of 2004, and the plan is that the B-EHR and the new terminology will be implemented in all hospitals by the year 2006. The impact of the Collaboration Server and the B-EHR are not part of this case study to evaluate the economic impact. However, the DHDN will have a considerable impact on the current processes, especially the impact of healthcare professionals being able to share data, as well as the current facility to transfer data. Achieving these changes is the challenge for each organisation within the DHDN and uses the MedCom standards to procure the appropriate and compliant e-Health applications for suppliers then deal directly with the process changes that are feasible. In this way, they carry the cost of e-Health and gain the benefits from improved processes.

The DHDN also has a continuous impact on healthcare processes, and, as a foundation for strategic goals, it avoids the need for additional information processes. The introduction of the e-Health Portal provides several functions. It informs citizens of health related issues and offers citizens opportunities to interact with the health services. Functions available to all users include:

- Prescription renewal
- E-Booking through patients' GPs
- Email consultation patients' GPs
- Information about health, illnesses and prevention
- Hospital patient information about examination, treatment, post-treatment
- Waiting list information
- Information about quality and performance
- Access to the current status of public reimbursement for personal medical expenses.

Healthcare professionals also have access to patient-sensitive information on the e-Health Portal. They use an electronic digital signature that is part of a national project giving a software-based signature to all citizens and employees in Denmark. The signature is distributed by Danish Telecom (TDC). A new top-domain was established, which is only available inside the DHDN. The top-domain secures that none of the health care services can be acceded via the Internet. Using VPN and the creation of the MedCom top-domain allow the partners and users in the DHDN to reuse the existing Internet connections:

- Starting with an effective vision of the potential of e-Health should be consistent with the political will to establish successful electronic communication.
- Support from all the healthcare stakeholders, authorities, system providers and healthcare professionals were crucial.
- Involving stakeholders effectively should seek to gain consensus, especially when communication on the network was being developed.
- Organisational and process change are critical to realising the benefits, but change occurs over time, not overnight, and changes and improvements will occur if there is a will to change and a consensus to follow.
- Installing technology and connecting hospitals is not enough; end users must be able to see the potential, and be willing to use it, so the principle of a very high degree of user influence has been adopted to ensure that after installing the technology, organizational changes have been achieved to realise the benefits.
- In addition to interoperability between different IT systems, the context of the communication also has to be created on a basis of consensus.
- Exchange of experience for the development work as more and more players were included in the project scope.
- Priority to setting and achieving sound, acceptable data standards is essential.
- Converting successful teamwork on a small scale to a large scale, complex healthcare setting across the whole country.
- Sequential national strategies that built from achievements and success.
- Avoiding a rush to adopt new technology when the old continued to deliver.
- Effective, persistent, consistent project management and leadership are essential when changing communication flows and seeking clarity to recognise and deal with victories and defeats

- Effective identification of internal effort, especially identifying and setting data standards, and seeking the appropriate external effort, such as enabling e-Health suppliers to deal with product development and compliance.

The MedCom already has an international dimension, reinforcing the potential transferability. Its approach to identifying, designing and defining data standards and protocols is well proven, and can be applied and adapted in all member states.

1.4.4 Case Study: The Norwegian Healthcare System

The National Insurance Scheme (folketrygden) is the cornerstone of the Norwegian welfare system. It provides a number of benefits to the Norwegian population through the National Insurance Service (Trygdeetaten). The National Insurance Service is the largest institution under the Ministry of Labour and Social Inclusion (Arbeids- og Inkluderingsdepartementet). It is responsible for the administration of the social security offices and the function utility centres. The national insurance service covers healthcare, old age and disability pensions, and unemployment benefits. Differently from some other countries, there is no private healthcare insurance system in Norway.

Norway has a population of only four and a half million people and is sparsely populated. It is therefore obvious that the responsibility for the Norwegian health service has historically been decentralized and operated through the nineteen counties (fylker) and 435 municipalities, each responsible for its part of the health service. In its present form, the healthcare system is the result of a reform which took place three years ago. Where previously the nineteen counties were directly owners of the 80 hospitals in the country, all hospitals are currently owned by the central government. With the exception of some private laboratories, all hospitals in Norway are therefore state-owned. This healthcare reform also created five larger regional healthcare service organizations that are responsible for healthcare service in each of five larger regions of Norway. All pharmacies are privately owned, except for pharmacies in hospitals, which are owned by the hospitals and therefore indirectly owned by the central government.

The national insurance service is organized under the management of a central directorate, the National Insurance Administration (NIA or Rikstrygdeverket), which runs its operations through its regional and municipal bodies. The NIA has overall authority over the Service and has the power to issue detailed regulations and general recommendation concerning the application of social insurance law. The National Insurance Administration is directly subject to the authority of the Ministry of Labour and Social Inclusion. On average, the National Insurance Service budget accounts for a third of the Norwegian national government budget. In recent years, this amounts to 260 billion Norwegian Kroner (equivalent to 32 billion EURO, 39 billion US Dollar).

The e-Health infrastructure discussed in this case study supports payments by the National Insurance Administration of healthcare services provided by the 80 hospitals, 550 pharmacies and 1850 general practitioners' offices in Norway worth ten percent of this amount, or approximately 26 billion Norwegian Kroner (3.2 billion EURO, 3.9 USD).

Norway has had a standardized communications infrastructure for healthcare insurance for over a decade. This infrastructure was based on EDIFACT messages and used the X.400 message protocol. It also made use of a proprietary Public Key Infrastructure (PKI). Architecture of the legacy infrastructure based on EDIFACT, X.400 and proprietary PKI The existing infrastructure covered communication between all pharmacies and hospitals and the National Insurance Administration. The existing system is in high volume use between GPs and hospitals for the transfer of medical results from the hospital to the general practioners EPJ (Electronic Patient Journal) systems. The system also connects each hospital directly to the National Insurance Administration. Although there were some diskette-based solutions, there was no networked electronic communication between general practitioners offices and the NIA. As a result of this, claims processing was still very much paper-based, time-consuming and labour-intensive.

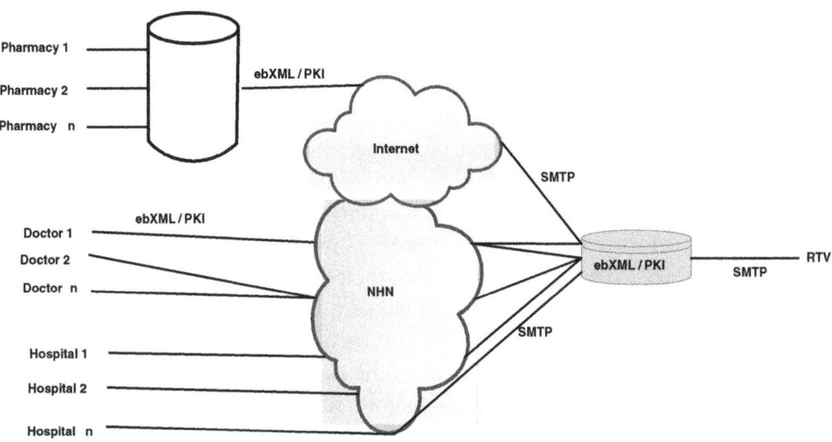

Figure 1.2 No Direct Connection between Individual Pharmacies and the NIA

The Figure 1.2 shows that there is no direct connection between individual pharmacies and the NIA. There is central hub, NAF Data, which connects to all pharmacies using a pharmaceutical computer network. This central system is connected, using EDIFACT batch file upload via X400, to the NIA systems.

In the new architecture, general practitioners offices are connected to the NIA and other organizations in the Norwegian healthcare using the National Health Network. This is one of the key differences from the existing architecture, where this communication is still very much paper-based. Unlike hospitals and pharmacies (which use company or "server" certificates), messages sent by general practitioners will be signed using the personal private key of the individual general practitioner. Sensitive messages sent to them will similarly be encrypted using their public key. The infrastructure provides on-line verification of signatures and also checks for revocation of certificates, using the standard Lightweight Directory Access Protocol (LDAP). The pharmacies remain connected using the existing interfaces and protocols to the national pharmacy system. However, this national pharmacy hub, acting as a kind of gateway, now connects using ebXML Messaging over the SMTP transport protocol over Internet Protocol to the NIA. The existing connections from hospitals to the NIA will continue to use the EDIFACT message format for existing message types. (Source Pim van der Eijk, 2005, Trygdeetaten Case Study, Norwegian e-Health Infrastructure based on XML, ebXML and PKI).

1.4.5 Case Study: Sweden

Prior to the e-Health investment, radiology services were provided in dedicated hospital departments with MRI and CT scanners. Tele-radiology services were provided during the evaluation by TMC in Barcelona and the objective of the Swedish hospitals is to use also other tele-care services in the future.

The planning, delivery and management of healthcare services in Sweden is carried out at three political levels: central government, county councils, and local authorities. Elected political representatives have a significant influence on health and welfare systems, and are generally responsible for strategic decisions and funding. The National Board of Health and Welfare is the government's central advisory and supervisory authority for health services, health protection and social services. The Board reviews and evaluates health services to establish their performance against goals laid down by central government. Whilst broad healthcare planning, guidance and supervision remain national responsibilities in Sweden, responsibility for healthcare delivery is decentralised to the 19 County Councils and the two Regions, a total of21 entities. The county councils are combined into 6 regions for specialised tertiary care, which are responsible for 8 university hospitals. The population of the 21 areas varies between 60,000 and 1.9 million people. County councils decide on the allocation of resources to the health services and are responsible for their overall planning. They also own and run hospitals, primary healthcare centres and other health institutions. Private providers usually have significant contracts with county councils to supply services that supplement services provided by county council healthcare entities.

Sjunet is an IP-based broadband network, connecting all Swedish hospitals, primary care centers and many other health services. It is built up of nodes connecting the firewalls in the 21 county councils and regions, and separate from the Internet. Users connected to a county council network can reach either the Internet or Sjunet depending on the service they need. In its first version Sjunet was set up as a virtual private network (VPN) with tunnels on the Swedish part of the Internet, and was delivered by the Swedish telecom company Telia. VPN technology guaranteed that information was not accessible from, or communicated through, the public Internet and the network provider guaranteed that the available bandwidth was sufficient for applications and services. From 2003 the network has been based on VLAN technology from Song Networks with built in redundancy, and technically separated from the Internet. The separation from the Internet means better availability what regards bandwidth. The bandwidth is determined by how much each county council purchase for access to Sjunet. Normally 10-100 Mbps is sufficient for most applications. For tele-radiology 4-10 Mbps is sufficient.

In 2001, Sweden recognised the need to establish a common IT infrastructure, to foster close co-operation between care providers and the IT industry and reinforce the IT areas of the care providers, Carelink and The Private Healthcare Suppliers Association. Swedish eHealth policies and strategies have largely evolved from this setting. By 2005, all county councils were members of the Carelink Cooperation dealing with IT strategy and investment. Currently, collaboration between the healthcare sector and industry is effective. Sjunet is now the accepted infrastructure backbone network for communication of healthcare data and services in Sweden, including various forms of telemedicine. This network is also currently being expanded through investment in e-Health to support healthcare in remote areas:

- Tele-radiology is sustainable as it is easier to integrate in clinical processes than other tele-medicine applications and the service provider (TMC) has a clear business model and work-flow process
- Tele-radiology is a solution to a specific problem, that is to say, a shortage of radiologists
- Main beneficiaries are citizens
- HPOs benefit
- ICT is a tool for providing a service in a better way, not as a goal in itself
- Costs reductions are significant, but the additional gains are more important in realizing a net benefit
- Links for Swedish hospitals to an independent out-sourcer is beneficial for patient access, quality, financing, technology obsolescence and capacity constraints
- HPOs can manage their mix of outsourcing and internal resources
- Flexibility in using tele-radiology is very important for the Swedish hospitals.

The tele-radiology has enabled the two Swedish hospitals (Sollefte and Bors) to expand their network of radiology specialists and have faster access to them through TMC. TMC has access to 60 specialists who are experts in different areas of radiology (although for legal reasons it only has access to 18 Swedish radiologists employed by TMC). Before tele-radiology, the two hospitals were limited to the range of expertise of their in house radiologists. Now, they have access to a number of subspecialities in radiology that were not available before. Images at the hospitals are now classified into emergency and non-emergency cases, with the latter sent to TMC. This provides resident specialists with more time to deal with the images they read.

It worth noting that Denmark, Norway and Sweden each have their own national healthcare networks, so the challenge of Baltic e-Health is to create a solution that enables Internet technology to be available to healthcare professionals working with their national networks. The Baltic Health Network will achieve this by utilising much of the existing equipment and infrastructure. The aims are to prove e-Health that will be secure and efficiently transmitted across regions, and so create benefits for citizens, patients and healthcare professionals.

1.4.6 Case Study: UK - NHS Direct Online (NHSDO) Information Service

Since the early 1990s, the United Kingdoms National Health Service (NHS) has adopted a more business-like ethos based mainly on a range of internal markets. This has driven several developments in the way it works. Introducing telephone call centres by NHS Direct was part of this, with an aim to support the unending search for improved patient focus and empowerment, and improved demand management. These can be seen in as part of the goal of the NHS to provide quality care that:

- Meets the needs of all citizens
- Is free at the point of need, apart from a small number of low charges
- Is based on citizens' clinical needs, not their ability to pay
- Enables people to make choices about their health and healthcare.

Patients access to information about their general health and conditions, and the most appropriate route to the healthcare they need, has been an important part of patient focus and empowerment. NHS Direct's call centres and its NHS Direct Online (NHSDO) services are contributing this. The NHS Direct call centres, were established in 1998. It provides health and healthcare information to citizens and healthcare professionals. The symptomatic service is for people who have signs or symptoms of illness, and may be unsure about dealing with them. It also enables them to make better choices about their use of the NHS. Whilst setting up the call centre services, NHS Direct was establishing other technologies and new media that would enable it to improve its information service to citizens and healthcare professionals. These included the use of the Internet and web-site technologies by NHSDO. These also enabled NHS Direct to develop its role in providing information about health and healthcare without relying on a spoken dialogue with citizens, a common approach in modern business. This is consistent with the development of other web-based information provided by, or through, the NHS, such as the National Knowledge service and National Electronic Library for Health and Directgov. Gradually, access to these types of web sites is being extended.

In a world where Internet and web-site access is routine, the technical innovation of NHSDO can be seen as the equivalent to a common feature of modern business organisations. Similarly, links to call centres for follow-up information can be found in many equivalent websites. The innovative aspect of NSHDO is applying these technologies in healthcare. The NHS Direct has developed and used NHS Direct Online (NHSDO) to provide citizens with access to information about health and healthcare. This enables them to improve their knowledge and choices about life styles, health and healthcare. The number of visitors to NHSDO has risen dramatically from about 1.5 million in 2000 to the forecast of some 24 million for 2008. The number of repeat visitors has risen too, from about one third of visits to about half. Information is provided by access to a range of facilities, including a health information enquiry service; an enquiry services; a health encyclopaedia; a best treatments website, self help guide; details of local NHS services, common health questions, interactive tools and a health space. Internet and web-based technology forms the basis of NHSDO, and is consistent with rise in Internet access in the UK. This also provides an e-Health dynamic underpins the continuous development of the service. The NHS Direct is a special health authority within the NHS. The NHSDO is an integrated part of the NHS Directs services (see Figure 1.3).

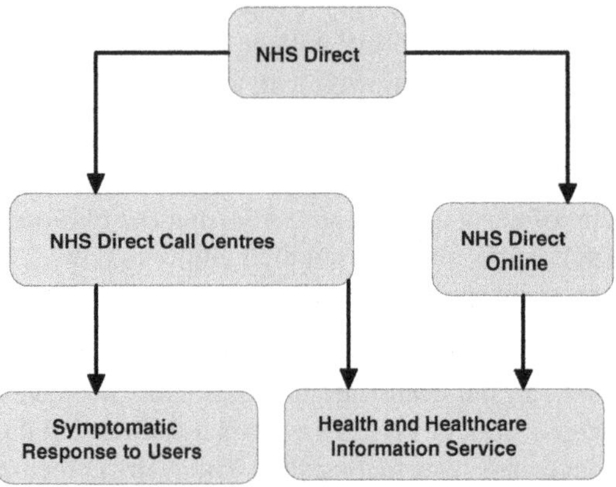

Figure 1.3 The Role of NHSDO

The NHSDO is a web portal providing citizens with health and healthcare information to help them to understand health and healthcare issues relevant to them, and to indicate the potential benefits they may gain from change. As for the call centres, NHSDO also enables citizens to make better choices about their use of the NHS. It is a service in addition, and complementary to, the NHS Direct call centres. Both NHSDO and the NHS Direct call centres are 24 hour services that provide healthcare information to users. Some NHSDO users may not find all they want or need on NHSDOs web pages, and may want further help or clarification after using NHSDO, and so may rely on the NHS Direct call centre service:

- The NHSDO provided a new service to citizens by providing information using the technology that citizens are increasingly using.
- The focus is on citizens and providing them with health and healthcare information to empower them to take more informed decisions and choices.
- Using Internet and web-based technologies enabled the productivity of NHSDO to improve dramatically over a relatively short period of time.

- The NSHDO relied on some external support in the earlier years, the NHSDO team is now extensively internal and effective and developing both the technology and content of the NHSDO.
- The e-Health dynamic of NHSDO expands citizens access to information as a continuous chain of developments and expansion.
- The economic focus of NHSDO is on providing information to citizens to enable them to make effective choices; it does not aim to reduce spending in healthcare.
- Critical success factors include providing health and healthcare information that citizens value, providing it with Internet technologies that citizens are increasingly using, managing the changing relationship between external and internal expertise, adopting an effective e-Health dynamic, and not marketing NHSDO, but allowing it to grow organically.
- Potential barriers to success were managed by NHSDO to ensure that the information in NHSDO is valued and accurate, that technologies work promptly and that its resources are strictly managed to avoid project overruns.
- Another lesson, derived from the nature of the e-Health application, is that the net economic benefits NHSDO are estimated to occur quickly compared to other e-Health applications in other, more conventional healthcare settings.

The NHSDO's reliance on Internet and web is directly transferable to other member states. Access to health and healthcare information to provide the content is also available elsewhere. Unusually for an e-Health project, change management is minimal for NHSDO. Having designed the e-health facility, released it, continued to develop it and set up an effective information review, evaluation and release function, the facility is ready to be implemented. Utilisation depends on citizens' access to, and use of, the Internet, and their perception of the value of the content. This enhances the transferability potential (see sub-section 4.3.2 for further details).

1.5 Securing e-Healthcare Information: Significance and Challenges

The extreme violations of health professional ethics and the Nuremburg Code have triggered determined efforts to ensure strict adherence to privacy and confidentiality safeguards. The nature of personal health information requires individual rights to be focused on privacy and confidentiality of managing information. The Electronic Health Records (EHR), Electronic Patient Records (EPR) and Electronic Medical Records (EMR) provide the basis for e-Health services. The information in these records (containing patient healthcare information) needs to be shared amongst multiple healthcare providers and healthcare professionals, but privacy issues have been a major inhibitor in the implementation of the EHR, EMR and EPR systems.

Information and communication technologies (ICTs) form the backbone for e-Health in delivering patient care services. The Internet offers affordable worldwide coverage, which makes it a favourable and popular platform for e-Healthcare.

As the technologies advance and the variety of Internet-enabled devices increase, the threats to e-Healthcare information also multiply. Hence, it is crucial that security technologies be harnessed to provide the privacy and security requirements to e-Healthcare information that is exchanged through the Internet. The establishment of the EHR privacy requirements in the context of standard e-Health frameworks, (HealthLink in Australia and HIPAA in USA) are both imperative (Ray and Wimalasiri, 2006). With regards to the above discussions, special attention needs to be paid towards the evolving web-based solutions, which offer special privacy and confidentiality challenges. Thus, within the e-Healthcare set-up, computer security engineers are charged to ensure individual privacy, confidentiality and trust in e-Healthcare information. Without securing e-Healthcare information, the key benefits of e-Health would not be fully realised.

The health information and systems are sensitive and generally require a higher degree of security than information and systems in other domains. The legitimate uses of health data are contentious and the balance between legitimate uses of e-Health information, the right to privacy and confidentiality is elusive. Thus, there is an uneasiness on the part of the individual about the maintenance, utilisation and transmission of the EHRs by healthcare service providers. Hence, the emerging calls for individual persons' choice and discretion captured in opt-in and opt-out provisions in the laws and policies governing healthcare service providers in the US and the UK would not be unexpected. The question of when it can be said that all security requirements for a given case have been attained and absolute assurance has been established is hard to resolve. We can measure only the degree of security requirement satisfaction rather than certainty. The problem in measuring the latter is one of the major challenges to attaining secure e-Healthcare information.

The complex nature of the healthcare environment renders the security of e-Healthcare information difficult to develop appropriate adaptable policy for securing individual patient EHR. However, it is noted that the unique capability of e-Health to transgress all existing geo-political and other barriers is a complicating factor in securing e-Healthcare information. The policy development initiatives continue to take place largely in an isolated manner and lacks convergence with other aspects of securing e-Healthcare information. Initiatives to develop and advance policy, standards, and tools in relation to the EHR access control and authorisation management must address this capability (Scott et al., 2004).

1.6 Concepts of e-Healthcare Information Security

The e-Healthcare information consists of digital multimedia and medical records. The concept of the EHR relates to e-Healthcare information that consists of a patient-centric, cross-institutional and longitudinal information entity that spans from cradle to grave. The EHR offers great promise for personalized medicine delivered through e-Health. It has been claimed to be probably the only vehicle through which we may truly realize the personalization of medicine beyond population-based genetic profiles that are expected to become part of medication and treatment indications in the near future (Shabo, 2005). The EPHRs consists of health information that is initiated, maintained, and owned by an individual. The sources of information contained in the EPHRs are from different healthcare service providers and accessible on-line by individuals who have been authenticated.

However, security has to do with excluding inappropriate and unauthorised people from access to e-Healthcare information. This includes both physical and electronic exclusion. This term also has different and often contradictory meaning. For instance, an organisation may regard security as ability to monitor and track message exchange to and from their employees while the employees regard it as total absence of such monitoring and tracking. Therefore, any restrictions that may be in place for the purpose of securing the data should be explicit. From an individual perspective, privacy is the ability and/or right of the individuals to exercise their free will and discretion in deciding when, how and to what extent information about them is communicated to others (Westin, 1983). Privacy concerns arise from an increasing occurrence of privacy violations. These privacy violations range from freak privacy accidents to privacy-breaching actions that are forbidden under the law, e.g., in the Emilio Calatayud Case in which over a six year period, Emilio, a US drug enforcement agent, searched various law enforcement computer systems and databases to obtain sensitive information, and then sold it to a private investigations firm.

Confidentiality in e-Healthcare is the duty or obligation imposed on one party to protect other secret, if those secrets are known and the trustworthiness to the first party. The trustworthiness within the context of e-Healthcare is the attribute that describes a system that will not fail. Thus, a trusted system may not be trustworthy. Some experts have viewed trust as having to do with official approval or integrity that is indeterminable through behavioural observation.

1.7 Frameworks and Approaches

The shared care and international information exchange require reliable and stable normative framework for managing e-Healthcare information. The framework should be based on the application of standardised solutions. However, most such standardised solutions are often not sufficient (Hildebrand et al., 2006). In addressing these problems, there is a need to create awareness about standardisation in e-Healthcare and to facilitate practical implementation. The desirable outcome of standardisation is a common concept of information security among healthcare providers. There is an urgent need to maintain security compliance requirements within the healthcare community. The demand for frameworks and approaches that establish a set of controls for e-Healthcare information security in a particular healthcare organisation should also be an integral part of the e-Healthcare development. Posthumus (Posthumus, 2004) has described the use of the Code of Practice for Information Security Management in ISO/IEC 17799.

The interoperability and information sharing between healthcare providers would require a distributed Peer-to-Peer (P2P) based framework that enables health operators of different hospitals to share and aggregate clinical information about patients Mario (Mario et al., 2008), mapped EHRs into a simple XML-based meta-EHR, a lightweight data structure that defined relevant and aggregate information extractions from the different EPRs adopted by each hospital. The sharing and interoperability are achieved by allowing hospital operators to formulate queries against meta-EPR schema and queries are distributed to the hospitals hosting meta-EPR instances using P2P infrastructure. The ARTEMIS project (Boniface and Wilken, 2005) is a good example of a semantic web service based P2P interoperability infrastructure for healthcare information systems. In ARTEMIS, healthcare providers define semantically annotated security and privacy policies for web services based on organisational requirements. The ARTEMIS mediator uses these semantic web service descriptions between organisational policies by reasoning over security and clinical concept ontologies. The strict legislative framework in which the systems deployed is based on interoperability of security and privacy mechanisms, which is an important requirement in supporting communication of electronic healthcare records across organisation boundaries. There is a growing recognition that socio-economic and cultural aspects of e-Healthcare must be evaluated and incorporated into e-Healthcare information management frameworks and approaches (Hildebrand et al., 2006). Therefore, particular attention must be paid to the emerging technologies. For example, health smartcards, biometrics, radio-frequency identification (RFID) and Near field communication (NFC) tags. Providing information and expert advice on standardisation and best practices will raise the acceptance on standardisation. Ethical and accessibility issues connected to identity management in e-Health must be investigated. It should be noted that ethics and accessibility, together with privacy, are the most significant obstacles for the adoption of e-Health processes.

Furthermore, the Grid Computing is receiving attention in e-Healthcare information management. The GEMSS Grid middle-ware project (Benkner et al., 2005) involved the creation of medical Grid service prototypes and secure service-oriented infrastructure for distributed on-demand supercomputing. Key aspects of the GEMSS Grid middle-ware include negotiable QoS support for time-critical service provision, flexible support for business models, and security at all levels in order to ensure privacy of patient data as well as compliance with the EU legislation.

Grant (Grant et al., 2006) describes the conceptual framework, design, implementation, and analysis plan for a diabetes patient web-portal linked directly to the EHR of a large academic medical center. The framework led to the design and implementation of Diabetes Patient portal that allows direct interaction with the EHR. Ultimate goal was to assess the impact of the resulting advanced informatics tool for collaborative diabetes care in a clinic-randomised controlled trial among 14 primary care practices within the existing integrated health care system. The aim of their framework was to address two key barriers to patient's care. These barriers are lack of patient engagement with therapeutic care plans, and the lack of medication adjustment by physicians ("clinical inertia") during clinical encounters. It was noted that these barriers may be amendable to informatics-based interventions.

Generally speaking, there is a lack of a comprehensive framework for evaluating the security engineering practices for e-Healthcare systems. The current trend that is characterised by the drive from institution-centred to patient-centred e-Healthcare information management introduces additional security and privacy concerns. The patient-centred e-Healthcare systems requires that information security and privacy should be assured not only by technologies and infrastructure but also by processes. Huang (Huang et al., 2008) developed a mapping from the Systems Security Engineering Capability Maturity Model (SSE-CMM) to process the patient-centred healthcare domain. The SSE-CMM established set of metrics to assess security risks based on the mapping.

To support clinical or medical research, e-Healthcare information access needs to establish methodologies and technical infrastructure for the next generation of integrated clinical and medical science research. In the CLEF approach (Kalra et al., 2005) robust mechanisms and policies were developed to ensure that patient privacy and confidentiality are preserved while delivering medically rich information for the purposes of scientific research. Scott (Scott et al., 2004) considered access and authorisation issues in an overall policy context within Canadian initiatives for a national guidelines for tele-health (National Initiative for Tele-health (NIFTE) Guidelines) framework; a unique tool that provides persistent protection of data (The Policy and Peer Permission (PPP) project); a pan-Canadian electronic health record solution ('Infoway'); and a tool with which to identify and describe the inter-relationships of e-Health issues amongst policy levels, themes, and actors (Glocal e-Health Policy). Such holistic considerations and security frameworks could help to minimise the cross boundaries issues in e-Health.

1.8 Issues in e-Healthcare Information Security

The emerging e-Health development and investment in national and organizational strategic visions and plans worldwide will no doubt pose a threat that will derail the plans for e-Healthcare information security. The identification of the key issues in e-Healthcare information security, privacy and confidentiality is crucial to the success of e-Healthcare (see Figure 1.4 for further details)

The misleading and controversial concepts that exist within the domain of computer security and the cross-fertilisation between this domain and other domains such as healthcare, law and organisational policy. This is an issue that is compounded within e-Healthcare environment as these concepts take on extra domain- and technology-specific connotations. Inter-disciplinary standardisation efforts that take a holistic approach could help in reducing this problem.

On a serious note, the issues of sharing and interoperability have continued to dominate e-Healthcare information management. From the legal perspective, this issue arises where one jurisdiction imposes the condition that healthcare information can only be transmitted to jurisdictions that have same information protection laws. The Personal Information Protection and Electronic Documents Act (PIPEDA) in Canada was a response to the legal compatibility requirements imposed by the the EU Directive on Data Privacy. From the technological perspective, the need to improve care quality and patient treatment outcomes, harnessing decision-support systems (DSS), evidence-based clinical practice guideline and clinical workflows has necessitated the demand for integration and interoperability between e-Healthcare systems.

The e-Healthcare information is diverse and complex with a wide variety of uses from billing and insurance to employment across disparate geographic and political boundaries. The aspects of e-Healthcare information that have issues in e-Healthcare are the EHRs and EPHRs. The EHRs are variably referred to as e-Patient health/healthcare records (EPRs) and/or e-Medical records (EMRs). The EPHRs are an emerging concepts that have attracted big ICT businesses attention. A typical example is the Google Health service (see Footnote 1). The sensitivity, diversity and complexity of e-Healthcare information are key issues that pose major modelling, implementation and security engineering challenges.

The e-Healthcare environments have raised major challenges for both e-Healthcare information security and management. The Internet and ubiquitous computing, which incorporate wireless, sensor-enabled and location-aware technologies, add an extra dimension to both security and management challenges to e-Healthcare information. These developments stretch to the limits and challenges of federated and distributed database technologies.

The standardisation of e-Healthcare information structure, communication and security has become a determinant factor for the success of e-Healthcare. Closely associated with standardisation is the enactment and harmonisation of laws, policies and regulatory frameworks. However, it is not clear whether there is a deliberate and targeted effort to align standards to laws, policies and regulatory frameworks for e-Healthcare information protection and vice versa. An important issue

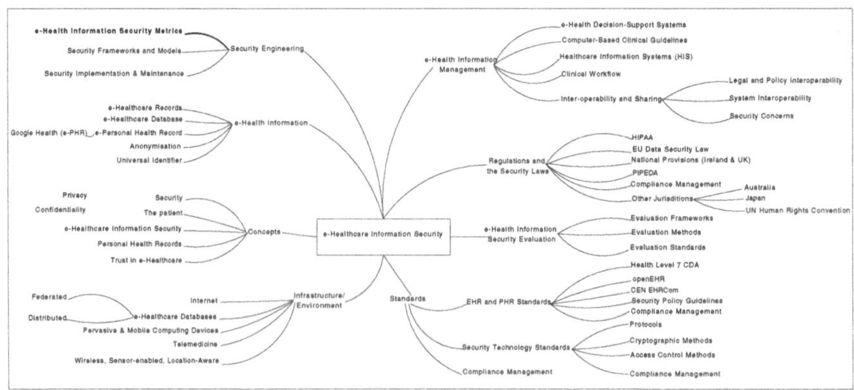

Figure 1.4 Major issues in e-Healthcare security

in e-Healthcare information security is the methods employed in the engineering of solutions for attaining implementations of privacy, confidentiality, measures and evaluation of information security safeguards. The investigation of the impacts of current methods in security engineering and evaluation would contribute to the success of e-Healthcare.

1.9 Summary

It has been noted that e-Healthcare information offers unique security, privacy and confidentiality challenges that require an examination of the mainstream concepts and approaches to information security. The issues of individual consent, privacy and confidentiality are the main factors for the adoption and successful utilisation of e-Healthcare information. The need for comprehensive incorporation of securing, privacy and confidentiality safeguards within e-Healthcare information management frameworks and approaches has been identified as one of the major trends. The e-Healthcare information security raises major challenges that demand a holistic approach spanning from legal, ethical, psychological, information and security domains. This chapter has focused on the major challenges in e-Healthcare information security, while the subsequent chapters will explore the societal impacts.

References

Karen M Albert. Integrating knowledge-based resources into the electronic health record: history, current status, and role of librarians. *Medical Reference Services Quarterly*, 26:1–19, 2007. ISSN 0276-3869. doi: 17915628. PMID: 17915628.

DB Baker and DR Masys. Pcasso: a design for secure communication of personal health information via the internet. *Int J Med Inform.*, 54(2):97–104, May 1999. URL http://www.ncbi.nlm.nih.gov/pubmed/10219949.

S Benkner, G Berti, G Engelbrecht, J Fingberg, G Kohring, S E Middleton, and R Schmidt. Gemss: grid-infrastructure for medical service provision. *Methods of Information in Medicine*, 44(2):177–81, 2005. ISSN 0026-1270. doi: 05020177. PMID: 15924170.

Mike Boniface and Paul Wilken. Artemis: towards a secure interoperability infrastructure for healthcare information systems. *Studies in Health Technology and Informatics*, 112:181–9, 2005. ISSN 0926-9630. doi: 15923727. PMID: 15923727.

Canada-Health-Research. Canada institute of health research, the future of public health in canada: Developing a public health system for the 21st century, june 2003, www.cihr-irsc.gc.ca/e/19573.html (access date 1 may, 2010), 2003.

Persephone Doupi and Johan van der Lei. Design and implementation considerations for a personalized patient education system in burn care. *International journal of medical informatics*, 74(2-4):151–7, March 2005. ISSN 13865056. PMID: 15694620.

eHealth-in Canada. e-health in canada, developing tomorrow's workforce today, current and future challenges, information and communications technology council, april 2009, 2009.

Richard W Grant, Jonathan S Wald, Eric G Poon, Jeffrey L Schnipper, Tejal K Gandhi, Lynn A Volk, and Blackford Middleton. Design and implementation of a web-based patient portal linked to an ambulatory care electronic health record: patient gateway for diabetes collaborative care. *Diabetes Technology & Therapeutics*, 8:576–86, October 2006. ISSN 1520-9156. doi: 10.1089/dia.2006.8.576. PMID: 17037972.

Jane Grimson. Delivering the electronic healthcare record for the 21st century. *International Journal of Medical Informatics 64 (2001) 111127*, 64:111–127, 2001.

Claudia Hildebrand, Peter Pharow, Rolf Engelbrecht, Bernd Blobel, Mario Savastano, and Asbjorn Hovsto. Biohealth–the need for security and identity management standards in ehealth. *Studies in Health Technology and Informatics*, 121: 327–36, 2006. ISSN 0926-9630. doi: 17095831. PMID: 17095831.

C. Derrick Huang, Qing Hu, and Ravi S. Behara. An economic analysis of the optimal information security investment in the case of a risk-averse firm. *International Journal of Production Economics*, 114(2): 793 – 804, 2008. ISSN 0925-5273. doi: DOI:10.1016/j.ijpe.2008.04.002. URL http://www.sciencedirect.com/science/article/B6VF8-4S98TWG-1/2/eef287240dcb9a1df7586d333781c21f. Special Section on Logistics Management in Fashion Retail Supply Chains.

D Kalra, P Singleton, J Milan, J Mackay, D Detmer, A Rector, and D Ingram. Security and confidentiality approach for the clinical e-science framework (clef). *Methods of Information in Medicine*, 44(2):193–7, 2005. ISSN 0026-1270. doi: 05020193. PMID: 15924174.

Deborah Beranek Lafky and Thomas A. Horan. Prospective personal health record use among different user groups: Results of a multi-wave study. *hicss*, 0:233, 2008. ISSN 1530-1605. doi: http://doi.ieeecomputersociety.org/10.1109/HICSS.2008.363.

M. Lalonde. A new perspective on the health of canadians, ottawa, health and welfare canada, 1974.

Peter Lennon. *Protecting Personal Health Information in Ireland: Law & Practice*. Oak Tree Press, 2005.

Kenneth D Mandl, William W Simons, William C R Crawford, and Jonathan M Abbett. Indivo: a personally controlled health record for health information exchange and communication. *BMC Medical Informatics and Decision Making*, 7: 25, 2007. ISSN 1472-6947. doi: 1472-6947-7-25. PMID: 17850667.

Mario, Domenico, Giuseppe, Paolo, and Pierangelo. Sigmcc: A system for sharing meta patient records in a peer-to-peer environment. *Future Generation Computer Systems*, 24:222–234, March 2008. doi: 10.1016/j.future.2007.06.006. URL http://www.sciencedirect.com/science.

Pew-Internet-Project. Pew internet and american life project, january 2009, www.pewinternet.org/pdfs/pip_generations_2009.pdf (access date 13 april, 2010), 2009.

Luuc Posthumus. Use of the iso/iec 17799 framework in healthcare information security management. *Studies in Health Technology and Informatics*, 103:447–52, 2004. ISSN 0926-9630. doi: 15747954. PMID: 15747954.

Pradeep Ray and Jaminda Wimalasiri. The need for technical solutions for maintaining the privacy of ehr. *Conference Proceedings: ... Annual International Conference of the IEEE Engineering in Medicine and Biology Society. IEEE Engineering in Medicine and Biology Society. Conference*, 1:4686–9, 2006. ISSN 1557-170X. doi: 10.1109/IEMBS.2006.260862. PMID: 17947109.

William H. Roach, Robert G.Hoban, Bernadette M. Broccolo, Andrew R. Roth, and Timothy P. Blanchard. *Medical Records and the Law*. Jones and Bartlett Publishers, 4th edition, 2006.

Richard E Scott, Penny Jennett, and Maryann Yeo. Access and authorisation in a glocal e-health policy context. *International Journal of Medical Informatics*, 73 (3):259–66, March 2004. ISSN 1386-5056. doi: 15066556. PMID: 15066556.

Amnon Shabo. The implications of electronic health record for personalized medicine. *Biomedical Papers of the Medical Faculty of the University Palack?, Olomouc, Czechoslovakia*, 149:suppl 251–8, December 2005. ISSN 1213-8118. doi: 16601821. PMID: 16601821.

Alan F. Westin. New issues of computer privacy in the eighties. In *IFIP Congress*, pages 733–739, 1983.

Zittrain and B. Edelman. Internet filtering in china. *Internet Computing, IEEE*, 1 (2):70 – 77, March-April 2003 2003.

Chapter 2
Securing e-Healthcare Information

2.1 Introduction

Securing personal e-Healthcare information aims mainly at protecting the privacy and confidentiality of the individual who receives healthcare services that are delivered through e-Health. Advances in security technologies have so far not eliminated the challenge posed by the need to secure e-Healthcare information. The rate of privacy and confidentiality breaches continue to increase unabated. These breaches pose challenges to all domains that converge on the task of securing information and building trust in e-Healthcare information management. Only a holistic approach that positions itself at the point of convergence of the domains of law, organisational policy, professional ethics and IT security could offer the promise to mitigate, if not eliminate, the major challenges to securing e-Healthcare information.

As efforts to digitize information are swiping across nearly all walks of life, healthcare providers are faced with a problem of protecting patients' privacy. While this is not a new problem, it is more difficult to protect patients' privacy in e-Healthcare due to sensitive and complex nature of the information to be protected and the increasingly sophisticated environment in which the protection is to operate. The e-Healthcare information management is a domain in which pro-actively securing and safeguarding the privacy of individual healthcare information is of fundamental importance. Several techniques have been devised to protect data such as encryption, digital signatures and anonymisation. By using these techniques healthcare providers become more competitive, trustworthy and increase use of e-Healthcare information systems. Healthcare service organisations that maintain e-Healthcare information systems are entrusted with the responsibility and duty to manage personal health information held in these systems. Thus, securing e-Healthcare information is a growing and on-going concern.

This chapter explores the main challenges in securing e-Healthcare information and the nature and theory of secure e-Healthcare information. These challenges and theoretical aspects of e-Healthcare are summarised in Figure 2.1. The ways in which technological frameworks are challenged in their efforts to secure e-Healthcare information is investigated. The chapter reviews the methods in the engineering of secure e-Healthcare information systems. The chapter concludes that only a holistic approach that positions itself at the point of convergence of the domains of law, organisational policy, professional ethics, and IT security could offer the promise to mitigate if not eliminate the major challenges to securing e-Healthcare information.

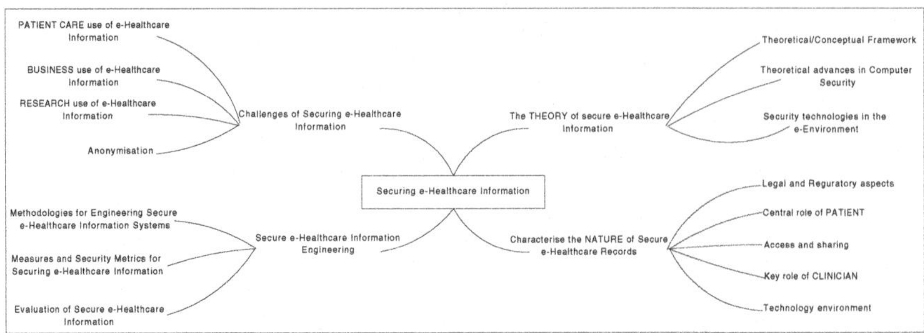

Figure 2.1 Major issues in Securing e-Healthcare Information

2.2 Breaches of Privacy and Confidentiality in e-Healthcare

The ever-growing catalogue of personal privacy and confidentiality breaches is posing major challenges as more and more healthcare organisations embrace e-Healthcare and computerise their healthcare information management processes. Some of these breaches are accidental, while others are the result of ethically questionable actions undertaken by business organisations, or a general laxity in securing sensitive e-Healthcare information that is controlled by the organisation. The data security includes both confidentiality and integrity. The confidentiality is required to keep sensitive information from being disclosed to unauthorised individuals, while integrity can be explained as having the data in the information system totally accurate and consistent. Privacy and confidentiality are two terms that have been considered synonymous and used interchangeably within the healthcare community.

2.2.1 Accidental Privacy and Confidentiality Breaches

In the case of Kaiser Permanente medical, some e-mails went astray (Brubaker, 2000) causing breach of confidentiality and integrity to personally identified health information that contains the appointment details, answers to patients' questions, medical advice for over 800 Kaiser Permanente (KP) members through KP Online, a web-enabled e-Health care portal. Beginning on 2 Aug 2000, Kaiser Permanente accidentally sent 858 e-mail messages from nurses and pharmacists (some including sensitive medical information) to the wrong people (Brubaker, 2000). The blame was placed on "human error" and a "technological glitch" in upgrading their Web site. However, in a study of this incident, Collmann and Cooper concluded that reasons at multiple levels account for the breach, including the architecture of the information system, the motivations of individual staff members, and differences among the subcultures of individual groups within as well as technical and social relations across the Kaiser IT program (Collmann and Cooper, 2007). They noted that none of these reasons could be strictly classified as security breaches. Their study led them to suggest that, to protect sensitive e-Healthcare information, health care organizations should put in place safe organizational contexts for complex e-Healthcare information systems. This is to be done in addition to complying not only with effective e-Healthcare information security practice, but also with laws and regulations such as the Health Insurance Portability and Accountability Act (HIPAA) 1996.

A Privacy breach incident reported by MSNBC on 19 January 2000 involved the GlobalHealthtrax web-based e-Healthcare information system. GlobalHealthtrax sell health products on-line. They inadvertently revealed customer names, home phone numbers, bank account, and credit card information of thousands of customers on their Web site (Bayardo and Srikant, 2003).

2.2.2 *Ethically Questionable Conduct*

Companies and organizations within the healthcare sector, that control e-Healthcare information databases, have been seen to make ethically questionable business decisions. For instance, pharmaceutical companies and medical doctors allow prescription data to be collected by data mining companies who then mine it and sell details of the information discovered (Cook, 2007).

CVS and Giant Food, chain drug stores in the US, made available patient prescription records for use by a direct mail and pharmaceutical company. In their investigation of such secondary use of patient prescription records, Lo and Alper (Lo and Alpers, 2000) noted that the use of personal health information in medication or drug benefits management is particularly important because of increasing pressure to control rising drug costs. However, the problem arises when such secondary uses of personal health information lead to the users seeking to derive financial benefit from selling access to the third parties. The resulting conflict of interest cast concerns on the non-primary usage motive for the collection of the information.

2.2.3 Breaches Due to Illegal Actions

In February 2008, the Irish Blood Transfusion Board (IBTS) experienced the theft, after a mugging of a laptop in New York that contained the data on over 170 000 Irish people who had used the services of the Irish Blood Transfusion Board between July and October of 2007 (Ryan et al., 2008). This is a typical example of the potential dangers of offshore outsourcing within the context of e-Healthcare and globalisation. The data were sent to a US software development company based in New York as part of an offshore outsourcing agreement on software upgrade of the IBTS systems (O'Regan, 2008). The data were sent by disc and encrypted with 256 AES encryption.

2.2.4 Laxity in Security for Sensitive e-Healthcare Information

Privacy breaches can occur as a result of incidents arising from laxity in securing sensitive e-Healthcare information. For example, in October 2007,the UK's NHS, a government agency, lost personal e-Healthcare information on all the nation's children and their families (BBC, 2007). Child benefit data were sent to the National Audit Office (NAO) by a junior official at Her Majesty's Revenue and Customs (HMRC). The data were sent by using the courier company TNT, which operates the HMRC's post system. The package contained two CDs, with details of 25 million individuals, was neither recorded nor registered, and failed to arrive. In another example of laxity in securing e-Healthcare information, a researcher at the Carnegie Mellon University retrieved health record of 69% voters in Cambridge, Massachusetts from an anonymous healthcare database. These breaches are a huge challenge to all domains that converge on the task of managing e-Healthcare information which include the law, organizational policies, professional ethics and IT security.

2.3 The IT Security Challenge for Securing e-Healthcare Information

The IT security focuses mainly on the protection of security and integrity of information and the prevention of information theft. Thus, systematic attempts are made and appropriate technical safeguards are mounted to prevent data loss anyhow and unauthorised individuals from inappropriately obtaining information in general without regard to domain-specific nuances. The major IT security challenges lies in the following areas:

1. authentication and authorisation;
2. security certification;

3. data security focusing on cryptography and;
4. integrity and non-repudiation.

The advances in computer storage, networking and information processing technologies have enabled increasingly massive collections of electronic data. Ability to communicate and process such data at high speed and access it remotely is a cause for security, privacy and confidentiality concerns. These concerns are further complicated by the existence of methods and technologies of analysing such data. In particular, data mining promises to efficiently discover valuable information and knowledge from massive electronic information sources. Thus, data mining is particularly vulnerable to misuse in breaching security, privacy and confidentiality.

The desire for the protection of the ownership and privacy of individual e-Healthcare information without impeding information flow during healthcare service delivery points to a challenge for the database community to design information systems that offer adequate protection (Agrawal et al., 2003).

The e-Healthcare distributed environment takes the issue of access control well beyond geographical locations. The shared care paradigm brings in many players and roles along an extended geographical dimension with the context of patient care. This complicates access control and creates risks of violations.

Presently, consensus has been reached that the patient owns personal e-Healthcare information. The existing irony is that the patient has no access control over personal e-Healthcare information held in the systems.

2.4 The Privacy and Confidentiality Challenge

The privacy challenges that are involved provide individuals with the ability to control how their e-Healthcare information should be managed and used by clinicians as well as other users in domains other than healthcare. Privacy is usually protected by the law, which imposes a duty on designated entities and systems to ensure that individuals are able to exercise their privacy rights. Privacy and confidentiality within the healthcare community are so closely related that the two have come to be considered as one and the same and are sometimes used interchangeably. Thus, Anderson observed that other authors view confidentiality as protecting the interest of the organisation and privacy as protecting the autonomy of the individual while privacy and confidentiality means the same in common medical usage (Anderson and Cardell, 2008).

Although e-Healthcare confidentiality governs the disclosure of personal healthcare information, but privacy grants a right to control disclosure to the individual patient while confidentiality imposes a duty on healthcare providers not to disclose the information and to ensure that individual patient exercise their privacy rights in controlling circumstances where they will allow disclosure by healthcare providers to happen. Thus, it would seem, from this distinction of the two terms, that while privacy is an individual's right, confidentiality is an obligation on trusted professionals and organisations to protect privacy and the exercise of the rights, it grants to the individual.

The major challenges arise from the fact that, on one hand, in practice, the individual is generally not in a strong position to control disclosure of personal e-Healthcare information, while, on the other hand, confidentiality within e-Healthcare is at risk under a multiplicity of threats occasioned by technological advances and organizational factors. The area of prescription data collection, processing and mining provides a typical example of a domain where, in practice, the patient currently is in a weak position to control the disclosure of their prescription-related information (Cook, 2007). This will remain so until certain conditions and developments occur within the e-Healthcare information management domain. One such major development is the wide adoption of the electronic personal health record (EPHR) by the individual, who will have full control. This will need to be accompanied by official recognition of EPHRs for use during daily patient care practice. Another major development would be the emergence of wholistic and comprehensive frameworks and their implementations for securing e-Healthcare information in a way that takes into account the information protection laws, security and healthcare record standards, appropriate computer security methods and technologies

The rapid evolution of e-Healthcare has a huge impact on the protection of patient information. Furthermore, the e-Healthcare environment has the capacity to facilitate rapid, massive, and potentially undetected breaches of patient privacy and confidentiality. Juxtaposing these potentialilties of e-Healthcare with the public concerns about privacy and confidentiality has led to the recognition by professional and state bodies that the protection of information given to healthcare providers is a fundamental ethical obligation to all healthcare professions.

The fact that the patient gives the information to healthcare providers in confidence and out of necessity is a key factor that adds ethical and moral dimensions to the information management activities of those in control of personal health information. Protecting the privacy of patients' identifiable health information is a significant issue for the success of e-Healthcare and realisation of its promises.

The patients disclose information to healthcare providers out of necessity to obtain treatment and improve their health. This information is given in-confidence. The patients' understanding is that the primary purpose for the disclosure, collection and storage of personal healthcare information is for their current and future medical care. When such personal healthcare information is used for other purposes that have nothing to do with their healthcare, it becomes a matter of serious privacy and confidentiality concern. The Government has invoked the common good to justify secondary uses of personal e-Healthcare information in endeavours that aimed at benefiting society as a whole. However, it is questionable whether profit motives in the secondary uses of personal e-Healthcare information is justifiable or not.

At a national level, personal healthcare information is important for use in computing vital statistics that are needed in planning and resource allocation. Furthermore,the national control of infectious and epidemic diseases largely involve close scrutiny and disclosure of personal healthcare information outside the patient care domain. The legal protection of personal privacy and confidentiality is of crucial significance to the advancement of democracy at a national level. However, this is in direct conflict with the national requirements outlined above.

2.5 Utilisation Challenges

The multi-purpose use of e-Healthcare information has given rise to chronic challenges for securing e-Healthcare information. The e-Healthcare information is personal and its primary purpose is to aid in decision-making of clinical care of an identified individual. Thus, for primary use purposes, the correct and accurate identification of individual subject of healthcare information is of fundamental importance. Furthermore, the individual and the information benefit privacy and confidentiality protection from both medical professional ethics and the law. Other uses of e-Healthcare information are referred to as secondary uses. The veil of protection essentially precludes secondary purposes or uses of personal health information, which help in the management of diseases outbreaks.

The secondary uses of healthcare information can be viewed as a trade-off between individual privacy and society's necessity to reduce healthcare costs and improve quality and efficiency of the healthcare service. It is necessary to use the EHRs in clinical or epidemiological research, assessment of care quality and healthcare service planning and management. Therefore, the secondary uses of e-Healthcare information have led to enhance patients' benefits through a well-managed healthcare service.

Any secondary use of e-Healthcare information, whether it does or does not bring benefits to the individual or the public, e.g., the use of information to deny employment or health insurance, gives rise to privacy and confidentiality concerns as well as legal and ethical considerations. Ethical considerations are managed through the various healthcare professions. Legal considerations are managed through information protection laws such as HIPAA 1996 in the US; and Directive 95/46/EC, Article 29 Working Party and Article 8 ECHR within the EU. Thus, secondary use of e-Healthcare information requires informed consent and complete removal of personal identifiable information (PII) of the individual who is the subject of such information. The removal of PII is a key challenge for e-Healthcare that is being addressed by anonymisation and pseudonymisation of e-Healthcare information (section 2.11).

Lo and Alper (Lo and Alpers, 2000) identified the specific confidentiality challenges from business-oriented secondary use of e-Healthcare information to include the issues of whether the goal of benefiting patients will be achieved and whether the means are appropriate. They recognised that the means may be problematic because of financial conflicts of interest, lack of patient authorization, inappropriate access to information by third parties, and inadequate safeguards for confidentiality. Lo and Alper made a call for policies to be put in place in order to protect confidentiality while allowing appropriate use of personal e-Health information in drug benefit management. They characterised sound policies to be those that include clear evidence of benefit to patients, an oversight committee, patient authorization, disclosure or prohibition of conflicts of interest, additional safeguards for sensitive medical conditions, strong confidentiality protections, and restrictions on advertising (Lo and Alpers, 2000).

2.6 Legal Protection Challenges

The challenges that occur at the boundary of the law and utilisation of e-Healthcare information for research purposes is the conflict between technical security on one hand and consent on the other hand. Technical security of healthcare information may receive undue priority over consent in the e-Healthcare information collection. Arnason (Arnason, 2004) decries that where the issue of consent enjoys priority, it has often appeared in confidential form, i.e., the demand for informed consent before participation in research. This has led Arnason (Arnason, 2004) to propose an alternative replacement for consent or presumed consent, which requires written authorisation based on general information to be used in research.

The challenges in the legal protection of e-Healthcare information relate to the enforcement and mandate of data protection agencies. In many countries the data protection is very weak. Therefore, incentive for industries and public bodies to incorporate privacy principles into their IT systems and services should be encouraged (EPTA, 2006).

2.7 The Nature of Secure e-Healthcare Information

The nature of secure e-Healthcare information is characterised in terms of security, privacy and confidentiality requirements from the domain of healthcare as well as the legal protections. The principles for personal information held in a database that proclaim to be Hippocratic (Agrawal et al., 2002) clearly express one proposal for the key elements of the secure management of e-Healthcare information. An attractive feature of these principles is their derivation from the law, guidelines and policy for the healthcare domain. An implementation of these principles as proposed for Hippocratic databases represents a convergence of law and technology for securing e-Healthcare information.

The ten principles were presented by Agrawal (Agrawal et al., 2002) and can be expressed within the context of e-Healthcare information management as follows:

1. The purpose for which an individual's e-Healthcare information has been collected shall be associated with that information (purpose specification);
2. The purposes associated with personal e-Healthcare information shall have the consent of the donor of the information (consent);
3. The e-Healthcare information collected shall be limited to the minimum necessary for accomplishing the specified purpose (limited collection);

4. The e-Healthcare information shall be subjected to only those queries that are consistent with the purpose for which the information has been collected (limited use);
5. The e-Healthcare information shall not be communicated outside the database for purposes other than those for which there is consent from the donor/owner of the information (limited disclosure);
6. The e-Healthcare information shall be retained only as long as necessary for the fulfillment of the purpose for which it has been collected (limited retention);
7. The e-Healthcare information about an individual shall be accurate and up-to-date (accuracy);
8. Personal e-Healthcare information shall be protected by security safeguards against theft and other forms of appropriation (safety);
9. An individual or a patient shall be able to access all e-Healthcare information about himself or herself (openness); and
10. The donor/owner of e-Healthcare information shall be able to verify compliance with these principles. Similarly, an e-Healthcare information system shall be able to address a challenge concerning compliance.

The modern adoption of the shared care paradigm in healthcare necessitates the need to share e-Healthcare information. The technical solution to supporting sharing e-Healthcare information is the interoperability between e-Healthcare information systems. It has been suggested that information exchange, supported by computable interoperability, is the key to many of the initiatives in e-Healthcare (Orlova et al., 2005). The openEHR community has recognised two forms of interoperability: syntactic interoperability and semantic interpretability. It has been suggested that semantic interoperability is a key requirement to enable the EHRs operations. The openEHR Foundation's archetype approach enables syntactic interoperability and semantic interpretability (Garde S, 2007).

The legal framework of e-Healthcare operations is increasingly becoming insecure, interoperability in e-Healthcare needs to be extended to accommodate security and privacy mechanisms (Boniface and Wilken, 2005). The interoperability of security and privacy mechanisms in e-Healthcare systems ensures legal compliance. It is also an important requirement for supporting secure communication of electronic healthcare records across local, national and international boundaries. The on-line data protection awareness and the coordinated application of privacy legislation become even more critical when referring to medical environments and thus to the protection of patients' privacy and medical data (Gritzalis, 2004). The legal protections of electronic health records involves the challenging issues of consent and security (Ries and Moysa, 2005). Consent and protections to privacy and confidentiality are usually in conflict with each other (Arnason, 2004). Raising awareness and providing guidance to on-line data protection as well as applying privacy-related legislation in a coherent and coordinated way are crucial issues to e-Healthcare. Early integration of privacy protection services into the e-Healthcare based on grid technologies, e.g., HealthGrid, has been noted to bring a synergy that is beneficial for the development and technologies themselves (Claerhout and Moor, 2005). In the light of the recent Italian Consolidation Act (2004) on privacy, *sensitive data* are considered different from *health data* (Conti, 2006). However, the Italian Act respects the rights that the fundamental freedom and the dignity of a person associated with health data should be regulated and controlled.

The data controllers collect, process and use personal health data owned by individuals. Hence, data controllers should recognise both moral and legal obligations to protect e-Healthcare information, such as birth defects (Mai et al., 2007) data, by employing numerous safeguards. Birth defects surveillance systems address the needs of the community and they are aimed at preventing birth defects or alleviating the burdens associated with them. In Australia and the USA, it has been noted that the use of state and federal public health and legal mandates against population-based surveillance can severely limit the ability of public health agencies to accurately access the health status of a group within a defined geographical area (Mai et al., 2007). Thus, protective safeguards on e-Healthcare information may be in conflict and need to be balanced with the common good, which Baeumen (den Bumen T., 2007) suggests should be based on medical criteria.

Yang (Yang et al., 2006) examines what constitutes an effective legal framework in protecting both the security and privacy of e-Health information. Their contribution was exemplified by the Health Insurance Portability and Accountability Act (HIPAA) 1996 of the U.S. However, the boundary issue in computerized health information needs further attention.

The collection and use of genetic data is a sensitive matter and the increasing incorporation of patient-specific genomic data into clinical practice and research, raises serious privacy concerns (den Bumen T., 2007) and (Malin and Sweeney, 2004). Therefore, the implications of genetic data are multi-faceted having relevance to different types of genetic diseases and to its multi-personal nature, since one person's genetic data also holds information about other people. Data protection is widely seen as the tool to address the latter issues. Baeumen (den Bumen T., 2007) states that the balance between the information needs of society and the right to privacy requires a *medically driven criteria* based on the concept of an *indication* as the balancing tool, which is equivalent *data protection.* Many system proposals have been made to protect privacy of genomic data by pseudonymisation, which involves the removal and encryption of explicitly identifying personal information, such as name or social security number (Malin and Sweeney, 2004).

2.8 The Principles for Securing e-Healthcare Information

The main concepts for e-Healthcare information security are reviewed. The objective is to formalise the theory of security, privacy, trust and confidentiality from the point of view of applications in e-Healthcare Information Management. A more formal and clear distinction is drawn among the key concepts of security, privacy, confidentiality and trust. The security challenges posed by the presence or absence of individual Unique Identifier in e-Healthcare information management is investigated as part of the theory. Privacy is the right to freely control the disclosure of personal e-Healthcare information (Rindfleisch, 1997) in a democratic society. The right to privacy protects the autonomy of the individual with respect to controlling access to personal e-Healthcare information.

The key fields, that affect privacy, are security, access to information and services, societal interaction, convenience and economic benefit (EPTA, 2006). These fields are evolving and hence subject to rapid change.

Since the Internet lies at the core of e-Healthcare, IT security is now recognised to be of key significance in e-Healthcare, although the fight for the protection of patient privacy and confidentiality would seem new in e-Healthcare information management. The security principles that are promulgated by the International Information Security Foundation are:

- *accountability principle* - information is not disclosed to unauthorised persons or processes;
- *awareness principle* - owners, providers and users of information systems should easily be able to gain knowledge of and information about the existence and extent of security measures, practices and procedures;
- *ethics principle* - the security of information should be provided in such a way that respects the rights and legitimate interest of others;
- *multi-disciplinary principle* - security measures, practices and procedures should consider and address all issues and viewpoints including technical, administrative, organisational, operational, commercial, educational and legal aspects;
- *proportionality principle* - the overall investment and resource allocation to security should be proportionate and appropriate to the value and degree of reliance on the IT system and to severity, probability and extent of potential harm envisaged;
- *integration principle* - security measures should be coordinated and integrated with each other as well as with other organisational measures on other areas so as to create a coherent security system;
- *timeliness principle* - all parties at all levels should act in a timely manner in preventing and responding to security breaches;
- *re-assessment principle* - security risk assessments should be carried out periodically as security requirements vary with time;
- *equity principle* - security of IT systems should be compatible with legal use and flow of data and information in a democracy.

Without doubt, the challenges facing e-Healthcare include the following threats: viruses, Trojans, worms causing denial-of-service attacks, impersonation, information theft, insiders privileged access to network operations and a grudge against their employer. IT security is never absolute and measures can only be mitigatory. These measures include policies, procedures and employment of technology as well as performing information risk assessments and can be classified into administrative, physical and technical with legal (e.g., HIPAA 1996 and EU Directives) and standards compliance falling into administrative measures. The main aspects that should be covered by IT security within e-Healthcare are based on the following generic factors:

1. authentication, authorisation and
2. security certification;
3. data security focusing on cryptography and;
4. integrity and non-repudiation.

Secure databases could play a key role in realising secure e-Healthcare information. The same could be said for the use of e-privacy policies to formally specify a healthcare organisation's e-Healthcare information management practices using XML-based policy definition language such as P3P (platform for privacy policy preferences) and EPAL (enterprise privacy authorisation language). The e-privacy policies could also formally specify an individual's privacy and confidentiality preferences. The alignment of privacy laws and organisational privacy policies to individual privacy concerns could be addressed by matching an organisation's privacy policy with individual's privacy preferences for healthcare information access and use. Since most e-Healthcare information is held in databases, an interesting technological intervention is required that will enable database queries to automatically be modified, through query re-writing, that will conform to combined privacy scheme based on both privacy policy and user's privacy preferences.

Generally speaking, e-Healthcare is not possible without distributed computing systems, because *shared Care* is the core paradigm for e-Healthcare. At the centre of the shared care paradigm is a model of patient care that envisages a healthcare service that is delivered by different clinicians, organisations, times and locations, using appropriate methods and tools that allow patient mobility. The e-Healthcare records form the informational foundation of communication and cooperation while a distributed computing infrastructure forms the technological foundation for such a complex shared care paradigm. Security within the distributed computing infrastructure for e-Healthcare is complex, as it extends beyond both physical and conceptual domains in healthcare. It is further complicated by the sensitivity of personal e-Healthcare information and must provide strong mutual authentication and accountability between communicating entities. While applications security is the second arm of distributed system security, it must provide services for accountability, authorisation and access control for information and functions.

2.9 Combining Security with Privacy and Confidentiality

The extended nature of security domain in e-Healthcare-supported shared care makes it impractical to grant authorisation for access to the EHRs on an individual basis. Privacy is the source of requirements, while IT security enables the realisation of these requirements. Therefore, there has to be a deliberate and targeted effort to ensure that patient privacy and confidentiality based on prevailing organisational policies and laws are implemented by means of IT security engineering. Confidentiality is enabled when IT security and privacy are combined. In other words, privacy and security is based on e-Healthcare management of confidentiality. Thus, it is possible for e-Healthcare information systems to offer elements of IT security without protecting patient privacy and confidentiality. It should be noted that privacy has been well established in the healthcare domain much longer than IT security.

Shoniregun (Shoniregun et al., 2004) has explored how to be effective in managing customer relationship and advocated trust-based approach to viewing eCRM. Their research work demonstrated the organisational value of eCRM and trust in eC within a multinational organisation and proposed the eC trust model, which incorporates people trust, technology trust and law and policy trust. These elements are also directly relevant as components of an e-Healthcare trust model. The question Shoniregun et al posed can be mapped into the e-Healthcare domain as: How can e-Healthcare information systems improve healthcare quality through information sharing and interoperability in a patient-centred managed care set-up while also securing higher level of patient trust on e-Healthcare information management?

The public assessment of trust tends to address the views of patient care at the grass-root level. Policy makers who are concerned with the erosion of public trust need to target aspects associated with patient-centred care and professional expertise (Calnan and Sanford, 2004), as these impact patient care quality. It has been noted that quality and trust are intertwined yet distinct concepts and their relation is not always straightforward (Lampe et al., 2003). Trust is generally a function of perceived quality, which in turn is a function of perceived professional expertise among other factors. Trust in physicians and medical institutions has been investigated in terms of what it is, whether is can be measured and whether it does matter (Hall et al., 2001). The significance of trust is also illustrated by efforts that explore the relationship between continuity, trust in regular doctors and patient satisfaction with consultations with family doctors (Baker et al., 2003). Thus, problems that are encountered in the ambulatory settings are found to be strongly related to lower trust (Keating et al., 2002). Also elements of trust in hospitals have been found to include vulnerability to financial loss as well as expectations of competence and, hence, patient care quality (Goold and Klipp, 2002). Trust is a basis for an alternative care quality-enhancing approach suggested by Davies et al (Davies and Lampel, 1998), which involves fostering greater trust in professionalism as a basis for quality enhancements instead of counter-productive mandatory publication of health outcomes. Therefore, Keating concluded that efforts to improve patients' experiences may promote more trusting relationships and greater continuity and should be a priority for physicians, educators, and health care organizations (Keating et al., 2002).

Study results have shown that more patients are looking for information online before talking with their physicians (Hesse et al., 2005). Despite newly available communication channels, the same studies reveal that physicians remained the most highly trusted information source to patients. The existing on-line communities and services have been found to fail to meet requirements upon which trust is established (Ebner et al., 2004). For instance, HealthConnect, an electronic health record system, was found to lack critical record-keeping functionality and that inadequate policy with regards to ownership, consent and privacy impacts on the business and systems architecture, and consequently its ability to deliver trustworthy records (Iacovino, 2004). Due to the sensitivity of personal medical data and psychological implications, e-Healthcare must be provided in a trustworthy environment (Blobel et al, 2001). The e-Healthcare communication and cooperation need to be based on established and sound engineering and technological paradigms with a strong emphasis on security, privacy and confidentiality. Typical examples of established and sound engineering and technological paradigms include object orientation, component and model-based architectures, secure socket layer (SSL) protocol and XML standards.

2.10 Identifiability in Securing e-Healthcare Information

In many countries, frustration has been expressed based on the difficulties encountered in coordinating multiple sources of e-Healthcare information in the absence of a unique personal identifier. The ability to breach individual privacy and confidentiality has caused major concerns especially when modern data analysis and mining techniques are used as tools for this purpose. The universal personal identifier (UPI), anonymisation and pseudonymisation are emerging concepts that impact the security of e-Healthcare information.

Unresolved problem in e-Healthcare is how the widely proposed standardize nationwide EHR system would uniquely identify and match a distributed composite of an individual's recorded healthcare information to an identified individual patient out of approximately 300 million people to a 1:1 match (Leonard, 2008). Integrating systems without a reliable unique personal identifier (UPI) in many countries (Grimson et al., 2000) and between health (person-based records) and social care (care-based records-e.g. child protection) has been singled out as one of the major challenges for using routinely collected primary care data in e-Healthcare and research (de Lusignan and van Weel, 2006). Arellano and Weber (Arellano and Weber, 1998) paint a particularly grim picture of this problem. The absence of a UPI has also been associated with problems of identifying potential participants for trial, access to records to confirm events, continued follow-up of patients during and after the trial, and secondary use of the trial data (Armitage et al, 2008).

The advantage of the UPI is to enable a model, whereby Electronic Health Records (EHRs) are stored on a remote central server. The EHRs can be accessed by doctors using a smart-card, which contains unique identifiers that facilitate secured, remote, transportable access by consulting physicians at the discretion of the patient (Dalley et al., 2006). The major disadvantage of the absence of the UPI is that patients' identities may not be reconcilable across institutions, and individuals with records held in different institutions will be falsely "counted" as multiple persons when databases are merged (Berman, 2004).

The major concern with UPIs is privacy and confidentiality risks. If the UPI gets into the hands of the third party, it will create a severe security risk. The possible solution for reducing the UPI security risks is the Master Patient Index (MPI) file (Freriks, 2000). Even though anonymisation and pseudonymisation are used to remove personally identifiable information, it is not enough to preserve the data confidentiality (Chiang et al., 2003).

The need for Universal Identifier in e-Healthcare is best illustrated by the French Personal Medical Record (PMR), which has raised many important questions regarding duplicates and the quality, precision and coherence of the linkage with other health data coming from different sources. The currently planned identifying process in the French ministry of Health raises questions with regards to its ability to deal with potential duplicates and to perform data linkage with other health data sources. Using the electronic health records, Quantin et al developed and proposed an identification process to improve the French PMR (Quantin et al., 2007).

2.11 Anonymisation and Pseudonymisation

The near complete removal of the PII from the EHRs is achieved either through anonymisation or pseudonymisation. These two concepts are introduced in this subsection. The problem and approaches to solutions for e-Healthcare information anonymization and pseudonymisation are discussed:

(a) Anonymisation

Anonymisation (which is also called sanitization or de-identification) is a result of the need to share or exchange information because of the business, standards or regulatory requirements. Anonymisation promotes information sharing and shared analysis among trusted or untrusted parties, while making sure that the probability of being able to make inference on personal identified information is low. The essence of anonymisation is to hide private information, promote sharing, analysis and foster trust from individuals whose data is being anonymised. The anonymised data is useful in a number of applications such as healthcare research, business marketing campaigns and information exchange between organisations in the same market segment or across multiple organisations. We are currently witnessing generation, collection, storage and shared analysis (in some cases we need restricted analysis) of a huge amount of data worldwide.

There are cases where information must be stored without allowing any modification (e.g. information on the taxes) in such a case data encryption and access policies are one of the ways to protect data. There are situations where information can be altered in order to protect the privacy of the data owners (e.g. medical data can be modified previous to their release, so that researchers are able to study the data without jeopardising the privacy of patients). The main challenge in the latter case is the problem on how data can be modified to minimise or prevent the possibility of information inference, thus guaranteeing the privacy of individuals. The anonymisation is used to remove or obfuscate any identifying information about a patient in a data set, making the re-identification or inference of an individual very difficult. In other words, the data should be shareable by adhering to privacy (what you cannot reveal?) and analysis (what you must reveal?) constraints. Data anonymisation can be applied to collection, retention and disclosure in a healthcare environment.

Data anonymisation is a long term problem. Therefore, before applying any of the techniques, a thorough threat analysis must be carried out. This is important, because what we want to protect today may not be what we may need to hide in the future. It is important to understand the trade-off of anonymisation and threat modelling not only from scientific and engineering point of view, but from society.

The need for sharing personal data play a crucial role in driving anonymisation efforts. Microsoft and Google both agreed to be part of the Networking Advertising Initiative that provides the data anonymisation. Customers in healthcare environment expect free, convenient and private way in which their vital e-Healthcare information is maintained. It is important to note that even when data is anonymised, there is always a possibility of being able to infer on personal information. Therefore, the optimal solution for anonymity is difficult (currently only heuristic solutions is possible). Some of the lingering questions in the area of anonymisation are: Is there any need to anonymise data that is stored? Do we just need secure storage using encryption? Are there any best practices in anonymisation? And is this just a research exercise?

(b) Pseudonymisation

We have noted that anonymisation removes PII of the individual from the EHRs mainly because the identity of the individual is not required for secondary use of the EHRs. However, situations exist where it may be required to re-create the link between the EHR and the individual to which the EHR belongs (Iacono, 2007). Such situations include handling follow-up data, individual's request to withdraw their information, further treatment of a patient in light of new discoveries and quality control. Maintaining privacy while allowing such re-identification of the individual is achieved through pseudonymisation. Neubauer and Riedl (Neubauer and Riedl, 2008) define the concept of pseudonymisation as:

> a technique where identification data is transformed into, and afterwards replaced by, a specifier, which cannot be associated with the identification data without knowing a certain secret.

The pseudonymisation allows re-identification of the individual associated with an EHR subject. This involves the identification and separation of personal data from other data in the EHRs. Riedl (Riedl et al., 2008) considers de-personalisation of EHRs as a process that precedes and is necessary for pseudonymisation. Iacono (Iacono, 2007) identifies two pseudonymisation schemes that are based on the ability to be reversible. The first is the one-way pseudonymisation scheme, which generate pseudonyms which are impossible to be used to re-identify the patients. This type of scheme requires the maintenance of a mapping database to store associations between pseudonyms and PII. The second is the reversible pseudonymisation scheme, which allows the patient to be re-identified through the use of cryptographic mechanisms applied to the pseudonyms. The latter does not require a mapping database.

There are a number of e-Healthcare information management instances where pseudonymisation has been applied to address the challenges of permitting secondary usage of information while ensuring patient privacy and confidentiality. Here we outline some key applications of pseudonymisation in emerging domains for e-Healthcare. Henrici (Henrici et al., 2006) proposed a pseudonymisation infrastructure in which they used one-way hash functions in addressing the demands of resource scarce tags. Their approach is better than approaches based on public key cryptography.

Clinical E-science Framework (CLEF) is an E-Science programme that aims to support integrated clinical and bioscience research (Kalra et al., 2005). CLEF applied pseudonymisation to a repository of histories of cancer patients so that the repository can be accessed for secondary use by researchers. The pseudonymisation was used in CLEF to preserve patients's privacy and confidentiality while delivering a repository of medically rich cancer information for the purposes of scientific research. For research purposes, especially clinical trials, patient is usually monitored during a long period of time. The disease progression and the diagnostic evolution represent extremely valuable information for researchers in clinical trials. Noumeir (Noumeir et al., 2007) set the objective of building a research database from de-identified clinical data while enabling the data set to be easily incremented by importing new pseudonymous data, acquired over a long period of time. They sought, through pseudonymisation, to enable the implementation of an imaging research database that can be incremented in time and propose a pseudonymisation scheme that closely follows Digital Imaging and Communication in Medicine (DICOM) standard recommendations. Noumir et al proposed the secondary usage of a radiology image electronic health record (EHR), while maintaining patient confidentiality using pseudonymisation.

Malin and Sweeney (Malin and Sweeney, 2004) state that anonymisation and pseudonymisation lack formal proofs and expose the erosion of privacy when genomic data, either pseudonymous or anonymous, are released into a distributed e-Healthcare environment. In their study, Malin and Sweeney applied several algorithms, which they collectively named RE-Identification of Data In Trails (REIDIT). The REIDIT algorithms linked genomic data to named individuals in publicly available records by leveraging unique features in patient-location visit patterns. Malin and Sweeney developed algorithmic proofs of re-identification and demonstrated the susceptibility to re-identification using real world data, which is used for testing privacy protection capabilities. Their work clearly illustrates further challenges, for anonymisation and pseudonymisation, which are important elements in data analysis, data mining and knowledge discovery techniques.

2.12 Technological Frameworks in Securing e-Healthcare Information

The revolutionalisation of healthcare through Information Technology (IT) is illustrated in most national government strategies for the healthcare sector (PITAC, 2004). A general consensus exists on the potential of harnessing information technology for e-Healthcare to reduce medical errors, lower costs, and improve patient care (Grimson, 2001). There is also a general recognition for the requirement for a technological framework for decommissioning manual, paper-based health records and their replacement with modern e-Healthcare information infrastructures (Agrawal and Johnson, 2007) and (Grimson, 2001). Securing e-Healthcare information within technological frameworks is an unresolved challenge.

The e-Healthcare phenomenon involves: 1) the move from paper records to electronic records; 2) changes of paradigms especially the move to patient-centric, shared and managed care paradigms as well as the introduction of strict legal information protection requirements; 3) the use of emerging and disruptive technologies; and 4) introduction of new procedures. Emerging technologies include health cards, biometrics, genomics, radio-frequency identification (RFID) and near-field communication (NFC) tags. The patient-centric healthcare paradigm involves heavy patient interaction with the e-Healthcare information system. There is a need for reliable, stable and secure e-Healthcare frameworks to comprehensively support these paradigm shifts, especially privacy protections, shared care and the extended patient mobility. The application of standardized solutions in this framework is a major challenge due to their unfamiliarity and lack of widespread adoption and implementation.

Securing e-Healthcare in a scenario of patient-centric healthcare paradigm can only be attained by paying attention to all of technologies, infrastructures and processes (Huang et al., 2008). Interoperability at both legal/policy and systems-levels is a significant challenge. Security, privacy and confidentiality are at the core of this scenario and have become prerequisite challenges for the acceptance and support of these new approaches and e-Healthcare.

The frameworks for supporting communication of e-Healthcare records across organisation boundaries within the shared care set-up must comply with strict legislative protection of e-Healthcare information. The interoperability of security and privacy mechanisms is an important requirement for such frameworks. Semantic web services are being used in peer-to-peer (P2P) interoperability infrastructures for e-Healthcare information systems. For instance, in the ARTEMIS project (Boniface and Wilken, 2005) healthcare providers define semantically annotated security and privacy policies for web services based on organisational requirements. These security and privacy policies are used by broker (application agent) between organisational policies and clinical concept ontologies.

Placing privacy and confidentiality at the core of the underlying computing technological solutions promises to offer substantial contributions to the challenge of securing e-Healthcare information. Most, if not all, EHR systems make use of database technologies. If database technologies were designed from the beginning to ensure privacy and confidentiality of the data stored in them, then the privacy and confidentiality challenges in e-Healthcare would be significantly reduced. The Hippocratic Database (HDB) (Agrawal et al., 2002) provides the technological framework and solutions for secure e-Health record maintenance, computer-assisted decision support and exchange of health information. HDBs claim to enable the secure management of e-Healthcare information and thus make the vision of revolutionizing health care through IT to be technically feasible (Agrawal and Johnson, 2007).

HDB technology is quite promising but it is yet to emerge, mature and be ready for use in e-Healthcare.

Technology developed in the European GEMSS project (Benkner et al., 2005) demonstrates that the Grid Computing can be used to provide medical practitioners and researchers with access to advanced simulation and image processing services for improved preoperative planning and near real-time surgical support. GEMSS uses standard Grid and Web technologies. The privacy risks of current Data Grid technologies are associated with the sharing of data in virtual organisations and the use of remote resources. These risks compromise widespread use of Data Grid technologies (Torres et al, 2006). However, the GEMSS Project claims to have managed these risks by combining negotiable QoS support for time-critical service provision, flexible support for business models, security and legal compliance at all levels (Benkner et al., 2005). Therefore, privacy of patient data together with compliance to laws are major challenges in frameworks that use Grid Computing infrastructures.

2.13 Engineering of Secure e-Healthcare Information

The progress towards full realisation of secure e-Healthcare information management has been hampered by a number of factors. Grimson has identified some of these factors: the lack of application of software engineering methodologies, the absence of usable standards, and the failure to acknowledge the impact of record systems on the healthcare system itself (Grimson, 2001). The e-Health heavily relies on the Internet, which was engineered to permit network resorces to be shared by all users. Network engineering involves performance trade-offs between the hardware, architecture, security and the budget available (Gemmill, 2005). The need for the use of sound software engineering principles and methods become clear given that e-Healthcare applications may run over a network whose design is unknown, being entirely under someone else's control and boundaries cross pollination. Clinicians and information technology experts are called upon to collaborate particularly in developing preventive engineering measures to protect information (Myers et al., 2008).

2.13.1 Methodologies for Engineering Secure e-Healthcare Information Systems

The healthcare domains have unique security requirements and re-visiting or innovatively using existing principles and methods of software and security engineering. Blobel and Pharow state that the existing methodologies for establishing requirements and solutions for securing applications are based on narrative descriptions about the use of available system (Blobel and Pharow, 2006). This leads to the risk of unforeseen security and privacy requirements.

Walker (Walker et al., 2008) proposes a coordinated set of steps to advance the practice and theory of safe EHR design, implementation, and continuous improvement. These include setting EHR implementation in the context of health care process improvement, building safety into the specification and design of the EHRs, safety testing and reporting, and rapid communication of EHR-related safety flaws and incidents, which Blobel et al also advocate. Xiao (Xiao et al., 2008) proposes an approach with several levels of security requirements based on software engineering principles, ethical regulations for healthcare data and the security requirements for distributed clinical settings.

The Unified Modeling Language (UML) is a non-proprietary general-purpose object modeling standard that is developed and maintained by the Object Management Group (OMG). OMG Security Specifications (OMG, 2008) provides security functionality at the API level using Common Secure Interoperability (CSIv2) and CORBA Security Service, Authorization Token Layer Acquisition Service (ATLAS) and Resource Access Decision (RAD). However, the beneficial effects of UML in specifying, visualizing, constructing, documenting, and communicating the model of a healthcare information system from the user's perspective have been investigated (Aggarwal, 2002), its benefits in engineering of secure e-Healthcare information systems are not yet fully established.

Aggarwal (Aggarwal, 2002) presented the process of object-oriented analysis (OOA) using the UML and demonstrated the practicality of application using UML in healthcare information system problems. The UML will accelerate advance usage of object-orientation, facilitate the capabilities of healthcare information systems and simplify their management and maintenance. Both UML and XML has been used for practical modelling of policy, authorisation management and access control (Blobel and Pharow, 2004). The UK NHS Information Authority used the UML model of authorisation to enhance the Healthcare Model (HcM) for Electronic Medical Records application (Longstaff et al., 2000).

An emerging and promising engineering methodology for e-Healthcare information was developed by the openEHR Foundation (Beale, 2002). The methodology model for e-Healthcare information proposed by Beale and Heard (Beale and Heard, 2006) was divided into two separate levels: the domain knowledge level (Beale et al., 2002), where healthcare concepts are modelled using archetypes, and the information level (Beale et al., 2005), where information structures are modelled. The key to this methodology is the concept of an *archetype* (Beale et al., 2002), which is a constraint-based model of a domain entity. Each archetype describes the structures of data instances whose classes comply with a reference information model. A small but generic reference information model allows an EHR system to handle many different medical concepts. However, these generic concepts are not enough to describe the semantics of all domain specific concepts.

2.13.2 Measures and Security Metrics for Securing e-Healthcare Information

Metrics provide the information needed in order to allow a controller of e-Healthcare information to prepare and to prevent privacy and confidentiality violations by establishing a quantitative basis for measuring security. Herrman (Herrmann, 2007) outlines three categories of security and privacy metrics:

1. **compliance metrics** - measure to applicable security and privacy standards and laws;
2. **resilience metrics** - measure the resilience (ability prevent,resist, withstand and recover) of all (physical, personnel, IT security and operational) controls before and after a system is put into production; and
3. **return-on-investment (ROI) metrics**- measure the ROI in all controls listed above to guide II capital investment.

Jaquith (Jaquith, 2007) formally characterises a good metric as a consistent standard for measurement that should be consistently measured without subjective criteria, cheap to gather, expressed as a cardinal number or percentage using at least one unit of measure and contextually specific. The significance of privacy and confidentiality in securing e-Healthcare information demands an adoption of the means of diagnosing and determing performance of security controls; quantifying security characteristics of the EHR implementations; and facilitating formal and structured enquiries such as *what-if* scenarios. Thus, the use of security and privacy metrics as tools that assists both the design, measuring and the evaluation of the effectiveness of security and privacy implementation mechanisms and systems is of fundamental importance.

Although most healthcare organisations recognise that e-Healthcare information privacy and confidentiality are a primary concern, few have adequate systems in place because securing information requires a risk-management approach with dependable, quantifiable metrics (Daniel Geer et al., 2003).

A key aspect of the implementation of e-Healthcare information in the EHRs is to meet the requirements of multipurpose users, reusability and inter-operability. The EHR systems have to meet special architectural requirements. Extended health networks are required to support inter-organisational communication and co-operation. Thus, multi-level authorisation management need to be put in place that extends beyond the individual user level. The first comprehensively deployed systems for security and privacy services in bio-genetic and health information systems was the model-driven architecture proposed by Blobel (Blobel and Pharow, 2006). The basic concept behind the approach is that models, methods and tools must be established to allow formal and structured policy definition, policy agreements, role definition, authorisation and access control (Blobel and Pharow, 2004). The structural roles define organisational entity-to-entity relationships and enable specific acts while the functional roles are bound to specific activities. But the aggregation of organisational, functional, informational and technological components are defined by rules.

2.13.3 Evaluation of Secure e-Healthcare Information

Evaluating the security engineering practices for healthcare information systems is vital for the success of e-Healthcare. The significance of e-Healthcare information security and privacy points to the challenging demand for a comprehensive framework. Huang (Huang et al., 2008) recently developed a mapping from Systems Security Engineering Capability Maturity Model (SSE-CMM) (Project, 2003) process areas to the patient-centered healthcare domain. They came up with a set of metrics to assess security risks for patient-centered healthcare systems. The resulting security risk assessment process was then applied in evaluating a typical patient-centered healthcare system. On a serious note, less work has been done in security evaluation frameworks within e-Healthcare Information systems. Therefore, we expect in the near future that most of the research in this area will be dominated by evaluation frameworks based on security risk assessment.

2.14 Discussion and Summary of Issues in Securing e-Healthcare Information

The increasing number of privacy and confidentiality breaches, whether accidental, based on ethically questionable decisions or due to illegal action, is a major challenge for domains that converge on the task of securing e-Healthcare information. These domains include but are not limited to law, organisational policy, IT security, and ethics. These breaches also point to the need for a more wholistic approach spans most of these relevant domains.

However, it is questionable, when it can be said that e-Healthcare information and its management environment are secure from breaches of privacy and confidentiality. Absolute security is impossible to attain. However, to be secure, e-Healthcare information must be managed within a technological environment that satisfy established security principles that are based on privacy laws and policies. The embedding and deliberate incorporation of security and privacy implementing features throughout all levels of the underlying technology stack is a promising approach to securing e-Healthcare information. Therefore, proposals such as Hippocratic databases would be of great beneft.

On a serious note, e-Healthcare is driven by requirements arising from the twin paradigms of shared and managed care within legal and policy environments that are increasingly becoming patient-centric. Shared care is characterised by a healthcare service that is delivered in multiple locations and by multiple carers who need to share information about patients. Managed care is characterised by cost reduction and quality enhancement techniques that are practiced by either healthcare service authorities or health insurance organisations. The two paradigms can be used in combination. In both paradigms, secure Internet-based communication and exchange of information and, hence, secure interoperability and cooperation among e-Healthcare information systems are a major requirement. Although e-Healthcare information is primarily for the purpose of patient care, secondary uses of this information are always necessitated by the need to benefit public health and planning. The key challenge is how to allow secondary uses of e-Healthcare Information without breaching individual privacy. Pseudonymisation and anonymisation are attempts to address this problem by de-personalisation of e-Healthcare information. However, both approaches are haunted by data analysis and mining or knowledge discovery techniques that can be used to undo their effects.

The issue of identifiability of e-Healthcare information also raises the question of a universal patient/personal identifier (UPI), which helps in linking the distributed e-Healthcare information to the correct rightful owner and thus ease systems integration while bringing huge privacy risks if it falls into the hands of third party. Methods based on patient master indices (PMI) attempt to reduce these risks by allowing localised multiple identifiers that are securely mapped to the UPI. Attaining secure e-Healthcare information would be impossible without proper engineering methodologies that place serious emphasis on the critical issues of security, privacy and confidentiality.

References

Vinod Aggarwal. The application of the unified modeling language in object-oriented analysis of healthcare information systems. *Journal of Medical Systems*, 26(5):383–397, October 2002. doi: 10.1023/A:1016449031753. URL http://dx.doi.org/10.1023/A:1016449031753.

Rakesh Agrawal and Christopher Johnson. Securing electronic health records without impeding the flow of information. *International Journal of Medical Informatics*, 76:471–479, June 2007. doi: 10.1016/j.ijmedinf.2006.09.015. URL http://www.sciencedirect.com/.

Rakesh Agrawal, Jerry Kiernan, Ramakrishnan Srikant, and Yirong Xu. Hippocratic databases. In *VLDB 2002, Proceedings of 28th International Conference on Very Large Data Bases, August 20-23, 2002, Hong Kong, China*, pages 143–154. Morgan Kaufmann, 2002.

Rakesh Agrawal, Alexandre Evfimievski, and Ramakrishnan Srikant. Information sharing across private databases. In *SIGMOD '03: Proceedings of the 2003 ACM SIGMOD international conference on Management of data*, pages 86–97, New York, NY, USA, 2003. ACM. ISBN 1-58113-634-X. doi: http://doi.acm.org/10.1145/872757.872771. URL http://portal.acm.org/citation.cfm?doid=872757.872771.

C. Lindsay Anderson and Judith B. Cardell. Reducing the variability of wind power generation for participation in day ahead electricity markets. *hicss*, 0:178, 2008. ISSN 1530-1605. doi: http://doi.ieeecomputersociety.org/10.1109/HICSS.2008.368.

M G Arellano and G I Weber. Issues in identification and linkage of patient records across an integrated delivery system. *Journal of Healthcare Information Management: JHIM*, 12(3):43–52, 1998. ISSN 1099-811X. doi: 10338786. URL http://www.ncbi.nlm.nih.gov/pubmed/10338786. PMID: 10338786.

Jane Armitage, Robert Souhami, Lawrence Friedman, Lutz Hilbrich, Jack Holland, Lawrence H Muhlbaier, Jane Shannon, and Alison Van Nie. The impact of privacy and confidentiality laws on the conduct of clinical trials. *Clinical Trials (London, England)*, 5(1):70–4, 2008. ISSN 1740-7745. doi: 5/1/70. PMID: 18283083.

Vilhjalmur Arnason. Coding and consent: moral challenges of the database project in iceland. *Bioethics*, 18(1):27–49, 2004. ISSN 0269-9702. doi: 15168697. PMID: 15168697.

R. Baker, A. G. Mainous, D. P. Gray, and M. M. Love. Exploration of the relationship between continuity, trust in regular doctors and patient satisfaction with consultations with family doctors. *Scandinavian Journal of Primary Health Care*, 21(1):27–32, 2003.

Roberto J Bayardo and Ramakrishnan Srikant. Technological solutions for protecting privacy. *IEEE Computer*, pages 115 – 118, September 2003. URL http://www.almaden.ibm.com/cs/projects/iis/hdb/Publications/papers/ieee03.pdf.

BBC. Uk's families put on fraud alert. *BBC News (Online)*, Tuesday, 20 November 2007, 2007. URL http://news.bbc.co.uk/1/hi/uk-politics/7103566.stm.

T. Beale. Archetypes: Constraint-based domain models for future-proof information systems. *OOPSLA 2002 workshop on behavioural semantics*, 2002.

T. Beale and S. Heard. *openEHR Architecture: Architecture overview.* openEHR Foundation. Retrieved, 2006.

T. Beale, A. Goodchild, and S. Heard. *EHR Design Principles. openEHR Foundation (Asia-Pacific) V2.2.* Feb 2002.

T. Beale, S. Heard, D. Kalra, and D. Lloyd. *The openEHR Data Structures Information Model.* Revision, 2005.

S Benkner, G Berti, G Engelbrecht, J Fingberg, G Kohring, S E Middleton, and R Schmidt. Gemss: grid-infrastructure for medical service provision. *Methods of Information in Medicine*, 44(2):177–81, 2005. ISSN 0026-1270. doi: 05020177. PMID: 15924170.

Jules J Berman. Zero-check: a zero-knowledge protocol for reconciling patient identities across institutions. *Archives of Pathology & Laboratory Medicine*, 128(3):344–6, March 2004. ISSN 1543-2165. doi: 14987147. URL http://www.ncbi.nlm.nih.gov/pubmed/14987147. PMID: 14987147.

B Blobel, P Pharow, V Spiegel, K Engel, and R Engelbrecht. Securing interoperability between chip card based medical information systems and health networks. *International Journal of Medical Informatics*, 64(2-3):401–15, December 2001. ISSN 1386-5056. doi: 11734401. URL http://www.ncbi.nlm.nih.gov/pubmed/11734401. PMID: 11734401.

Bernd Blobel and Peter Pharow. Mda-based ehr application security services. *Studies in Health Technology and Informatics*, 103:387–93, 2004. ISSN 0926-9630. doi: 15747945. PMID: 15747945.

Bernd Blobel and Peter Pharow. Formal policies for flexible ehr security. *Studies in Health Technology and Informatics*, 121:307–16, 2006. ISSN 0926-9630. doi: 17095829. PMID: 17095829.

Mike Boniface and Paul Wilken. Artemis: towards a secure interoperability infrastructure for healthcare information systems. *Studies in Health Technology and Informatics*, 112:181–9, 2005. ISSN 0926-9630. doi: 15923727. PMID: 15923727.

Bill Brubaker. Kaiser permanente medical e-mails go astray, the washingtonpost, 10 aug 2000. The WashingtonPost, August 2000. URL http://www.pubmedcentral.nih.gov/articlerender.fcgi?artid=2213471.

M. W. Calnan and E. Sanford. Public trust in health care: the system or the doctor?. *Quality & Safety in Health Care*, 13(2):92, 2004.

Yu-Cheng Chiang, Tsan sheng Hsu, Sun Kuo, Churn-Jung Liau, and Da-Wei Wang. Preserving confidentiality when sharing medical database with the cellsecu system. *International Journal of Medical Informatics*, 71(1):17–23, August 2003. ISSN 1386-5056. doi: 12909154. PMID: 12909154.

B Claerhout and G J E De Moor. Privacy protection for healthgrid applications. *Methods of Information in Medicine*, 44(2):140–3, 2005. ISSN 0026-1270. doi: 05020140. PMID: 15924163.

Jeff Collmann and Ted Cooper. Breaching the security of the kaiser permanente internet patient portal: the organizational foundations of information security. *Journal of the American Medical Informatics Association : JAMIA*, 14(2):239243, April 2007. doi: 10.1197/jamia.M2195. URL http://www.pubmedcentral.nih.gov/articlerender.fcgi?artid=2213471. PMC2213471.

A Conti. The recent italian consolidation act on privacy: new measures for data protection. *Medicine and Law*, 25(1):127–38, March 2006. ISSN 0723-1393. doi: 16681118. PMID: 16681118.

Robert M. Cook. Rx data mining: Improving health care or invading privacy? *Fosters Daily Democrat Sunday Citizen, Sep 30*, 2007. URL http://www.citizen.com/apps/pbcs.dll/article?AID=/20070930/GJNEWS01/709300094SearchID=73324675253076.

Andrew Dalley, Ken Lynch, Peter Feltham, and John Fulcher. The use of smart tokens to permit the secure, remote access of electronic health records. *International Journal of Electronic Healthcare*, 2(1):1–11, 2006. ISSN 1741-8453. doi: 8EG4WJG1KJ64B902. PMID: 18048231.

Jr. Daniel Geer, Kevin Soo Hoo, and Andrew Jaquith. Information security: Why the future belongs to the quants. *IEEE Security and Privacy*, 01(4):24–32, 2003. ISSN 1540-7993. doi: http://doi.ieeecomputersociety.org/10.1109/MSECP.2003.1219053.

H. T. Davies and J. Lampel. Trust in performance indicators? *British Medical Journal*, 7(3):159, 1998.

Simon de Lusignan and Chris van Weel. The use of routinely collected computer data for research in primary care: opportunities and challenges. *Family Practice*, 23(2):253–63, April 2006. ISSN 0263-2136. doi: cmi106. PMID: 16368704.

Schulte In den Bumen T. Human genetic data from a data protection law perspective, [article in german]. *Bundesgesundheitsblatt Gesundheitsforschung Gesundheitsschutz.*, 50(2):200–8, Feb 2007. URL http://www.ncbi.nlm.nih.gov/pubmed/17238055.

W. Ebner, J. M. Leimeister, and H. Krcmar. Trust in virtual healthcare communities: Design and implementation of trust-enabling functionalities. *Proceedings of the Hawaii International Conference on System Sciences (HICSS 37)*, 2004.

EPTA. Ict and privacy in europe: Experiences from technology assessment of ict and privacy in seven different european countries, final report, http://epub.oeaw.ac.at/ita/ita-projektberichte/e2-2a44.pdf, accessed: 2008.07.17, european parliamentary technology assessment network (epta). Online, October 2006. URL http://epub.oeaw.ac.at/ita/ita-projektberichte/e2-2a44.pdf.

G Freriks. Identification in healthcare. is there a place for unique patient identifiers? is there a place for the master patient index? *Studies in Health Technology and Informatics*, 77:595–9, 2000. ISSN 0926-9630. doi: 11187622. URL http://www.ncbi.nlm.nih.gov/pubmed/11187622. PMID: 11187622.

Hovenga EJS Heard S Garde S, Knaup P. Towards semantic interoperability for electronic health records: Domain knowledge governance for openehr archetypes. *Methods of Information in Medicine*, 46(3):332343, 2007. doi: http://dx.doi.org/doi:10.1160/ME5001.

Jill Gemmill. Network basics for telemedicine. *Journal of Telemedicine and Telecare*, 11(2):71–6, 2005. ISSN 1357-633X. doi: 10.1258/1357633053499822. PMID: 15829050.

S. D. Goold and G. Klipp. Managed care members talk about trust. *Social Science & Medicine*, 54(6):879–888, 2002.

Jane Grimson. Delivering the electronic healthcare record for the 21st century. *International Journal of Medical Informatics 64 (2001) 111127*, 64:111–127, 2001.

Jane Grimson, William Grimson, and Wilhelm Hasselbring. The si challenge in health care. *Commun. ACM*, 43(6):48–55, 2000. ISSN 0001-0782. doi: http://doi.acm.org/10.1145/336460.336474. URL http://portal.acm.org/citation.cfm?id=336460.336474.

Stefanos Gritzalis. Enhancing privacy and data protection in electronic medical environments. *Journal of Medical Systems*, 28(6):535–47, December 2004. ISSN 0148-5598. doi: 15615282. PMID: 15615282.

Ma Hall, E. Dugan, B. Zheng, and Ak Mishra. Trust in physicians and medical institutions: What is it, can it be measured, and does it matter?. *Milbank Quarterly*, 79(4):613, 2001.

D. Henrici, J. Gotze, and P. Muller. A hash-based pseudonymization infrastructure for rfid systems. *Security, Privacy and Trust in Pervasive and Ubiquitous Computing, 2006. SecPerU 2006. Second International Workshop on*, pages 6 pp.–, June 2006. doi: 10.1109/SECPERU.2006.2. URL http://ieeexplore.ieee.org/search/wrapper.jsp?arnumber=1644273.

Debra S Herrmann. *Complete Guide to Security and Privacy Metrics: Measuring Regulatory Compliance, Operational Resilience and ROI*. Auerbach Publications, NY, 2007.

B. W. Hesse, D. E. Nelson, G. L. Kreps, R. T. Croyle, N. K. Arora, B. K. Rimer, and K. Viswanath. *Trust and Sources of Health Information The Impact of the Internet and Its Implications for Health Care Providers: Findings From the First Health Information National Trends Survey*, volume 165. Am Med Assoc, 2005.

C. Derrick Huang, Qing Hu, and Ravi S. Behara. An economic analysis of the optimal information security investment in the case of a risk-averse firm. *International Journal of Production Economics*, 114(2): 793 – 804, 2008. ISSN 0925-5273. doi: DOI:10.1016/j.ijpe.2008.04.002. URL http://www.sciencedirect.com/science/article/B6VF8-4S98TWG-1/2/eef287240dcb9a1df7586d333781c21f. Special Section on Logistics Management in Fashion Retail Supply Chains.

Luigi Lo Iacono. Multi-centric universal pseudonymisation for secondary use of the ehr. In *Geneva 2007*, 2007. URL http://geneva2007.healthgrid.org/proceedings/proceedings/pdf/25.pdf.

Livia Iacovino. Trustworthy shared electronic health records: recordkeeping requirements and healthconnect. *Journal of Law and Medicine*, 12(1):40–59, August 2004. ISSN 1320-159X. doi: 15359549. PMID: 15359549.

Andrew Jaquith. *Security Metrics: Replacing Fear, Uncertainty and Doubt.* Addison-Wesley, 2007.

D Kalra, P Singleton, J Milan, J Mackay, D Detmer, A Rector, and D Ingram. Security and confidentiality approach for the clinical e-science framework (clef). *Methods of Information in Medicine*, 44(2):193–7, 2005. ISSN 0026-1270. doi: 05020193. PMID: 15924174.

N. L. Keating, D. C. Green, A. C. Kao, J. A. Gazmararian, V. Y. Wu, and P. D. Cleary. How are patients' specific ambulatory care experiences related to trust, satisfaction, and considering changing physicians? *J Gen Intern Med*, 17(1):29–39, 2002.

K Lampe, P Doupi, and M Jeroen van den Hoven. Internet health resources: from quality to trust. *Methods of information in medicine*, 42(2):134–42, 2003. ISSN 00261270. PMID: 12743649.

A.A.; Asfour S.S Leonard, D.D.C.; Pons. Realization of a universal patient identifier for electronic medical records through biometric technology. *Information Technology in Biomedicine, IEEE Transactions on*, PP(99):1, 2008. doi: 10.1109/TITB.2008.926438.

Bernard Lo and Ann Alpers. Uses and abuses of prescription drug information in pharmacy benefits management programs. *JAMA*, 283(6):801–806, February 2000. doi: 10.1001/jama.283.6.801. URL http://jama.ama-assn.org/cgi/content/abstract/283/6/801.

J. J. Longstaff, M. A. Lockyer, and M. G. Thick. A model of accountability, confidentiality and override for healthcare and other applications. In *Proceedings of the fifth ACM workshop on Role-based access control*, pages 71–76, Berlin, Germany, 2000. ACM. ISBN 1-58113-259-X. doi: 10.1145/344287.344304. URL http://portal.acm.org/citation.cfm?id=344287.344304.

Cara T Mai, David J Law, Craig A Mason, Bradley D McDowell, Robert E Meyer, and Debra Musa. Collection, use, and protection of population-based birth defects surveillance data in the united states. *Birth Defects Research. Part A, Clinical and Molecular Teratology*, 79(12):811–4, December 2007. ISSN 1542-0760. doi: 10.1002/bdra.20420. PMID: 18064713.

Bradley Malin and Latanya Sweeney. How (not) to protect genomic data privacy in a distributed network: using trail re-identification to evaluate and design anonymity protection systems. *Journal of Biomedical Informatics*, 37(3):179–92, June 2004. ISSN 1532-0464. doi: 15196482. PMID: 15196482.

Julie Myers, Thomas R Frieden, Kamal M Bherwani, and Kelly J Henning. Ethics in public health research: privacy and public health at risk: public health confidentiality in the digital age. *American Journal of Public Health*, 98(5):793–801, May 2008. ISSN 1541-0048. doi: AJPH.2006.107706. PMID: 18382010.

Thomas Neubauer and Bernhard Riedl. *Improving Patients Privacy with Pseudonymization*, pages 691–696. IOS Press, 2008. URL http://www.hst.aau.dk/~ska/MIE2008/ParalleSessions/PapersForDownloads/09.PS/SHTI136-0691.pdf.

Rita Noumeir, Alain Lemay, and Jean-Marc Lina. Pseudonymization of radiology data for research purposes. *Journal of Digital Imaging: The Official Journal of the Society for Computer Applications in Radiology*, 20(3):284–95, September 2007. ISSN 0897-1889. doi: 10.1007/s10278-006-1051-4. PMID: 17191099.

OMG. Object management group security, www.omg.org/technology/documents/, accessed 16 august. online, August 2008. URL http://www.omg.org/technology/documents/formal/omgsecurity.htm.

Michael O'Regan. Ahern to raise laptop theft with data agency. *The Irish Times*, Thu, Feb 21, 2008. URL http://www.irishtimes.com/newspaper/ireland/2008/0221/1203471491741pf.html.

Anna O Orlova, Mark Dunnagan, Terese Finitzo, Michael Higgins, Todd Watkins, Allen Tien, and Steven Beales. Electronic health record - public health (ehr-ph) system prototype for interoperability in 21st century healthcare systems. *AMIA ... Annual Symposium Proceedings / AMIA Symposium. AMIA Symposium*, pages 575–9, 2005. ISSN 1559-4076. doi: 58762. PMID: 16779105.

PITAC. (presidents information technology advisory committee), report to the president - revolutionizing health care through information technology,. Technical report, Executive Office of the President, USA, June 2004.

SSE-CMM Project. Systems security engineering capability maturity model (sse-cmm) model description document, version 3.0, june 15, 2003, carnegie mellon university. Standard Release, June 2003.

Catherine Quantin, Franois-Andr Allaert, Paul Avillach, Benot Riandey, Marius Fieschi, Maniane Fassa, and Olivier Cohen. Proposal of a french health identification number interoperable at the european level. *Medinfo. MEDINFO*, 12(Pt 1): 503–7, 2007. doi: 17911768. PMID: 17911768.

Bernhard Riedl, Veronika Grascher, Stefan Fenz, and Thomas Neubauer. Pseudonymization for improving the privacy in e-health applications. In *41st Hawaii International International Conference on Systems Science (HICSS-41 2008), Proceedings, 7-10 January 2008, Waikoloa, Big Island, HI, USA*, page 255. IEEE Computer Society, 2008.

Nola M Ries and Geoff Moysa. Legal protections of electronic health records: issues of consent and security. *Health Law Review*, 14(1):18–25, 2005. ISSN 1188-8725. doi: 16538772. PMID: 16538772.

Thomas C. Rindfleisch. Privacy, information technology, and health care. *Commun. ACM*, 40(8):92–100, August 1997. ISSN 0001-0782. doi: http://doi.acm.org/10.1145/257874.257896.

Jim Ryan, Barbara Doster, Sandra Daily, and Marty Heslin. Soft innovation as data-driven process improvement exploited via integrated hospital information systems. *hicss*, 0:246, 2008. ISSN 1530-1605. doi: http://doi.ieeecomputersociety.org/10.1109/HICSS.2008.405.

S. A. Shoniregun, A. Omoegun, D. Brown-West, and O. Logvynovskiy. Can ecrm and trust improve ec customer base? *e-Commerce Technology, 2004. CEC 2004. Proceedings. IEEE International Conference on*, pages 303–310, 2004.

Erik Torres, Carlos de Alfonso, Ignacio Blanquer, and Vicente Hernndez. Privacy protection in healthgrid: distributing encryption management over the vo. *Studies in Health Technology and Informatics*, 120:131–41, 2006. ISSN 0926-9630. doi: 16823130. PMID: 16823130.

James M. Walker, Pascale Carayon, Nancy Leveson, Ronald A. Paulus, John Tooker, Homer Chin, Albert Bothe Jr., and Walter F. Stewart. Ehr safety: The way forward to safe and effective systems. *Journal of the American Medical Informatics Association*, 15:272–277, June 2008. doi: 10.1197/jamia.M2618. URL http://www.sciencedirect.com/science.

Liang Xiao, Paul Lewis, and Alex Gibb. Developing a security protocol for a distributed decision support system in a healthcare environment. In *Proceedings of the 30th international conference on Software engineering*, pages 673–682, Leipzig, Germany, 2008. ACM. ISBN 978-1-60558-079-1. doi: 10.1145/1368088.1368184. URL http://portal.acm.org/citation.cfm?id=1368088.1368184.

Che-Ming Yang, Herng-Ching Lin, Polun Chang, and Wen-Shan Jian. Taiwan's perspective on electronic medical records' security and privacy protection: lessons learned from hipaa. *Computer Methods and Programs in Biomedicine*, 82(3):277–82, June 2006. ISSN 0169-2607. doi: S0169-2607(06)00073-3. PMID: 16730852.

Chapter 3
Laws and Standards for Secure e-Healthcare Information

3.1 Introduction

The legal developments in healthcare have been driven by the public concern for personal privacy and confidentiality within the context of an increasingly connected world centred on the Internet. The developments in standardisation within e-Healthcare have been influenced by the two key paradigms of patient-centred and managed care that necessitated demands for lowering costs and increasing quality of patient care. The technical challenge of these paradigm shifts is inter-operability for supporting the delivery of care at multiple locations by multiple carers who need to share the patient health record.

There has been an increasing tendency for governments to be involved in e-Healthcare information security (Moore, 2004). This has resulted in the emergency of laws regulating individual privacy and confidentiality of information through agencies such as data protection agencies or commissions.

The developments in standardisation within e-Healthcare, especially in the USA and Europe, have been motivated by patient-centred and managed care. These new ways of healthcare service delivery necessitate the inter-operability of healthcare information systems for supporting the delivery of care at multiple locations by multiple carers who need to share the patient e-Health record. The e-Healthcare information standards deal with a broad range of e-Healthcare record aspects including the architecture, content, storage, security, confidentiality, functionality, and communication of information. Standards cover policies for integrity and confidentiality and procedures that support the uses of data and healthcare decision making. Thus, these standards incorporate requirements that can be construed as meeting legal provisions.

The law is an effective formal basis for standardisation due to its ability to punitively enforce the standards. The standards can be a formal basis for the law in a persuasive and discretionary manner of influence on the legislature or law-makers. The formal convergence of the law, standards and technology is as significant to secure e-Healthcare information as to warrant serious investigation.

This chapter outlines the developments of privacy and confidentiality in e-Healthcare information and the standards for securing information. The laws and standards required for securing e-Healthcare information systems discussed in this chapter are summarised in Figure 3.1.

3.2 The Rationale for Laws and Standards in Securing e-Healthcare Information

The rationale for laws and standards in securing e-Healthcare information mainly addresses public interests. The standards for e-Healthcare information management mainly facilitate information sharing through fostering interoperability. The patient privacy and information sharing are at the core of the rationale for laws and standards.

Public concerns about the privacy of their health information have been justified by actual incidents and potential violations of individual privacy and confidentiality. These concerns together with use of personal e-Healthcare information on many aspects of daily life have led to the recent emergence in many countries of laws intended to protect personal health information and to regulate its primary and secondary uses (Armitage et al, 2008). Privacy has emerged as a basic and fundamental right for every human being and is associated with a number of values including (Lennon, 2005):

- inherent human dignity, freedom, autonomy and self-determination;
- vital protected space for personal comfort and growth; and
- exercise of freedom.

The collection and use of genetic data have caused much concern around the world including Germany where it is noted by Baeumen (den Bumen T., 2007) that the key solution lies in:

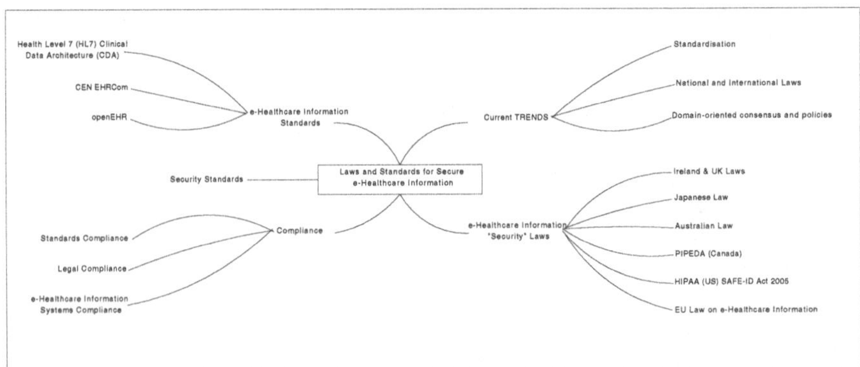

Figure 3.1 Major issues in Laws and Standards for Secure e-Healthcare Information

1. The legal protection of genetic data as defined with regard to the different sets of diseases;
2. In the fact that such protection needs to fit into the preexisting data protection legislation; and
3. In the consideration of the particularities of genetic data such as the multi-personal impact.

The lack of either comprehensive or effective legal protection of patient privacy, coupled with increasing cases of privacy breaches, is a concern to the public in most countries. It can be noted that privacy laws in most parts of the world are fragmented and tend to protect isolated portions of privacy instead of unifying legal protection to cover privacy in a holistic manner.

Effective product inter-operation without compatibility problems is emerging as a critical requirement and yet difficult to realise in ICTs for supporting patient-centred, shared and managed care health services. This is referred to as interoperability for e-Healthcare information. Standards can be de jure or formal, or they can be de facto or informal. De facto standards may block competition and promote monopolies, which may lead to poor privacy or low quality products. However, in general, formal standards benefit market growth and competition, vendors, healthcare establishments (HCEs) and healthcare service recipients. Generic information security standards can also cover areas of healthcare information security. Examples include: security standards for lower layers of the OSI standard. Rationale for healthcare-specific information security standards include:

1. special security requirements; and
2. urgent need for certain standards that may not exist but may be generic.

Standardisation facilitates and promotes inter-operability, portability, mobility, quality and trust in e-Healthcare.

3.3 Laws and Standards: Relationships, Roles and Interactions

Privacy laws, security standards and regulations are the main instruments for protecting e-Healthcare information privacy. Emerging privacy laws mandate that patients must have more control over their e-Healthcare information than before. Privacy law also governs the secondary use and disclosure of health information. Security standards and regulations specify requirements for building data integrity, confidentiality, and availability into e-Healthcare information systems, while other standards focus on supporting e-Healthcare information sharing through interoperability among e-Healthcare information systems.

The Laws and standards are produced by different types of representative bodies (elected/democratic vs appointed/aristocratic/elitist). The Laws follow public opinion, while standards attempt to direct technological innovation through persuasion. Both may lag behind technological advances or innovation due to an elaboration process that involves lengthy discussion and debates. Laws, in particular, are also subject to the slow pace of change in public opinion.

Popular products in the market can become *de facto* standards. Official standards cannot interfere with the market to affect a market-driven de facto standard. This has implications on the relationship between standards bodies and companies. However, a de facto standard can be affected by laws if it is in conflict with them.

It is of great importance to protect patient data, so that the privacy of the patient could be safe guarded and to protect the professional interests of health care providers. Many parties (employers, insurance companies, etc.) are interested in permanent patient data. These data should be extremely well protected in EPR systems. In Europe there may be more sensitivity toward the improper use of patient data than elsewhere. If the security issue is not addressed properly, then it could even impede the introduction of EPRS in some countries, end even hamper the use of EPR data. The right to privacy has been anchored in the Treaty for the Protection of Human Rights and Fundamental Freedom (Treaty of Rome, 1954) and in European law (EU, 1995).

3.4 Legal Protection of Privacy in e-Healthcare Information Management

There is a global move towards the introduction of legislation and legal enforcement of the protection of privacy and confidentiality of the personal health information. The right to privacy is at the core of the protection of e-Health information. Privacy is a fundamental human right that has been recognised throughout ancient civilisations and religions, and is at the centre of the state, the public interest and the individual control of e-Healthcare information. The on-going developments in the evolution of the right to privacy are now punctuated by the threats posed on the Internet and its increasing role in the delivery of healthcare information services. This section reviews legal developments focusing specifically on securing e-Healthcare information.

3.4.1 International and EU Law on Protection of e-Healthcare Information

At the international level the protection of privacy is generally recognised in a consistent manner by the United Nations (UN), the Organisation of Economic Corporation and Development (OECD), the Council of Europe and the European Community (EC). Thus, privacy and data protection has been a subject of international instruments. The most significant of these instruments are: *Guideline Governing the Protection of Privacy and Trans-border Flows of Personal Data* (1980) from the OECD; and the *Convention for the Protection of Individuals* with regard to the *Au-*

tomatic Processing of Personal Data (1981) from the Council of Europe (CE). The two instruments are similar in broad terms.

The Convention is open for signing by members other than those within the Council of Europe. The two instruments were prompted by concerns arising from the development of fast electronic processing and transmission of information. OECD Guidelines recognised that considerable disadvantages would arise from limiting the relevant protection rules solely to the automatic processing of personal data. The Data Protection Convention was based on Article 8 of the European Convention on Human Rights (ECHR) and has been subject to adaptations through the adoption of recommendations by the CE, which included those on medical databanks and the protection of medical and genetic data. The two instruments have had a huge impact on the development of privacy and data protection laws around the world. However, their European influence is being superseded by the growing European Union (EU) interest in the protection of privacy and data.

The EU's initial entry into data protection and privacy came in the form of the 1995 Directive 95/46/EC on the *Protection of Personal Data.* Since the EU functions and legal powers are limited to specific areas set out in the Treaty of Rome, Directive 95/46/EC is of a limited jurisdiction and is cast as a harmonisation measure under the treaty's Internal Market [1] provisions. The EU Directive was issued in order to create a common foundation of the protection of privacy among European Community (EC) members as a way to facilitate the implementation of the EC's Common Internal Market. Thus, this directive was a harmonisation measure to facilitate flow of information within the envisaged EU Internal Market.

The 72 recitals and 34 articles of the 1995 EU Directive are non-prescriptive but set a general framework for implementing measures of member states and for the exercise of the wide degree of discretion afforded to the members states. The Directive stipulates that:

- The processing of personal data must be *necessary;*
- The flow of personal data from EC members states to countries that do not provide *adequate* protection of personal data is prevented; and
- Member states are encouraged to adopt *suitable* measures to ensure the full implementation of the provisions of the Directive.

These stipulations of necessity of usage, adequacy of protections and suitability of measures form the basis of each EU member state's discretion over the content of its data protection laws. The discretion also means that there is bound to be wide variations in the data protection laws among EU member states.

The background setting for the EU Directive, besides the move towards a common internal market, included the shift towards managed care, the increase in secondary uses of health information, patient mobility leading to the fragmentation of the healthcare record. The introduction of the EU Directive brought into focus the

---

[1] The Internal Market is *"an area without internal frontiers in which the free movement of goods, persons, services and capital is ensured. "The Treaty of Rome, http://eur-lex.europa.eu/LexUriServ/site/en/oj/2006/ce321/ce32120061229en00010331.pdf, accessed 28th August 2008.*

argument from medical researchers that stringent legislative provisions would have adverse effects on vital research such as cancer registry-based research.

3.4.2 Irish Law on Protection of e-Healthcare Information

In Ireland there is no single privacy law as privacy provisions are found in the constitution, statutes and the common law. The Irish law protects the privacy of healthcare records. The data protection and privacy for e-Healthcare information in Ireland is governed by the following laws:

- The Data Protection Act (DPA) 1988 as amended by the 2003 Act;
- Data Protection (Access Modification) (Health) Regulations 1989;
- The Freedom of Information (FOI) Act 1997 [2] as amended by the 2003 Act [3];
- The European Data Protection Directive 1995;
- The European Communities (Data Protection) Regulation 2001;
- The Unenumerated Constitutional Right to Privacy (Kennedy v. Ireland decision); and
- Common law [4] (Hale and Runnington, 1820) relating to confidentiality, contractual, equitable and ethical duties.

The implicit or unenumerated constitutional right to privacy has been recognised in a number of judicial decisions. Example, *Kennedy v.Ireland* (1987) [5] where Judge Hamilton stated that:

> It [right to privacy] is not an unqualified right. Its exercise may be restricted by the constitutional rights of others, by the requirements of the common good and is subject to the requirements of public order and morality.

In Ireland, the right to privacy was characterised in 1998 as a fundamental human right which was not absolute but required the protection of the law (LRC, 1998). The Data Protection Acts 1988-2003, which also incorporate the provisions of EC Data Protection Directive 1995, now form the basis of the protection of privacy in Ireland.

[2] The Freedom of Information Act 1997 commenced on 21 April 1998 for Irish Government Departments and Offices and other Government bodies and on 21 October 1998 for Irish local authorities and health boards.

[3] The Freedom of Information (Amendment) Act 2003 came into force in Ireland on 11 April 2003. This Act introduced a number of important amendments to the 1997 Act notably in relation to Section 19 (Government Records), Section 20 (Deliberations of Public Bodies), Section 24 (Security, Defence and International Relations) and Section 47 (Fees).

[4] The common law, *leges non scripta* (unwritten law, i.e., the sources of such laws are not formally declared to be so although the laws are binding), is created and refined by judges: a decision in the case currently pending depends on decisions in previous cases and affects the law to be applied in future cases. When there is no authoritative statement of the law, judges have the authority and duty to make law by creating precedent. The body of precedent is called "common law" and it binds future decisions. (see also Marbury v Madison, 5 U.S. 137)

[5] Kennedy v. Ireland [1987] Irish Reports (IR) p. 587

The DPA 1988 has two primary purposes: first, the 1998 Act represented Ireland's ratification of the 1991 Data Protection Convention of the Council of Europe; and, second, the 1988 Act was also meant to create a legal foundation for the International Financial Services Centre, which was to be established in Dublin. The 1988 Act was prompted by economic considerations only (McMahon and Binchy, 2000), so that it has been described as minimalist (Lennon, 2005) with its scope limited to the protection of computerised personal information only while effectively disregarding the protection privacy of information in all its forms. Thus, the 1988 Act was felt to be particularly limited in healthcare due to the slow pace of adoption of e-Healthcare information management systems, the bulk of health records being paper-based at that time. The Act is not prescriptive and it does not preclude other laws especially the common law, as it imposes a common law duty of care on people who control and process e-Healthcare information, allowing litigation under the law of torts. The Section 4 of the 1988 Act also grants the right of access, rectification or deletion of personal data to individuals who are the subjects of the data.

The Data Protection (Access Modification) (Health) Regulations 1989, hereafter referred to as the 1989 Health Regulation, was introduced to protect the patients from the health and mental effects arising from awareness of health condition as a result of their exercise of the right of access to their health information under the 1988 Act. The 1989 Health Regulation creates a legal cul de sac by stipulating the right of access which should be denied to a patient if health experts determine that access to personal health information is likely to cause serious harm to the physical health of the patient. The Regulation permits information to be edited by health experts to mitigate the harmful effectss on the information that has been released.

The Freedom of Information (FOI) Act 1997 as amended by the 2003 Act has the purpose of asserting the right of members of the public to obtain access to official information subject to the public interest and the right to privacy. The Act creates three statutory rights, namely: 1) a right to access records held by public bodies; 2) a right to have personal information in a record amended where it is incomplete, incorrect or misleading; and 3) a right to obtain reasons for decisions affecting the person. Further to this, the Act provides the establishment of an independent Office of Information Commissioner to review most decisions made by public bodies under the Act.

The amended DPA 1988 and the FOI Act 1997 grant the right of access to information. Firstly, the DPA 1988 does not apply to manual files until the 2003 Act amendments such that both the DPA and the FOI Act applies to both manual and electronic files. Secondly, the DPA applies to personal information held by a either a private or a public data controller, while the FOI Act applies only to information held by a public body. Therefore, health records held by private healthcare service providers cannot be accessed under the FOI Act. Thirdly, the FOI Act has more exclusions and exemptions that restrict access to information than the DPA. The 1989 Health Regulation under the DPA restricts access to personal data associated with physical or mental health, while the FOI Act restricts access to records of a psychiatric or medical nurture. Fourthly, the granting of access to information that may potentially harm the requestor is discretionary under the FOI Act while it is mandatory under the DPA Regulations.

3.4.3 UK Law on Protection of e-Healthcare Information

In the UK, the right to privacy was implicitly protected as far back as the 14th century as the Justices of Peace Act 1361 made eavesdropping a criminal offence. The right to privacy in the UK did no exist explicitly but was protected indirectly through other common law torts such as defamation and libel. By 1990, there was no statutory definition of privacy. The possibility of deducing the definition from the common law was suggested and yet privacy could not be recommended for explicit statutory protection (Calcutt, 1990). The UK Data Protection Act (DPA) 1998, which gives effect to the European Community Data Protection Directive 1995, regulates the processing of information relating to individuals but does not define privacy.

3.4.4 Australian Law on Protection of e-Healthcare Information

Australia, like the UK, did not recognise the general right to privacy under the common law until a 2001 High Court decision, which was not uniformly received by state courts throughout Australia (Hughes et al, 2008). However, the 1988 Privacy Act lays out the statutory framework for the protection of the right to privacy in Australia although there is a general lack of uniformity of privacy laws among Australian states. The recent Australian Privacy Law and Practice Report (ALRC, 2008), which followed the 2007 massive review of Australian privacy laws (ALRC, 2007) conducted by the Australian Law Reform Commission, proposes to harmonise the complex privacy laws through a statutory cause of action for invasion of privacy and a set of unified privacy principles.

3.4.5 New Zealand Law on Protection of e-Healthcare Information

New Zealand's Privacy Act (PA) 1993, as amended in 1993, 1994 and 2000, implements the twelve principles of the OECD Guidelines. The PA 1993 also mandates the Privacy Commissioner (PC) to publish sector-oriented privacy codes of practice. The Health Information Privacy Code 1994 now forms the primary privacy practice code for the domain of healthcare in New Zealand. As a result of the 2000 amendments, the PA incorporates data export controls that are required as adequate level of privacy protection under Article 25 of the EU Data Protection Directive 1995. Therefore, the PC is empowered to ban the transfer of personal information from

New Zealand to foreign states where the PC deems the states not to have adequate data protection measures in place.

3.4.6 Japanese Law on Protection of e-Healthcare Information

Japan's newly enacted data privacy laws arose out of public concerns, especially consumer and employee concerns, that personal data - such as name, address, identification number, and credit card information - are being misused or transferred to others without regard to privacy or security. Consequently, the Japanese Personal Data Protection (PDP) Act was passed by the Japanese bi-cameral legislature, the Diet, in May of 2003. It came into effect against companies only on April 1 in 2005. The PDP Act 2003 applies to all business organisations that collect and store personal information on more than five thousand individuals, which could be worldwide.

Under the 2003 PDP Act, a business is required to specify and publicly announce a "purpose of use" that clearly describes how the business uses personal data in Japan. The "purpose of use" is at the core of the new law. What a business can and cannot do with its own personal data depends on what is its "purpose of use". Every multinational business organisation with large databases that operates in Japan now needs a thorough "purpose of use" tailored to its specific Japanese data processing activities.

Besides the "purpose of use", the 2003 PDP Act also requires businesses to prevent unauthorised disclosure, loss, or destruction of personal data (making critical strict security measures and employee oversight). Furthemore, the 2003 PDP Act limits the transfers of personal data to third parties - whether in Japan or abroad - unless "principals" (data subjects) consent. Principals can tell business not to disclose their data to others, and businesses have to explain to principals their right to "opt out."

The new Japanese law's emphasis on "purpose of use" differs substantially from regulatory approaches in Europe, Canada, Hong Kong, Argentina, and many other countries. It would seem that, with such radically different approaches, a unified single strategy for international privacy law compliance may not be functional.

3.4.7 US Law on Protection of e-Healthcare Information

The US 1791 constitutional Bill of Rights is not explicit on providing for the right to privacy leading to Warren and Brandeis (Warren and Brandeis, 1890-91) to consider whether the existing law in 1890 afforded a principle which could properly be invoked to protect the privacy of the individual; and, if it did, what the nature and extent of such protection was, which they deemed should be at the level of constitutional protection. Ultimately, states constituting the USA made provisions for the right to privacy in their constitutions. The most significant privacy protection law to affect the area of securing e-Healthcare information in the US is the Health Insurance Portability and Accountability Act (HIPAA) of 1996, which is discussed from section 3.4.7.1 to 3.4.7.5.

3.4.7.1 Health Insurance Portability and Accountability Act (HIPAA) in 1996

When the US Congress passed the Health Insurance Portability and Accountability Act (HIPAA) in 1996, the goal was to:

1. create a simpler, more standardised system that would eventually lower healthcare costs;
2. reduce errors through safe, universally accepted electronic communication of health care transactions; and
3. eliminate paper claims (Edlin and Johns, 2006).

Consequently, HIPAA 1996 mandates the US Department of Health and Human Services (HHS) to specify and promulgate rules that spell out in greater detail than the Act, the healthcare privacy requirements that must be met by specified healthcare service providers in order to be in compliance with the Act. Sections 261 to 264 of HIPAA, the Administrative Simplification provisions, require the Secretary of HHS to publicize standards for the electronic exchange, privacy and security of health information.

3.4.7.2 HIPAA Rules

The HIPAA rules have been developed and implemeted in a gradual and evolutionary manner and currently consist of the following rules:

1. the Privacy Rule;
2. the Security Rule;
3. the Transactions and Code Sets Rule;
4. the Enforcement Rule; and
5. the Unique Identifiers Rule (National Healthcare Provider Identifier(NPI)).

The Privacy Rule titled *"The Standards for Privacy of Individually Identifiable Health Information"*, sets out, the US national standards for the protection of certain health information. The Privacy Rule standards address the use and disclosure of individuals health information called *protected health information* (PHI) by organisations subject to the Privacy Rule called *covered entities,* as well as standards for individuals' privacy rights to understand and control how their health information is used.The Privacy Rule defines PHI as all *individually identifiable health information* held or transmitted by a covered entity or its business associate, in any form or media, whether electronic, paper, or oral.

The security rule adopts standards for the security of *electronic protected health information* EPHI to be implemented by covered entities, which include health plans, health care clearinghouses, and certain health care providers. All covered entities are required to be in compliance with the HIPAA Security Rule, which includes, reviewing and modifying, where necessary, security policies and procedures on a regular basis. This is particularly relevant for organizations that allow remote access to EPHI through portable devices or on external systems or hardware not owned or managed by the covered entity.

The Transactions and Code Sets Rule adopts standards for eight electronic transactions and for code sets to be used in those transactions. It also contains requirements concerning the use of these standards by health plans, health care clearinghouses, and certain health care providers - the covered entities.

The Unique Identifiers Rule establishes the standard for a unique health identifier for health care providers for use in the health care system and announces the adoption of the National Provider Identifier (NPI) as that standard (FederalRegister, 2004). It also establishes the implementation of specifications for obtaining and using the standard unique health identifier for health care providers. The implementation specifications set the requirements that must be met by covered entities who transmit any health information in electronic form in connection with a transaction for which the Secretary has adopted a standard. Covered entities must use the identifier in connection with standard transactions.

The Enforcement Rule sets out the regulations that establish how HHS Department regulators will determine liability and calculate fines for health-care providers found to have violated any of the HIPAA rules following an investigation and administrative hearing. Privacy complaints are investigated by regulators from the HHS Office for Civil Rights (OCR).

3.4.7.3 HIPAA Privacy and Security Rules

The distinct differences between the Privacy Rule and the Security Rule are so important and informative that they need to be noted.

Firstly, the security standards adopted in the Security Rule require covered entities to implement basic safeguards to protect electronic protected health information from unauthorized access, alteration, deletion, and transmission. Hence, the Security Rule defines administrative, physical, and technical safeguards to protect the confidentiality, integrity, and availability of electronic protected health information.

Secondly, the Privacy Rule sets standards for how protected health information should be controlled. The rule sets forth what uses and disclosures are authorized or required. It also stipulates what rights patients have with respect to their health information.

Thirdly, the Privacy Rule narrows the scope of the information to which the security safeguards must be applied. The scope is narrowed from electronic health information pertaining to individuals to protected health information in electronic form. Thus, the scope of information covered in the Security Rule is consistent with that in the Privacy Rule, which addresses privacy protections for *protected health information.*

Fourthly, the scope of the Security Rule is more limited than that of the Privacy Rule, though it is consistent with it. The Privacy Rule applies to protected health information in any form. The Security Rule applies only to protected health information in electronic form. As a result, security standards for health information in non-electronic form are not included in the Security Rule.

3.4.7.4 The Impact of HIPAA 1996

Advances in Securing e-Healthcare Information Security under HIPAA: HIPAA is a legal, standard and official rule for healthcare privacy and security. It requires security services that support implementation features including access control, audit controls, authorisation control, data authentication and entity authentication (Chen et al, 2005). Audit controls proposed by HIPAA Security Standards are audit trails. Audit trails monitor activities. The aim of audit controls is to assess compliance with a secure domain's policies, to detect instances of non-compliant behaviour, and to facilitate detection of improper creation, access, modification and deletion of Protected Health Information (PHI). The strength of HIPAA derives from its mandatory and punitive nature. Hence, it represents an exceptional significant advance in securing e-Healthcare information. Progress has been observed to be fairly rapid although some things have also been noted to have remained much the same (Edlin and Johns, 2006).

HIPAA 1996 Compliance: HIPAA officers' perceptions of security compliance in 2004 and 2005 are compared in this article Davis and Having (Davis and Having, 2006). The security standards for achieving the highest level of compliance in both 2004 and 2005 were obtaining required business associate agreements and physical safeguards to limit access to electronic information systems. Respondents indicated least compliance in performing periodic evaluation of security practices governed by the Security Rule. Roadblocks, threats, problems and solutions regarding HIPAA compliance are discussed.

3.4.7.5 Merits and De-Merits of HIPAA Approach

The HIPAA 1996 has demanded the time, energy, and financial investment for the health insurance industry, but the challenges arise from difficulties in its implementation aimed at attaining compliance to its rules (Edlin and Johns, 2006). However, its enactment has brought about both benefits and new challenges. The stated aims and objectives of HIPAA 1996 are clearly beneficial to the patient and the public.

Firstly, as a standard, HIPAA enjoys the advantages that have already been discussed in relation to standards.

Secondly, a significant challenge that emerged from HIPAA is to integrate and enable interoperability between proprietary claims systems and legacy software with the new HIPAA standards that took effect in October 2003.

Thirdly, HIPAA's privacy and security rules and the standard identifiers have demanded more upgrades and improvements. The rules and standards have also required payers to spend millions of additional dollars over the first three years of HIPAA compliance (Edlin and Johns, 2006).

Fourthly, the often cited fore-most barriers to compliance with HIPAA are as follows:

1. The *comprehension and interpretation of the legal requirements*;
2. *The achievement of successful integration of new policies and procedures*; and
3. *The resolution of issues arising with third parties.*

The difficulty in comprehending and interpreting the law has been deemed to be the most difficult aspect of the implementation of HIPAA precautionary measures and actions. This and other barriers to HIPAA progress are most likely to remain the same until security education and training become widely adopted as a core aspect of securing e-Healthcare information.

Apart from the recent Japanese Personal Data Protection (PDP) Act 2003, HIPAA 1996 is probably the only first modern large scale e-Healthcare information protection legislation that has been seriously put into operation at a federal level accompanied by enforcement measures and punitive sanctions for non-compliance. The HIPAA rules constitute a mandatory framework that has given rise to a massive drive towards adoption of computerisation of e-Healthcare information systems that seriously implement existing and otherwise ignored standards, especially, security and privacy protection standards.

3.4.8 Canadian Law on Protection of e-Healthcare Information

The Canadian strategy for information privacy protection is layered and sectoral while assuming that privacy protection requires multiple solutions. At the higher layer, the federal legislation for the protection of information consists of banking, telecommunications and transportation, while at the lower layer, provincial privacy and information protection laws covering other domains. Permeating through these layers is the adoption of the Model Code for the Protection of Personal Information (MCPPI) 1996, which was developed by the Canadian Standards Association.

The federal information privacy laws are: the Privacy Act (PA) 1980 and the Personal Information Protection and Electronic Documents Act (PIPEDA) 2000. The PA 1980 applies to Canadian Federal Government bodies and requires to respect personal privacy right of individuals. These bodies are required to limit the collection, usage and disclosure of personal information. The PA further grants individuals the right of access and rectification of errors in personal information held by federal bodies. Similar protection of personal information within the private sector is provided through PIPEDA 2000.

Health Information Privacy Code (HIP Code) 1994 was developed by the Canadian Medical Association in corporation with the Data Protection Commissioner. The HIP Code sets twelve specific rules for agencies in the health sector to better ensure the protection of individual privacy. The code addresses the health information collected, used, held and disclosed by health agencies (in terms of the rights to privacy and access; special nature of health information; limits on collection, use, disclosure and access, non-therapeutic use; patient's consent; accuracy in recording; security safeguards; accountability to patients; transparency; retention and unique identifiers). The HIP Code has been recently amended by the HIP Code 1994 Amendment No. 6 to align it with other laws. For the Canadian national health sector, the HIP Code is effectively a set of information privacy principles on which national laws are based. For example, the Personal Health Information Protection Act (PHIPA) 2004, which is based on the HIP Code 1994, has been in effect in Ontario, Canada since November 1, 2004. PHIPA creates rules for the collection, use and sharing of personal health information by "health information custodians" (HIC). Examples of HICs are doctors, pharmacists and other health care providers. PHIPA also grants patients rights of access to their health records. The Act provides for patient involvement in determining how their health information is used.

Other countries with long traditions of legal protection of the right to privacy are Sweden and France. The 1776 Access to Public Records Act brought openness to Swedish government, while the 1789 French Declaration of the Rights of Man and the Citizen protected private property paving the way for the 1858 provisions for the punitive protection of private information in France.

3.5 Standards for Secure e-Healthcare Information

The majority of e-Healthcare information systems maintain e-Healthcare information about patients in electronic healthcare records (EHRs) using proprietary formats. This has led to interoperability problems at both local and inter-organisational units in healthcare. As a way to fight this problem, several EHR standards that enable structured clinical content and easy exchange have emerged during the last few years. This section reviews the most relevant EHR standards with a focus on their provision for security and privacy protection.

3.5.1 Health Level 7 (HL7) Standardisation

The Health Level 7 (HL7) is a Standards Developing Organisation (SDO), which is accredited to the American National Standards Institute (ANSI). HL7 standardisation efforts focus on clinical and administrative data, which are increasingly occurring in e-Healthcare. HL7 is an international community made up of members, who are healthcare experts and information scientists. HL7 members, who constitute the HL7 Working Group, have interests in the development and advancement of clinical and administrative standards for e-Healthcare and work together to create these standards, which also facilitate the integration of electronic healthcare information. HL7 standards, or specifications, have tended to focus on enabling e-Healthcare applications to exchange key sets of clinical and administrative health information.

The ISO-OSI(International Standards Organisation's Open Systems Interconnection) network model has a "Level 7" as the top level. Thus OSI Level 7 is the network application layer, which is concerned with applications, end user processes, quality of service, authentication, privacy, constraints, and the semantics of information. Hence, HL7 focuses on e-Healthcare standards at the 7th layer of the OSI model. The key standard for the HL7 is the Clinical Document Architecture (CDA), which is a document architecture standard for representing medical and legal health care encounter documents in a standardised format. The HL7 Care Record Summary (CRS), while not yet a HL7 standard, was proposed as a special use-case of the CDA as a care record summary like the ASTM Continuity of Care Record (CCR). It has now been revised and presented as a Discharge Summary, a medical legal document, and a Referral Document, a quasi-medical legal document.

The HL7 CDA/CRS security takes a transactional security approach. This approach is similar to the Internet-based SSL when applied to a document that is sent from a web server to a client or from the client to the web server. In HL7 CDA/CRS security, e-Healthcare information in standard format has a known health care sender and a known health care recipient. The recipient and the sender would have agreed to the security mechanisms needed for that exchange. The aim of HL7 CDA/CRS security is to secure the resulting transaction.

In the area of Role Based Access Control (RBAC), the HL7 Security Technical Committee has formalised a set of permissions. The engineering and role definition content models for HL7 RBAC are compliant with the ANSI RBAC standard. In the HL7 RBAC model, the elements of the permissions contain only one object and at least one operation. A scenario-based role engineering process was used to come up with the permissions set.

The HL7 CDA Version 3 relegates most of the security and privacy functionality to the technological platforms with the standard merely requiring ascertaining platform compliance. For *confidentiality of patient information*, the technological platforms are required to provide functions that limit the right to view or transfer selected data to users with specific kinds of authorisation and auditing access to patient data. HL7 CDA Version 3 standard contains the necessary data objects, attributes and transaction contents to support conveying the necessary information from one healthcare application system to another, so that these systems may perform the confidentiality functions. For *authenticated authorisation for services,* the technological platforms are required to provide functions that may include, but are not limited to, electronic signature and authentication of users based on technologies more advanced than passwords. For *transactional security, privacy, non-repudiation and integrity,* the technological platforms upon which HL7 CDA Version 3 information systems developers implement applications that use HL7 are required to have significantly more capability to protect the confidentiality and integrity of patient information than is common. The required platform functions are public- and private-key encryption, and correspondent system authentication and non-repudiation.

3.5.2 Committee for European Normalisation (CEN) Technical Committee (TC) 251 Standardisation

CEN is the European Committee for Standardisation. TC 251 is a CEN Technical Committee that identifies its domain of focus as:

> the application of information and communication technology in healthcare, social care and wellness. Until recently, predominantly the playing field of well established players with a background in medical or health informatics. e-Health is attracting new players from other sectors such as the telecommunication. CEN/TC 251 has some distinct characteristics from other standards organisations. It is a regional (EU) Standards Development Organisation (SDO) among international or domain specific SDOs and its focus is almost exclusively content technology and not communication technology. [6]

The EHR communications standardisation in CEN TC 251 occurs at a European level with main communication constructs being specified in the four standards, CEN 13606-1-4 (see Table 3.4). Similar and complementary work is on-going in both ISO and HL7. These developments are paving the way to cross fertilisation of standards. Blobel (Blobel, 2004) observed the existence of a strong prospect for an agreement on a generic EHR interoperability standard in Europe and internationally. Tables 3.1, 3.2, 3.3, 3.4, 3.5 and 3.6 [7] present the published standards of the CEN TC 251. Some of these standards are complementary to those of ISO and HL7.

Table 3.1 Published CEN TR XXXXX Standards of CEN/TC 251

STANDARD	GENERAL DESCRIPTION
CEN/TR 15212:2006	Vocabulary - web-based terms and concepts database
CEN/TR 15253:2005	QoS requirements for health information interchange
CEN/TR 15299:2006	Identification of patients & related objects
CEN/TR 15300:2006	Formal modelling of healthcare security policies
CEN/TR 15640:2007	Patient safety of health software

[6] CEN TC251 Executive Summary, http://www.cen.eu/nr/cen/doc/ExecutivePDF/6232.pdf, accessed: 15 August 2008

[7] CEN/TC 251- Published standards, http://www.cen.eu/CENORM/Sectors/Technical CommitteesWorkshops/CENTechnicalCommit tees/Standards.asp?param=6232&title=CEN%2FTC+251#, accessed: 16 August 2008

Table 3.2 Published CEN TS XXXXX standards of CEN/TC 251

STANDARD	GENERAL DESCRIPTION
CEN/TS 14271:2003	File exchange format for vital signs
CEN/TS 14796:2004	Data Types
CEN/TS 14822-4:2005	General purpose information components
CEN/TS 15127-1:2005	Testing of physiological measurement software
CEN/TS 15211:2006	Mapping of hierarchical message descriptions to XML
CEN/TS 15260:2006	Safety risks from health informatics products

Table 3.3 Published CR XXXXX Standards of CEN/TC 251

STANDARD	GENERAL DESCRIPTION
CR 12069:1995	Profiles for medical image interchange
CR 12161:1995	Defining profiles for healthcare
CR 12587:1996	Development of healthcare messages
CR 12700:1997	ENV 1613:1994 - Exchange of Laboratory Information
CR 1350:1993	Syntaxes for existing interchange formats
CR 13694:1999	Safety & Security Related Software Quality Standards
CR 14300:2002	Interoperability of multimedia report systems
CR 14301:2002	Security protection of healthcare communication
CR 14302:2002	Security for intermittently connected devices

3.5.3 The openEHR Specification Standard

The openEHR [8] is an international not-for-profit Foundation, working towards making *the inter-operable, life-long electronic health record a reality* and improving health care in the information society. The Foundation seeks to achieve its mission by developing *open EHR specifications* (openEHR, 2007), open-source software and knowledge resources; engaging in clinical implementation projects; participating in international standards development and supporting health informatics education.

The stable release for the openEHR Specification standard at this time is Revision 1.1, which was issued on 12 April 2007. In essence, the openEHR standard is a specification for an openEHR Health Computing Platform and consists of *requirements, abstract specifications, implementation technology specifications (ITSs), computable expressions and conformance criteria.* The detailed aspects of the openEHR standard are available on the Foundations website. These aspects focus on *security and confidentiality* provisions of the openEHR standard, which are presented in Section 7 of the Architecture Overview document of the openEHR specification (openEHR, 2007).

The openEHR identifies key security requirements that provide:

- Privacy and confidentiality within openEHR is required to be patient consent-driven. The main requirement for protecting privacy in openEHR is stated thus: *data sharing must be controlled by patient consent* while allowing differential ac-

[8] The openEHR Foundation is a not-for-profit organisation led by the University College London, UK, and Ocean Informatics Pty, Australia. http://www.openehr.org, accessed: 15 August 2008

Table 3.4 Published EN XXXXX standards of CEN/TC 251

STANDARD	GENERAL DESCRIPTION
EN 1064:2005+A1:2007	Communication protocol - Computer-assisted ECG
EN 1068:2005	Registration of coding systems
EN 12052:2004	Digital imaging - Communication, workflow and data management
EN 12251:2004	Secure User Identification - Authentication by Passwords
EN 12264:2005	Categorical structures for systems of concepts
EN 12381:2005	Time standards for healthcare specific problems
EN 12435:2006	Expression of results of health measurements
EN 12967-1:2007	Service architecture 1: Enterprise viewpoint
EN 12967-2:2007	Service architecture 2: Information viewpoint
EN 12967-3:2007	Service architecture 3: Computational
EN 13606-1:2007	EHR communication 1: Reference model
EN 13606-2:2007	EHR communication 2: Archetypes interchange specification
EN 13606-3:2008	EHR communication 3: Reference archetypes & term lists
EN 13606-4:2007	EHR communication 4: Security
EN 13609-1:2005	Supporting information 1: coding schemes update
EN 13940-1:2007	Concepts to support continuity of care 1: Basic concepts
EN 14463:2007	Syntax for medical classification systems - ClaML
EN 14484:2003	Health data transfer, EU DP directive - High-level security policy
EN 14485:2003	Handling health data - international applications - EU DP directive
EN 14720-1:2005	Service request/report messages 1: Basic services - referral, discharge
EN 14822-1:2005	General purpose information components 1: Overview
EN 14822-2:2005	General purpose information components 2: Non-clinical
EN 14822-3:2005	General purpose information components 3: Clinical
EN 15521:2007	Categorical structure for terminologies of human anatomy
EN 1614:2006	Dedicated kinds of property in laboratory medicine
EN 1828:2002	Classifications and coding systems of surgical procedures

cess to aspects of health information depending on sensitivity of the information as perceived by the patient. The specification notes the complexity in allowing differential access while preserving privacy when inter-related health information enables inferences to be easily drawn from any revealed portions of the EHR.

- The need for fast access to health information during emergencies and the large numbers of care-givers under normal and abnormal situations in various aspect of the care of a patient is recognised in openEHR as requiring general consent since care-givers may not be known. Secondary uses of data such as for on-going research purposes also require patient consent. The openEHR specification identifies the requirement of implementing the system.
- The rationale for the requirement of general consent is also the rationale for the requirement for some access control to be specified in terms of roles or categories. The status of a user or care-givers is based on the role or category at the time when rights of access are being decided. Complexity in this requirement arise from the fact that healthcare roles are liquid and ever-changing from one moment to the next, from one location and jurisdiction to the next and due to temporary replacements. The openEHR specification recognises that the role-based access control mechanism for healthcare must be highly flexible to suit the real clinical setting.

Table 3.5 Published ISO-Related Standards of CEN/TC 251

STANDARD	GENERAL DESCRIPTION
EN ISO 11073-10101:2005	PoC device comm 10101: Nomenclature
EN ISO 11073-10201:2005	PoC device comm 10201: Domain information model
EN ISO 11073-20101:2005	PoC device comm 20101: Application profiles - Base std
EN ISO 11073-30200:2005	PoC device comm 30200: Transport profile - Cable connected
EN ISO 11073-30300:2005	PoC device comm 30300: Transport profile - Infrared wireless
EN ISO 18104:2003	Reference terminology model for nursing
EN ISO 18812:2003	Clinical analyser interfaces to LIS - Use profiles
EN ISO 21549-1:2004	Patient healthcard data 1: General structure
EN ISO 21549-2:2004	Patient healthcard data 2: Common objects
EN ISO 21549-3:2004	Patient healthcard data 3: Limited clinical data
EN ISO 21549-4:2006	Patient healthcard data 4: Extended clinical data
EN ISO 21549-5:2008	Patient healthcard data 5: Identification data
EN ISO 21549-6:2008	Patient healthcard data 6: Administrative data
EN ISO 21549-7:2007	Patient healthcard data 7: Medication data
EN ISO 27799:2008	Information security - ISO/IEC 27002 (ISO 27799:2008)

Table 3.6 Published ENV XXXX standards of CEN/TC 251

STANDARD	GENERAL DESCRIPTION
ENV 12443:1999	Healthcare Information Framework (HIF)
ENV 12537-1:1997	Registration of information objects - EDI 1: The Register
ENV 12537-2:1997	Registration of information objects - EDI 2: Procedures
ENV 12610:1997	Medicinal product identification
ENV 12611:1997	Categorical structure of systems of concepts - Medical devices
ENV 12612:1997	Exchange of healthcare administrative information
ENV 13607:2000	Exchange of information on medicine prescriptions
ENV 13608-1:2000	Security for healthcare communication 1: Concepts and terminology
ENV 13608-2:2000	Security for healthcare communication 2: Secure data objects
ENV 13608-3:2000	Security for healthcare communication 3: Secure data channels
ENV 13609-2:2000	Supporting information 2: Updating of medical laboratory-specific information
ENV 13730-1:2001	Blood transfusion related messages 1: Subject of care messages
ENV 13730-2:2002	Blood transfusion related messages 2: Production messages (BTR-PROD)
ENV 13734:2000	Vital signs information representation
ENV 13735:2000	Interoperability of patient connected medical devices

- This flexibility must also extend to supporting usability within the clinical setting of the security and privacy mechanism.
- The openEHR specification also assumes the following set of threats as a basis of security and privacy model: human error in patient identification, inappropriate access, malicious theft of health information generic threats (viruses, worms, Trojans, denial-of-service attacks) and system failures.

As a solution to the requirements outlined above, openEHR provides a minimalist security policy profile which it recognises to be necessary, but insufficient for securing e-Healthcare information. The general security policy principles include: indelibility of health records, i.e., nothing must be deleted; audit trailing with user identity, timestamp, reason, digital signature and version information; and anonymity based on separation of identifying personal information from content of the health record.

The rest of the security policy profile embodied in openEHR deals with issues of access control. Ultimately, the security policy is required to scale to distributed environments.

The minimalist policy in openEHR is supported by models for integrity, anonymity and access control. Integrity is ensured through comprehensive versioning and a digital signing scheme that allows parts or versions of the EHR to be signed separately. Anonymity is implemented through separation of patient demographic information and using a pseudonymisation scheme, where a patient is represented by a special system object called PARTY_SELF.

3.5.4 International Standards Organisation Technical Committee (ISO/TC) 215 Healthcare Informatics Standardisation

The ISO/TC 215 is the Technical Committee (TC) of the International Organisation for Standardisation (ISO), which develops and maintains standard on Health Informatics. TC 215 works on the standardisation of Health Information and Communications Technology (ICT). The standards allow compatibility and interoperability between independent systems.

Shared care implies sharing information. For information sharing to be secure, there is a requirement for a common concept of information security among healthcare information users. There is also a requirement for a system to maintain compliance to the security requirements within the healthcare community (Posthumus, 2004). Implementing standards-based e-Healthcare information security could be difficult and security specifications cannot be rigorously verified. The use of formal methods in the verification of security specifications is important, as the methods are based on standards-based security criteria. Motimoto (Morimoto et al, 2006) proposes a security specification verification technique based on the international standard ISO/IEC 15408. The formalisation was first applied to the security criteria of ISO/IEC 15408. The verification technique of security specifications was then developed based on the formalised criteria with formal methods. The resulting verification technique allows the formal verification to define the security specifications in order to satisfy the security criteria of ISO/IEC 15408. Another interesting aspect of Morimoto et al's technique is that the ambiguity and/or oversight in security specifications written in natural language could also be detected.

At the European level, the Committee for European Normalisation (CEN) is focusing on the EHR communications standardisation with the major EHR constructs for communication being defined in the CEN 13606 standard model (Kalra, 2006). Complementary activity is part of the component of ISO and in HL7.

The Code of Practice for Information Security Management specified in the ISO/IEC 17799 standard has been used as a general framework for establishing a set of controls for information security in a particular organisation (Posthumus, 2004). This could provide a foundation for a standard-based compliance monitoring.

The ISO/IEC 17799 standard has also been used as a framework for standards on information security in healthcare and their implementation (Posthumus, 2004), providing a foundation for a common concept of information security in e-Healthcare.

Barlette et al (Barlette and Fomin, 2008) suggest that the legislative environment can play a crucial role for further growth of security standards adoption. The latter has been demonstrated in HIPAA 1996 in the USA.

3.5.5 ASTM Committee E31 on Healthcare Informatics Standardisation

The American Society for Testing and Materials (ASTM) Committee E31 standardisation efforts focus on the architecture, content, storage, security, confidentiality, functionality and communication of e-Healthcare information and knowledge from a patient-specific perspective.

3.5.5.1 ASTM Committee E31 Standards for Security and Privacy in Healthcare Informatics

The Table 3.7 presents the main security and privacy standards, while Tables 3.8 - 3.10 presents some of the key e-Healthcare standards that are developed and maintained by the ASTM Committee E31 on Healthcare Informatics. (See Table 3.7 for further details).

Table 3.7 ASTM Committee E31 Standards for Security and Privacy in Healthcare Informatics

CATEGORY	STANDARD	DESCRIPTION
Security & Privacy	E1714	Universal Healthcare Identifier (UHID)
	E1762	Electronic Authentication of Health Information
	E1869	Confidentiality, Privacy, Access & Data Security
	E1985	User Authentication and Authorisation
	E1986	Health Information Access Privileges
	E1987	Individual Rights over Health Information
	E1988	Training of Persons accessing Health Information
	E2017	Amendments to Health Information
	E2084	Authentication Using Digital Signatures
	E2085	Security Framework for Health Information
	E2086	Internet and Intranet Healthcare Security
	E2147	Audit and Disclosure Logs for Health IS
	E2212	Healthcare Certificate Policy

E1714 is an ASTM standard for Universal Healthcare Identifier (UHID) and it specifies the creation of a national health care identifier. The standard describes the desired properties of identifier and existing identifier schemes. The standard also

Table 3.8 ASTM Committee E31 Standards for Healthcare Vocabularies

CATEGORY	STANDARD	DESCRIPTION
Vocabularies	E2087	Quality indicators for health vocabularies
EHR Content	E1239	Hospital Functionality for EHR Systems
	E1384	Content and Structure of the EHR
	E1633	Coded Values Used in the EHR
	E1715	OO Models in EHRs
	E1744	View of Emergency Medical Care
	E2171	Rating-Scale Measures Relevant to the EHR
	E2436	Human Characteristics Data in Healthcare IS
	E2473	Occupational/Environmental Health View of EHR

Table 3.9 ASTM Committee E31 Standards for Documentation in Healthcare

Documentation	E1902	Secure Dictation, Transcription & Transcribed EHRs
	E1959	Medical Transcription Services
	E2117	QA for Medical Transcription
	E2185	Digital Voice Data Transfer
	E2344	Data Capture through the Dictation
	E2364	Speech Recognition Technology Products

Table 3.10 ASTM Committee E31 Standards for Modelling and E-Healthcare Records

Modelling	E1340	Rapid Prototyping
	E2145	Modelling in Health Informatics
EHRs	E2182	Clinical XML DTDs
	E2183	XML DTD Design, Architecture & Implementation
	E2184	Healthcare Document Formats
	E2210	Clinical Practice Guideline Elements Model (GEM)
	E2211	E-Personal Health Record Consumers & Suppliers
	E2369	Continuity of Care Record (CCR)

specifies a proposed identifier scheme, descriptions of how the proposed scheme would function, and an evaluation of how well the proposed scheme meets the properties outlined in the standards document.

ASTM E1762 (95(2003)) is the Standard Guide for Electronic Authentication of Health Care Information. Its purposes are:

- To serve as a guide for developers of computer software providing, or interacting with, electronic signature processes,
- To serve as a guide to healthcare providers who are implementing electronic signature mechanisms, and
- To be a consensus standard on the design, implementation, and use of electronic signatures.

The standard defines a document structure for use by electronic signature mechanisms, as well as the characteristics of an electronic signature process. It also defines the minimum requirements for different electronic signature mechanisms, as well as the signature attributes for use with electronic signature mechanisms. Furthermore, after describing acceptable electronic signature mechanisms and technologies, the standard then defines the minimum requirements for user identification, access control, and other security requirements for electronic signatures. ASTM E1762 outlines technical details for all electronic signature mechanisms to allow interoperability between systems supporting the same signature mechanism. The standard was intended to be complementary to standards emerging from efforts in other standards organisations. ASTM E1762 does not incorporate the determination of which documents require signatures, since it deems such an issue to be addressed by law, regulation, accreditation standards, and an organisation's policy.

ASTM E1869 is a standard guide for Confidentiality, Privacy, Access, and Data Security Principles for Health Information Including Electronic Health Records. It covers the principles in these areas while focusing on the person identifiable health information. This standard is applicable to computer-based systems. However, many of the principles also apply to health information and patient records that are not in an electronic format. The ASTM E1869 standard does not cover the basic principles and ethical practices for handling confidentiality, access, and security of health information. It assumes that the latter are contained in laws, rules and regulations, and in ethical statements of professional conduct.

ASTM E1985 - 98(2005) is a standard for User Authentication and Authorisation. It covers mechanisms that may be used to authenticate healthcare information (both administrative and clinical) users to computer systems, as well as mechanisms to authorise particular actions by users. These actions may include access to healthcare information documents, as well as, specific operations on those documents (for example, review by a physician). ASTM E1985 addresses both centralised and distributed environments, by defining the requirements that a single system shall meet and the kinds of information, which shall be transmitted between systems to provide distributed authentication and authorisation services. The standard addresses the technical specifications for how to perform user authentication and authorisation. The standard is silent on the actual definition of who can access what, as is based on organisational policy.

ASTM E1986 (98(2005)) is a standard for Information Access Privileges to Health Information. It focuses on the process of granting and maintaining access privileges. It directly addresses the maintenance of confidentiality of personal, provider, and organisational data in the healthcare domain. The standard also deals with specific requirements for granting access privileges to patient-specific health information during health emergencies. The ASTM E1986 standard applies to all individuals, groups, organisations, data-users, data-managers, and public and private firms, companies, agencies, departments, bureaus, service-providers, and similar entities that collect individual, group, and organisational data related to health care. It also applies to all collection, use, management, maintenance, disclosure, and access of all individual, group, and organisational data related to health care. ASTM E1986 broadly covers all methods of collection and use of data whether paper-based, written, printed, typed, dictated, transcribed, forms-based, photocopied, scanned, facsimile, telefax, magnetic media, image, video, motion picture, still picture, film, microfilm, animation, 3D, audio, digital media, optical media, synthetic media, or computer-based. The standard does not address specific legislative and regulatory issues regarding individual, group, and organisational rights to protection of privacy. The standard also does not directly define explicit disease-specific and evaluation/treatment-specific data control or access, or both. ASTM E1986 assumes that the confidential protection of elemental data elements in relation to which data elements fall into restrictive or specifically controlled categories, or both, is set by policies, professional practice, and laws, legislation and regulations.

ASTM E1987-98 is a standard for Individual Rights Regarding Health Information. This standard was Withdrawn in 2007 and has not been replaced by any other standard. This is probably because individual rights are not absolute and are always subject to change through legislation and policy. This is a typical example of standards bodies shying away from rights-based standards. However, it is clear from the scope of other standards that matters that have legal implications are generally placed outside the scope of standardisation, even though standards may depend on them. Another standard, which was also withdrawn in 2007 without replacement, the ASTM E1988-98 standard for Training of Persons who have Access to Health Information.

ASTM E2017-99(2005) is a standard for Amendments to Health Information and addresses the criteria for amending individually-identifiable health information. Certain criteria for amending health information is found in laws, rules and regulations, and in ethical statements of professional conduct. Such criteria are not addressed by any current standard.

ASTM E2084 is a standard specification for Authentication of Healthcare Information Using Digital Signatures. The use of digital signatures to provide authentication of healthcare information, as described in ASTM E1762, is specified in this standard. ASTM E2084 also describes how the components of a digital signature system meet the requirements specified in ASTM E1762. The description in the standard also covers the specification of allowable signature and hash algorithms, management of public and private keys, and specific formats for keys, certificates, and signed healthcare documents. It is intended that ASTM E2084 standard should be read in conjunction with ASTM E1762, which describes the scope of, and requirements for, authentication of healthcare information. ASTM E2084 specification also describes one implementation of digital signatures that meets all of the requirements of ASTM E1762. It should be noted that ASTM E2084 does not prescribe any particular policy regarding which documents should be authenticated, and by whom.

ASTM E2085 is a standard for Security Framework for Healthcare Information, which specifies a framework for the protection of healthcare information. The framework includes both storage and transmission of information. ASTM E2085 describes existing standards used for information security, which can be used in many cases. It also describes, which (healthcare-specific) standards are needed to complete the framework. Appropriate background information on security (and particularly cryptography) is included. The framework is designed to accommodate a very large (national or international), distributed user base, spread across many organisations, and it therefore recommends the use of certain (scaleable) technologies over others.The framework in ASTM E2085 does not address policy issues, which are addressed by standardisation work, that is being undertaken by the ASTM Subcommittee E31.17.

The ASTM E2086 Standard for Internet and Intranet Healthcare Security deals with mechanisms that can be used to protect healthcare information, which is being transmitted over networks using the Internet Protocol Suite (IPS). The Internet, as well as corporate intranets, use off-the-shelf components to implement the protocols covered by the standard. The question of when these mechanisms are used is based on risk analysis, by an organisation's security policy. The Internet Engineering Task Force (IETF) defines security standards for use with the IPS. The ASTM E2086 Standard covers the relevant IETF standards and recommends, where needed, particular options, such as cryptographic transformations, to be used with in conjunction with the standards.

ASTM E2147 is a standard for Audit and Disclosure Logs for Use in Health Information Systems. It is for the development and implementation of security audit/disclosure logs for health information. The standard specifies how to design an access audit log to record all access to patient identifiable information maintained in computer systems. It also includes principles for developing policies, procedures, and functions of health information logs to document all disclosure of health information to external users for use in manual and computer systems. The process of information disclosure and auditing should confirm, where relevant, with the privacy laws.

3.5.5.2 ASTM E31 Security Model for e-Healthcare Information

The ASTM Continuity of Care Record (CCR) is a standard for a comprehensive data summary that aggregates data from multiple sources, health care records, medical legal documents, and health care encounters. The CCR design was aimed at projecting a comprehensive overall clinical picture of a patients current and relevant historical health care status. The CCR standard is officially balloted and approved as ASTM Standard E2369-05. Instead of taking a transactional approach, like the HL7 CDA security model, the ASTM CCR security demands security and confidentiality at all times. The ASTM CCR is a summary record produced by a physician, patient, or institution/system that exists in its own right, irrespective of who its intended target is. The ASTM CCR security demands, that it must be secure and confidential at all times, not merely during a transaction.

For instance, an ASTM CCR is generated by a healthcare unit. The unit generating the CCR will give the data to the patient or save it as a data source. In most instances the healthcare unit is not aware who the patient will see next and, hence, the next end-user of the CCR will be unknown. A CCR is, therefore, required to exist as a secure and confidential document in its own right. This is regardless and in addition to the technical transport security mechanism through which it might be sent. Hence, ASTM CCR security aims at securing e-Healthcare information, so that all transactions, including open Internet transactions and data on portable digital media, such as USB drives, are secure.

3.5.6 Generic IT Security within e-Healthcare Information Management

It is commonly recognized that security and privacy are inextricably linked. The protection of the privacy of e-Healthcare information depends in large part on the existence of IT security measures to protect that information. When security requirements for securing e-Healthcare information are spelt out, IT security experts generally respond by saying that *"health systems with the characteristics thus described are technically feasible and should be generally implemented and deployed"* (Falcao-Reis et al, 2008). It is generally accepted that security approaches, standards and laws that are designed for e-commerce inherited security weaknesses, financial liability and, hence, not sufficient for personal health data, where the personal damage caused by unintentional disclosure may be far more serious. Generic IT security standards have the tendency to be targeted towards applications in e-commerce. The complexity of the healthcare domain means that generic security solutions cannot just be easily dropped in to meet the unique security and privacy requirements of health care applications (Baker and Masys, 1999). This section explores the use of generic IT security standards in e-Healthcare information management and how they interact with healthcare security standards and laws.

3.5.6.1 Authentication and Authorisation in e-Healthcare

It is becoming increasingly important that patients should be able to view their electronic health records (EHRs). The EHR access by patients is here to stay is clear from the legal underpinnings based on laws such as Freedom of Information Acts. It has been argued that with simple precautions, record access is safe and affords many benefits to both patients and clinicians as they could pave the way towards health records might be written as a co-produced document (Fisher et al, 2006) possibly incorporating patient contributions. Since patient now has access to his or her records, standards for record sharing and access control authentication need to be written.

Robust, reliable and standards forms of authentication are a particularly important requirement for protecting the privacy of personal e-Healthcare records (PEHRs). The personal e-Healthcare record will often contain sensitive and protected health information maintained by the patient.

The Health care industry is unlikely to be expected to successfully single-handedly develop and deploy a large scale, national or international authentication infrastructure. Consequently, it would seem to be pragmatic to not only leverage existing hardware, software, and networks, but also implement and comply with security standards and privacy protection laws.

3.5.6.2 Identity and the Unique Position of Biometric Methods for Authentication

Identity plays a key role in authenticating patients in order to enable their access to EHRs. Strategies for manual identity management mostly utilise some aspect of the patient's body as well as biographical techniques, e.g., birth and location of birth and mother's maiden name. When the patient is ill, being able to make proper identification becomes crucial for proper treatment. Identity techniques during periods of serious illness and hospitalisation may be rendered difficult, especially in this global age of e-Health characterised by mobility (Mordini and Ottolini, 2007). The e-Healthcare is a sector that is increasingly embracing biometric methods of identification that include fingerprint authentication even within network-based access (Fisher et al, 2006). Biometric security ensure secure identification, which is critical in the health care domain for controlling access to centralised archives of digitised patients e-Healthcare information; for limiting physical access to buildings and hospital wards; and for authenticating medical and social support personnel; and identifying patients accurately.

Among biometric-based personal identification systems, which include fingerprinting and iris recognition, DNA has been found to provide the most reliable personal identification (Hashiyada, 2004). It is intrinsically digital and unchangeable whether the person is alive or death. Are there any standards on this form of authentication? if they are, what do they say?

Biometric authentication seems to be a return to classical approach where the human body is central to identity. However, Mordini and Ottolini (Mordini and Ottolini, 2007) argue that biometric authentication devices can significantly reveal health information and calls for a careful ethical, political and ultimately legal scrutiny before widespread adoption of biometric authentication. This points to the need for using IT security standards within e-Healthcare information management standards within the context of the legal framework for allowing biometric authentication to be beneficially utilised.

3.5.6.3 Authentication and Authorisation in Emerging Technologies for e-Healthcare Information Management

Mobile Devices: Ubiquitous wireless mobile devices are transforming e-Healthcare to emerging mobile healthcare (m-healthcare) (Istepanian et al, 2006) with further new complications to the security and privacy of health information. This is a new area where laws and standards are yet neither stable nor sometimes available. Sax (Sax et al, 2005) proposed a new model for authentication of users to e-Healthcare information systems that exploits wireless mobile device technologies. Sax et al further state that cell phones are not only widely distributed and have high user acceptance but that they also offer advanced security protocols. They address the challenge for the strong authentication of individuals in m-healthcare by creating a registration authority and an authentication service. While generic IT security and healthcare standards may exist to protect privacy in e-Healthcare, the challenges from m-healthcare arising from the uniqueness and immense possibilities brought about by ubiquitous wireless mobile devices may necessitate going to the drawing-board. The advanced security protocols referred to by Sax et al are generic IT security protocols that have not helped in abating reported breaches in e-commerce, especially, when attacks use a combination of ubiquitous wireless mobile devices with social engineering and other methods.

Smartcards: The use of crypto-processor cards for authentication and authorisation has been investigated with huge national adoption proposals in Europe (Broek and Sikkel, 1997; Kleinebreil et al, 2003; Kohler et al, 1996), particularly in Germany (Blobel et al, 2001) and France (Kleinebreil et al, 2003). For example, Bales et al (Bales, 2005) report that from 2006 onwards all members of the German health insurance system were to be issued a new electronic health card . The new health card differed from the old card, as it was designed to either include patient-related health data or provide access to such data in addition to its administrative functions. Bales et al noted that for maximum data safety, security and privacy, a crypto-processor card was to be used so as to permit authentication (electronic identity check), encryption and the electronic digital signature. The only biometric aspect to the card was a photograph of the card holder on the e-Health card for easy identification of the insured person by a human agent. Personal e-Healthcare information stored in a networked e-Healthcare environment allows fast access to information and supports advanced shared care requirements. Security token-like smart cards have been noted to be more suitable for identification purposes, data protection, privacy protection, access rights, and limited person-based information storage, e.g., for emergency procedures (Pharow and Blobel, 2006). However, linking networked e-Healthcare environment with crypto-processor or smart card enables making beneficial use of different technologies without ignoring their existing weaknesses (Pharow and Blobel, 2006). EAP smart cards can enhance security and privacy in emerging wireless network infrastructures, i.e., m-health, because they ensure strong authentication in IP networks based on the Extensible Authentication Protocol (EAP) [9]. For example, EAP smart cards (Urien and Pujolle, 2008) could be in the form of Java cards [10] deployed on clients' terminals (such as IEEE 802.1X supplicants) or in RADIUS servers. The preferred way to deal with the challenges of modern healthcare and welfare requirements shall be a well-balanced combination of cards and networks that are secured based on standards such as the ISO 20301:2006, which is designed to confirm the identities of both the healthcare application provider and the health-

[9] Extensible Authentication Protocol (EAP) is a universal authentication framework that is mostly used in wireless networks as well as in Point-to-Point connections. EAP is developed and maintained by the Internet Engineering Task Force (IETF) RFC 3748. The strength of EAP lies in its ability to support multiple authentication methods.Although the EAP protocol is not limited to wireless LANs and can be used for wired LAN authentication, it is mostly used in wireless LANs. RFC3748 is available at http://www.ietf.org/rfc/rfc3748.txt?number=3748, accessed: 18 August 2008.

[10] Sun Microsystems, Inc., Java Card Technology, http://java.sun.com/javacard/, accessed: 18 August 2008

card holder in order that information may be securely exchanged by using cards issued for healthcare service.

Radio-Frequency Identification (RFID): RFID tagging is an emerging ubiquitous wireless technology, which has been proposed for use in authorisation and authentication. The technology is based on embedding the RFID tags [11] in objects including implantation in human beings, e.g., the VeriChip. According to Halamka (Halamka et al, 2006) the proposed uses of the VeriChip include identification of medical patients, physical access control, contactless retail payment, and even the tracing of kidnapping victims. RFID tags have serious security privacy weaknesses problems and their increasing use require regulations and standardisation (Karygiannis et al, 2007). For example, Halamka et al noted that the VeriChip is vulnerable to simple, over-the-air spoofing attacks where an attacker could be capable of scanning a VeriChip, eavesdropping on its signal, or simply learning its serial number and create a spoof device whose radio appearance is indistinguishable from the original. As a result of the high security vulnerability, Halamka et al recommended that the VeriChip should serve exclusively for identification, and not authentication or access control.

3.5.6.4 Data Integrity and Non-repudiation

Data integrity refers to the assurance that data is consistent and correct. From the IT security perspective, data integrity refers to the validity of data, which can be compromised by malicious alterations, such as an attacker altering an account number in a bank transaction, or forgery of an identity document; or by accidental alterations, such as a transmission error, or a hard disk crash.

Non-repudiation [12], in ordinary terms, is the concept of ensuring that a party in a dispute cannot repudiate, or refute the validity of a statement or contract. The concept of non-repudiation is most commonly applied in the verification and trust of signatures. In IT security, non-repudiation refers to situation where a service can provide proof of the integrity and origin of data or where there is an authentication that can be asserted to be genuine with high degree of assurance.

---

[11] An RFID tag is an object that can be applied to or incorporated into a product, animal, or person for the purpose of identification using radio waves. Passive RFID tags have no internal power supply. The minute electrical current induced in the antenna by the incoming radio frequency signal provides just enough power for the CMOS integrated circuit in the tag to power up and transmit a response. Active RFID tags have their own internal power source that is used to power the integrated circuits and to broadcast the response signal to the reader. Communications from active tags to readers is typically much more reliable, i.e., has fewer errors, than from passive tags due to the ability for active tags to conduct a "session" with a reader. See http://csrc.nist.gov/publications/nistpubs/800-98/SP800-98_RFID-2007.pdf, accessed 18 August 2008.

[12] In law, a signature on a paper contract or memorandum may always be repudiated by the signatory. However, such repudiation can be mounted in two ways: 1) The signatory may claim fraud or forgery, e.g., saying, "I never signed that!"; and 2) The signatory may accept the signature as legitimate but dispute its validity due to unjustified or unlawful coercion, for instance under blackmail or confessions made under torture.

The e-Healthcare information for a particular individual can be preserved for a century. During this long period of preservation of health information, non-repudiation as well as the availability, integrity and confidentiality of stored information over these lengthy preservation periods are required to be completely demonstrated and thoroughly proved to avoid loss and to ensure that the ability to manipulate the information remains possible (Ruotsalainen and Manning, 2007).

3.5.6.5 Dominant Encryption Standards for Protecting Confidentiality

Encryption is the process in cryptography for transforming information, the *plaintext,* using an algorithm, the *cipher,* to produce unreadable output, the *cyphertext,* to anyone except those possessing special knowledge, the *key.* The encryption applies a cipher to plaintext to create cyphertext, which can only be decrypted by using the key. In the medical and legal perspective, patient confidentiality is an obligation placed on the clinicians to ensure that information about a patient will not be disclosed to other parties without the patient's consent. Encryption provides a way to protect the confidentiality of messages in e-Healthcare, especially during the transmission of the messages.

The Data Encryption Standard (DES): The DES is the US Federal Information Processing Standard (FIPS PUB 46). It have been used for over 20 years by the U.S. Government organisations and in commerce to protect sensitive (unclassified) information. DES was designed in the 70s. The DES was replaced by the Triple DES, which is a block cipher that improves on the DES cipher by applying it three times. TDES is slowly also being replaced by the *Advanced Encryption Standard (AES)* (NIST, 2001). However, the electronic payments industry still uses TDES extensively. It would be expected that TDES will remain an active cryptographic standard for some time to come. The DES family of encryption algorithms has been used almost universally by financial institutions (Fls) around the world (Garon and Outerbridge, 1991). In 1991, it was noted that for the foreseeable future there were no alternatives to its continued use. Within ten years, that is by year 2000, unmodified single-key DES was deemed to be breakable for a cost of about 3,500 per solution in under one day. Many financial systems which relied at that time on single-key DES were predicted to be vulnerable to attack in the 2000s.

The Advanced Encryption Standard (AES): The AES, which is also called *Rijndael,* is a block cipher adopted as an encryption standard by the U.S. government after it was announced by National Institute of Standards and Technology (NIST) as US FIPS PUB 197 (FIPS 197) on November 26, 2001 (NIST, 2001). The Belgian cryptographers, Joan Daemen and Vincent Rijmen, developed AES and submitted it to the AES selection process under the name "Rijndael", a portmanteau of the names of the two inventors (Daemen and Rijmen, 2002). In October, 2000, NIST selected Rijndael as the AES (FIPS-197) and destined it for massive world-wide usage.

Being a *substitution-permutation (SP) network* [13], the AES is fast, easy to implement, and requires little memory. As a new encryption standard, it is currently being deployed on a large scale.

Discussion: Despite the general availability of AES, the Data Encryption Standard is not yet fully obsolete. According to Courtois et al (Courtois and Bard, 2007), DES has never been broken from the practical point of view. Its extension, Triple DES, is believed to be very secure and is widely used in the financial sector. Courtois at al point out that TDES should remain in use for the foreseeable future, especially, when some doubts have been raised about whether its replacement, AES, is secure. These doubts arise as a result of the extreme level of *"algebraic vulnerability"* of the AES S-boxes (their low I/O degree and exceptionally large number of quadratic I/O equations). The AES has been selected for use by U.S. Government organisations to protect sensitive (and even secret and top secret) information (NIST, 2001). It is also becoming a (de facto) global standard for commercial software and hardware that use encryption or other security features. The AES encryption standard has also been widely adopted in e-Healthcare information management as the section 3.5.6.6 reveals.

3.5.6.6 Encryption for Protecting Confidentiality in e-Healthcare

The adoption of the AES encryption in e-Healthcare information management is growing and could be seen beyond the US into other healthcare jurisdictions. For example, the Irish Blood Transfusion Service (IBTS) laptop that was stolen (Honan, 2008) in New York while holding data, which was sent to the US on a CD and encrypted with 256 AES encryption. The data contained over 170,000 individuals' information who had used the services. In this scenario, the protection of privacy and confidentiality could rely only on the strength of the AES encryption if the data on the laptop was still encrypted.

The use of encryption within emerging computing infrastructures

1. Mobile devices: The mobile devices have increased their penetration in the healthcare sector. Some of the reasons given for their increased penetration include enhanced functionality, low cost, high reliability and easy-to-use nature (Weerasinghe et al, 2007). A major challenge in this aspects arises from the wireless nature of communication links in mobile networks. Applications that use the mobile device infrastructure require a concrete security framework based on encryption and long-term security keys, e.g., keys found in a mobile Subscriber Identity Module (SIM). Weerasinghe (Weerasinghe et al, 2007) developed a novel protocol that will send the information securely while including the access privileges to the authorised recipient. The increasing use of mobile phones has led us to the use of SMS messages

[13] In cryptography, an SP-network, or substitution-permutation network (SPN), is a series of linked mathematical operations used in block cipher algorithms like the AES.These networks consist of S-boxes and P-boxes that transform blocks of input bits into output bits. Generally, these transformations are to be operations that are efficient to perform in hardware, such as exclusive OR (XOR) gates.

in the electronic interactions between health care professionals and patients. Hassinen (Hassinen and Laitinen, 2005) demonstrated that it is possible to send, receive and store text messages securely with a mobile phone with no additional hardware required using encryption methods only.

2. Grid Computing: In an e-Healthcare application of grid technology, it was shown that the security mechanisms in Intensive Care Grid (ICGrid) [14] are not enough to provide a comprehensive solution, mainly because the data-at-rest is still vulnerable to attacks coming from untrusted Storage Elements where an attacker may directly access them (Luna et al, 2008). Luna et al solved this problem through a new privacy-oriented protocol which uses a combination of encryption and fragmentation to improve data's assurance while keeping compatibility with current legislations and Health Grid security mechanisms. Encrypted storage of confidential data effectively reduces the risk of disclosure. A self-enforcing scheme for encrypted data storage could also be achieved by combining Grid security systems with distributed key management and classical cryptography techniques. Virtual Organisations, as the main unit of user management in Grid, can provide a way to organise key sharing, access control lists and secure encryption management (Torres et al, 2006).

3. Database security: In database security, data encryption is often supported for the sole purpose of protecting the data in storage and assumes trust in the server, that decrypts data for query execution. Damiani et al (Damiani et al, 2003) introduce a simple yet robust single-server solution for remote querying of encrypted databases on untrusted servers. Their approach is based on the use of indexing information attached to the encrypted database which can be used by the server to select the data to be returned in response to a query without the need of disclosing the database content. In the Hippocratic Database approach, securing electronic health records involves information sharing across autonomous data sources using cryptographic protocols (Agrawal and Johnson, 2007). Encryption also plays a key role in the Healthcare Data Card or Health Card (Bales, 2005). The card is fitted with a microprocessor that permits authentication, encryption and the electronic digital signature. It ensures maximum data safety and security and ultimately the confidentiality of information.

The use of encryption in health research

In the secondary usage of healthcare information for research purposes, linking different e-Healthcare records for the purpose of cohort studies may require matching with personal names and other personally identifiable data. Okamoto (Okamoto, 2004) examined the possibility of performing this privacy-sensitive procedures in a *linkable anonymising* manner using encryption. Thus, cancer records are matched without revealing patient identifiers to the user.

Okamoto (Okamoto, 2004) noted that, on one hand, *bidirectional communication* entails encryption and deciphering, necessitating both senders and receivers sharing

[14] The Intensive Care Grid (ICGrid) is a Grid application that enables: the retrieval of data from patient attached medical sensors found in modern Intensive Care Units; the filtering and annotation of these; data by ICU medical staff; the storage and replication of annotated data-sets; and the distributed searching of stored meta-data annotations and the retrieval of data-sets.

a common secret *key*. On the other hand, *record linkage* in research use of healthcare information entails only encryption and not deciphering because researchers do not need to know the identity of the linked person. It was concluded that this unidirectional nature relieves researchers from the historical problem of *key sharing* and enables data holders such as municipal governments and insurers to encrypt personal names in a relatively easy manner.

The limitations and alternatives to encryption

The standards and security features such as encryption have also been singled out as sources of bottlenecks in the EHR systems. An example bottleneck scenario investigation includes the estimation of the delays created in queues during the exchange of the EHRs between different health service points (Orfanidis et al, 2007). Delays have been observed to derive from LAN and Internet technologies, the EPR encryption/decryption, the HL7 message generation/parsing, and the databases.

Pseudonymisation has been proposed as an alternative to encryption. For example, in PIPE (Pseudonymisation of Information for Privacy in e-Health) (Riedl et al, 2007), a new EHR architecture for primary and secondary usage of health data incorporates security model that is based on Pseudonymisation as an alternative to encryption. Riedl (Riedl et al, 2007) stated that the need for presenting pseudonymisation and encryption as alternatives arises from concerns and the lack of existing approaches that provide a sufficient level of security, thus, raising the need for a system that guarantees data privacy and keeps the access to health data under strict control of the patient.

The Bermans scenario (Berman, 2004) detailed below eliminated the need for encryption in protecting privacy and confidentiality in e-Healthcare:

> Institution A and Institution B each create a random character string and send it to the other institution. Each institution receives the random string from the other institution and sums it with their own random string, producing a random string common to both institutions (RandA+B). Each institution takes a unique patient identifier and sums it with RandA+B. The product is a random character string that is identical across institutions when the patient is identical in both institutions. A comparison protocol can be implemented as a zero-knowledge transaction, ensuring that neither institution obtains any knowledge of its own patient or of the patient compared at another institution (Berman, 2004).

The resulting protocol is considered to be executable at high computational speed and requires neither the use of encryption algorithm nor a one-way hash algorithm. Berman et al also pointed out that there is no need to protect the protocol from discovery. They further characterise it as a zero-knowledge protocol for reconciling patients across institutions.

3.5.6.7 Security Certification

The e-Healthcare is inter-jurisdictional in the sense that it is Internet-based. Therefore, e-Healthcare poses risks to patient health information that involve not only technology and professional protocols but also laws, regulations and professional security cultures. Secure e-Health requires not only national standardisation of professional education and protocols, but also global interoperability of regulations and laws.

Pretty Good Privacy (PGP) encoding is based on the Public-Key Procedure. PGP claims to allow the safe transmission of medical data. If the used keys belong to the key owner and the key owner's identity is guaranteed by a trusted third party, PGP allows the use of an electronic signature. For example, the digital signatures based to the certified keys correspond to the advanced signature according to German Signature Law (Schütze et al, 2006).

3.5.6.8 Security in Web-based Contexts

Providing authentication and authorisation services in web-based distributed e-Healthcare systems require well-engineered security architectures that cater for the unique requirements of the modern healthcare environment. For instance, user roles are an important characteristic of healthcare domain and hence the architecture may require to be partly based on a role-based access (RBAC) scheme. Gritzalis (Gritzalis and Lambrinoudakis, 2004) incorporates a RBAC scheme with the implementation of an intelligent localised security agent capable of authenticating the local and remote users that can access the local resources; assigning, through temporary certificates, access privileges to the authenticated users in accordance a RBAC scheme; and communicating vital information to other sites, via local security agents. Possible solutions to avoid possibly risky biometric authentication and establish a survivable authentication framework in e-Health may include temporary one-time passwords (OTPs) (Bicakci and Baykal, 2003), which should be accompanied by a new convenient method to generate these OTPs, and using temporary certificates in assigning access privileges to the authenticated users in accordance with a RBAC scheme.

The limitations of the e-commerce targeted generic IT security standards and technologies, and the need to overcome security and privacy limitations, have been recognised for over a decade. For example, Baker (Baker and Masys, 1999) focused on Internet-based communications systems in an effort to apply the state of the art security to e-Health information. To achieve patient-centred and secure online access to secure e-Healthcare information systems, it was necessary for them to innovatively combine existing generic IT security strategies and technologies into solutions that would meet the healthcare domain requirements. It included role-based access control, multi-level security, strong device and user authentication, session-specific encryption and audit trails. Baker et al also noted that unlike Internet-based electronic commerce security and privacy solutions, e-Healthcare solutions required e-Healthcare information to be secured end-to-end: in the server, in the data repository, across the network and on the client.

In the web services environment within the context of unprecedented emerging privacy law mandate, confidentiality of e-Healthcare information could be protected by having all patient records and medical images using AES encryption with 256-bit keys. Weaver (Weaver et al, 2003) applied encryption in the context of web services. In their work authentication Web service was used to manage trust levels, issue authorization tickets, and use biometric devices to establish identity. An authorization Web service was used to determine what data may be accessed, in what way, and by whom. The principles, guidelines and recommendations compiled by the OECD protection of privacy and trans-border flow of personal data are described and considered within health information system development by Falcao-Reis (Falcao-Reis et al, 2008). The technical implementation of a policy based on these OECD guidelines would provide technical support for patient empowerment which society should encourage and governments should promote. Falcao-Reis (Falcao-Reis et al, 2008) introduced a technical solution based on web security standards.

Public Key Infrastructures (PKIs) that use Trusted Third Party (TTP) services have been singled out as one of the appropriate options for addressing Internet-based e-Healthcare information security and privacy risks. Enhanced Trusted Third Party (ETTP) services are now believed to offer secure authentication as well as authorisation of users. Blobel (Blobel, 2001) achieved this through associating role profiles and security attributes to standard Web-based interactions. Their final result was the provision of what they called *an initial degree of 'automation' in building certified secure medical Internet-based applications.* Such applications would be capable of securely deploying established standard-based paradigms such as object orientation, component architecture, secure socket layer (SSL) protocol, and XML standards.

3.5.6.9 Conclusion

The differences in security technologies may need to be innovatively exploited to address e-Healthcare's unique security and privacy requirements. For example, combining security policy schemes with encryption technologies creates new encryption technologies such as the *policy-based encryption* due to Garson (Garson and Adams, 2008), which they proved to be quite useful within a health care environment for providing both encryption and access control.

3.6 Discussion and Summary of the Legal and Standardisation Challenges

The role of privacy laws, policies and technologies in securing e-Healthcare information (Bomba et al, 1995) was proposed where three elements are involved in the formulation and implementation of privacy. These elements are:

1. Public policy - what level of privacy does society want?
2. Legal structure - does the law adequately provide for society's privacy requirements?

3. Technical tools - how much privacy can technical tools provide, at what cost, and with what effects on the system?

While these elements constitute the canonical set of elements in the formulation and implementation of privacy, standardisation could be considered to be a unifying enabling factor that allow these canonical elements to be robust and scalable.

For instance, current medical imaging systems generate activity logs to create large volumes of log data. However, Chen (Chen et al, 2005) noted that there was a lack of regular description to integrate these large volumes of log data into generating HIPPA compliant auditing trails. In coming with a solution to this problem, Chen et al applied Supplement 95 of the DICOM Standard on Audit Trail Messages to developing a security monitoring system that supported a HIPAA-compliant and standard-based auditing system for medical imaging systems.

If we examine technical tools alone, it might seem to be apparent that the necessary technologies are generally available for providing the security of medical records required by public policy. Such tools may include encryption, user and data authentication methods, authorisation schemes and mechanisms for the prevention of data inference. While none of these available measures are full-proof, they would seem to be suitable for most applications where the encryption mechanism can provide protection for a given length of time. However, without standardisation supporting policy relating to a networked, patient-centric and managed care environment may not be nearly achievable.

Healthcare organisations are now placed in a dilemma that requires balancing between patient privacy and the requirements of public benefits which mostly occur in the form of legal requirements to disclose information to the government or to research projects. Healthcare information protection laws allow the use of patient information in the public interest, including the use of health information collected to improve or monitor public health or as part of medical research. The impact of these laws could be dramatic as regulatory bodies' interpretations of the law could affect the conduct of work that utilises this information (Brous, 2007). Armitage (Armitage et al, 2008) observed that unnecessarily restrictive interpretation of the law may be a serious impediment to:

1. identification of potential participants for a clinical research or clinical trial;
2. access to e-Healthcare records to confirm events;
3. continued follow-up of patients after the trial has been concluded; and
4. secondary use of the trial data for purposes not directly related to the original purpose of the study.

The new healthcare information protection laws have often confused and unnecessarily alarmed many conscientious health care providers. For instance, Levine (Levine, 2006) noted that nurses in particular are likely to be on the front line of family caregivers' inquiries, as physicians are often difficult to reach and family caregivers look to nurses as sources of reliable information.

Laws and standards mandate privacy policies to exist within e-Healthcare information systems. Patients must be made aware and must acknowledge these policies and be empowered to opt-in/out of their information being shared with third parties.

Laws and standards demand IT security to design, implement and safeguard e-Healthcare information. The security tools and mechanisms must be put in place to prevent unauthorised access to e-Healthcare information. Also internal controls and audit trails must be put in place to monitor access to and operations on the information.

Laws and standards bring in the issue of compliance in areas of administrative procedures, physical safeguards, technical security services and measures. The main effect of compliance is to increase the cost of delivering e-Healthcare.

A key impact of the law in e-Healthcare information security is the enforcement of the legal provisions. The enforcement of the law can happen in two ways, namely, by the state and by individuals through lawsuits or litigation.

A positive effect of laws and standards for securing e-Healthcare information is increasing awareness and budget allocations towards security and privacy. The resources are allocated to security and privacy and more focus is turned on efforts and cooperation to enhance this area which has been neglected. This could increase trust and trustworthiness of e-Healthcare information systems.

3.7 Summary

Privacy and information protection laws that stipulate the adoption of IT security and other standards as well as provide for sanctions for non-compliance are increasingly becoming a common feature in securing e-Healthcare information. Compliance with privacy protection laws and standards can only be attained by putting IT security and privacy measures in place.

Encryption and access control are necessary for ensuring proper authorization and confidentiality for patient records. Strong authentication and audit logs are required to ensure that access is granted. Compliance to security and privacy protections laws in e-Healthcare information systems could be made easier through the deliberate use of standards-based implementation of mechanisms and tools that assist in the auditing task. This is an area where security and healthcare standards and technologies could be combined to support the legal requirements.

Compliance requires defining a security policy governing secure storage of e-Healthcare information. The policy would ensure patient's privacy and confidentiality in ways that comply with the law, e.g. HIPAA, and regulations, e.g. EU Directives. It will require the adoption of a set of standards for data acquisition, storage, information communication and authentication and authorisation management that meet the set of requirements arising from the privacy protection laws.

All this may not be adequate unless security and privacy protection awareness is fostered among staff and users through proper and standards-based policies and procedures for training and notifications. This process will result in a strong foundation for both legal and standards compliance.

Patient privacy and the sharing of healthcare information may give rise to conflict. The law seeks to protect patient privacy. Standards, with the exception of privacy and security standards, seek to facilitate interoperability for healthcare information sharing. Consequently, the law and standards have disparate perspectives, that conflict. However, they also cooperate and complement each other in privacy protection.

The law could be an effective formal basis for adoption and compliance to these standards due its capability for punitive enforcement. A typical example is HIPAA 1996. Standards could also be a formal basis for the law in a persuasive and discretionary manner of influence on law-makers. The formal convergence of the law, standards and technology is significant to secure e-Healthcare information and warrants serious investigation.

This chapter has examined the developments in the law on the protection of privacy and confidentiality of e-Healthcare information. The chapter has also reviewed the standards for securing e-Healthcare information while emphasising the emerging patterns for the convergence of the law, standards and technology in the realisation of secure e-Healthcare information.

References

Agrawal R, Johnson C (2007) Securing electronic health records without impeding the flow of information. International Journal of Medical Informatics 76:471–479, DOI 10.1016/j.ijmedinf.2006.09.015

ALRC (2007) (australian law reform commission), lrc discussion paper 72 - review of australian privacy law, vol. 1-2. Tech. rep., Commonwealth of Australia, URL http://www.austlii.edu.au/au/other/alrc/publications/dp/72/

ALRC (2008) (australian law reform commission), australian privacy law and practice report, vol. 1-3. Tech. Rep. 1, Commonwealth of Australia

Armitage J, Souhami R, Friedman L, Hilbrich L, Holland J, Muhlbaier LH, Shannon J, Nie AV (2008) The impact of privacy and confidentiality laws on the conduct of clinical trials. Clinical Trials (London, England) 5(1):70–4, DOI 5/1/70, pMID: 18283083

Baker D, Masys D (1999) Pcasso: a design for secure communication of personal health information via the internet. Int J Med Inform 54(2):97–104, URL http://www.ncbi.nlm.nih.gov/pubmed/10219949

Bales S (2005) [the introduction of the electronic health card in germany]. Bundesgesundheitsblatt, Gesundheitsforschung, Gesundheitsschutz 48(7):727–31, DOI 10.1007/s00103-005-1080-z, URL http://www.ncbi.nlm.nih.gov/pubmed/16003565, pMID: 16003565

Barlette Y, Fomin VV (2008) Exploring the suitability of is security management standards for smes. hicss 0:308, DOI http://doi.ieeecomputersociety.org/10.1109/HICSS.2008.167

Berman JJ (2004) Zero-check: a zero-knowledge protocol for reconciling patient identities across institutions. Archives of Pathology & Laboratory

Medicine 128(3):344–6, DOI 14987147, URL http://www.ncbi.nlm.nih.gov/pubmed/14987147, pMID: 14987147

Bicakci K, Baykal N (2003) Survivable authentication for health information systems. AMIA Annual Symposium Proceedings / AMIA Symposium AMIA Symposium p 791, DOI 14728296, URL http://www.ncbi.nlm.nih.gov/pubmed/14728296, pMID: 14728296

Blobel B (2001) Trustworthiness in distributed electronic healthcare records-basis for shared care. In: ACSAC, pp 433–441, DOI http://doi.ieeecomputersociety.org/10.1109/ACSAC.2001.991560, URL http://doi.ieeecomputersociety.org/10.1109/ACSAC.2001.991560

Blobel B (2004) Authorisation and access control for electronic health record systems. International Journal of Medical Informatics 73:251257

Blobel B, Pharow P, Spiegel V, Engel K, Engelbrecht R (2001) Securing interoperability between chip card based medical information systems and health networks. International Journal of Medical Informatics 64(2-3):401–15, DOI 11734401, URL http://www.ncbi.nlm.nih.gov/pubmed/11734401, pMID: 11734401

Bomba B, Cooper J, Miller M (1995) Working towards a national health information system in australia. Medinfo 1995 8:Pt 2:1633, DOI http://www.ncbi.nlm.nih.gov/pubmed/8591519

Broek LVD, Sikkel AJ (eds) (1997) Health Cards '97. IOS Press

Brous EA (2007) Hipaa vs. law enforcement. a nurses' guide to managing conflicting responsibilities. The American Journal of Nursing 107:60–3, DOI 10.1097/01.NAJ.0000282298.26312.3c, pMID: 17667394

den Bumen T SI (2007) Human genetic data from a data protection law perspective, [article in german]. Bundesgesundheitsblatt Gesundheitsforschung Gesundheitsschutz 50(2):200–8, URL http://www.ncbi.nlm.nih.gov/pubmed/17238055

Calcutt D (1990) Report of the committee on privacy and related matters, cm 1 102 (london, hmso, 1990)

Chen X, Zhang J, Wu D, Han R (2005) Hippa's compliant auditing system for medical imaging system. Conference Proceedings: Annual International Conference of the IEEE Engineering in Medicine and Biology Society IEEE Engineering in Medicine and Biology Society Conference 1:562–3, DOI 17282242, pMID: 17282242

Courtois N, Bard GV (2007) Algebraic cryptanalysis of the data encryption standard. In: 11-th IMA Conference, Cirencester, UK, URL http://eprint.iacr.org/2006/402

Daemen J, Rijmen V (2002) The Design of Rijndael. Springer, ISBN 3-540-42580-2

Damiani E, Vimercati SDC, Jajodia S, Paraboschi S, Samarati P (2003) Balancing confidentiality and efficiency in untrusted relational dbmss. ACM, Washington D.C., USA, pp 93–102, DOI 10.1145/948109.948124, URL http://portal.acm.org/citation.cfm?id=948109.948124

Davis D, Having K (2006) Compliance with hipaa security standards in u.s. hospitals. Journal of Healthcare Information Management: JHIM 20(2):108–15, DOI 16669594, pMID: 16669594

Edlin M, Johns S (2006) High standards. a decade after the law went into effect, there is still debate about the pros and cons of the hipaa privacy and electronic transaction regulations. AHIP Coverage 47(6):26–9, DOI 17175737, pMID: 17175737

Falcao-Reis F, Costa-Pereira A, Correia ME (2008) Access and privacy rights using web security standards to increase patient empowerment. Studies in Health Technology and Informatics 137:275–85, DOI 18560089, pMID: 18560089

FederalRegister (2004) Hipaa administrative simplification: standard unique health identifier for health care providers. final rule. Federal Register 69(15):3433–68, DOI 14968800, pMID: 14968800

Fisher B, Fitton R, Poirier C, Stables D (2006) Patient record access–the time has come. Studies in Health Technology and Informatics 121:162–7, DOI 17095813, pMID: 17095813

Garon G, Outerbridge R (1991) Des watch: an examination of the sufficiency of the data encryption standard for financial institution information security in the 1990s. SIGSAC Rev 9:29–45, DOI 10.1145/126569.127016, URL http://portal.acm.org/citation.cfm?id=126569.127016

Garson K, Adams C (2008) Security and privacy system architecture for an e-hospital environment. ACM, Gaithersburg, Maryland, pp 122–130, DOI 10.1145/1373290.1373306, URL http://portal.acm.org/citation.cfm?id=1373290.1373306

Gritzalis D, Lambrinoudakis C (2004) A security architecture for interconnecting health information systems. International Journal of Medical Informatics 73(3):305–9, DOI 15066563, pMID: 15066563

Halamka J, Juels A, Stubblefield A, Westhues J (2006) The security implications of verichip cloning. Journal of the American Medical Informatics Association: JAMIA 13(6):601–7, DOI M2143, pMID: 16929037

Hale M, Runnington C (1820) The History of the Common Law of England: And An Analysis of the Civil Part of the Law. H. Butterworth, URL http://books.google.ie/books/pdf/

Hashiyada M (2004) Development of biometric dna ink for authentication security. The Tohoku Journal of Experimental Medicine 204(2):109–17, DOI 15383691, pMID: 15383691

Hassinen M, Laitinen P (2005) End-to-end encryption for sms messages in the health care domain. Studies in Health Technology and Informatics 116:316–21, DOI 16160278, pMID: 16160278

Honan B (2008) Data on over 170,000 irish blood donors and patients lost; security watch, bh consultings security watch blog, february 20th, 2008, http://bhconsulting.ie/securitywatch/?p=207; accessed: 2008-07-17. Online, URL http://bhconsulting.ie/securitywatch/?p=207

Hughes G, Dawson S, Brookes T (2008) Considering new privacy laws in australia. Security & Privacy, IEEE 6(3):57–59, DOI 10.1109/MSP.2008.60

Istepanian RSH, Laxminarayan S, Pattichis CS (eds) (2006) M-Health: Emerging Mobile Health Systems. Topics in Biomedical Engineering (Int. Book Series), Springer

Kalra D (2006) Electronic health record standards. Yearbook of Medical Informatics pp 136–44, DOI me06010136, pMID: 17051307

Karygiannis T, Eydt B, Barber G, Bunn L, Phillips T (2007) Guidelines for securing radio frequency identification (rfid) systems: Recommendations of the national institute of standards and technology. Tech. rep., National Institute of Standards and Technology (NIST), Depatment of Commerce, USA Government, URL http://csrc.nist.gov/publications/nistpubs/800-98/SP800-98, nIST Special Publication 800-98

Kleinebreil L, Saba R, Razafindramanana N (2003) Health cards as a part of french health telematics. Studies in Health Technology and Informatics 96:224–8, DOI 15061549, URL http://www.ncbi.nlm.nih.gov/pubmed/15061549, pMID: 15061549

Kohler CO, Rienhoff O, Schaefer OP (1996) Health Cards '95: Proceedings of the Health Cards '95 Conference, Frankfurt, Germany, 23-26 October 1995. IOS Press

Lennon P (2005) Protecting Personal Health Information in Ireland: Law & Practice. Oak Tree Press

Levine C (2006) Hipaa and talking with family caregivers: what does the law really say? The American Journal of Nursing 106:51–3, DOI 00000446-200608000-00022, pMID: 16905933

LRC TLRC (1998) Report on privacy: Surveillance and the interception of communications (lrc 571998). Tech. rep., The Law Reform Commission, IRELAND, URL http://www.lawreform.ie/publications/data/lrc99/

Luna J, Dikaiakos MD, Kyprianou T, Bilas A, Marazakis M (2008) Data privacy considerations in intensive care grids. Studies in Health Technology and Informatics 138:178–87, DOI 18560120, pMID: 18560120

McMahon BME, Binchy W (2000) Irish Law of Torts, 3rd edn. BUTTERWORTHS/Tottel Publishing

Moore C (2004) The growing trend of government involvement in it security. In: InfoSecCD '04: Proceedings of the 1st annual conference on Information security curriculum development, ACM, New York, NY, USA, pp 119–123, DOI http://doi.acm.org/10.1145/1059524.1059551

Mordini E, Ottolini C (2007) Body identification, biometrics and medicine: ethical and social considerations. Annali dell'Istituto Superiore Di Sanit 43(1):51–60, DOI 17536154, pMID: 17536154

Morimoto S, Shigematsu S, Goto Y, Cheng J (2006) A security specification verification technique based on the international standard iso/iec 15408. ACM, Dijon, France, pp 1802–1803, DOI 10.1145/1141277.1141701, URL http://portal.acm.org/citation.cfm?id=1141277.1141701

NIST (2001) Fips-197: Advanced encryption standard, national institute of standards and technology (nist). NIST Website, http://csrc.nist.gov/publications/fips/fips197/fips-197.pdf, accessed 20 August 2008, URL http://csrc.nist.gov/publications/fips/fips197/fips-197.pdf

Okamoto E (2004) [encryption technique for linkable anonymizing]. Nippon Ksh Eisei Zasshi] Japanese Journal of Public Health 51(6):445–51, DOI 15296025, pMID: 15296025

openEHR F (2007) openehr architecture - architecture overview, revision 1.1, pages: 87. Specification Release,, URL http://www.openehr.org/releases/1.0.1/html/architecture/overview/Output/security.html\#1121809

Orfanidis L, Bamidis PD, Eaglestone B (2007) A simulation-based performance analysis of a national electronic health record system. Medinfo MEDINFO 12:302–6, DOI 17911727, pMID: 17911727

Pharow P, Blobel B (2006) Benefits and weaknesses of health cards used in health information systems. Studies in Health Technology and Informatics 124:320–5, DOI 17108543, pMID: 17108543

Posthumus L (2004) Use of the iso/iec 17799 framework in healthcare information security management. Studies in Health Technology and Informatics 103:447–52, DOI 15747954, pMID: 15747954

Riedl B, Grascher V, Neubauer T (2007) Applying a threshold scheme to the pseudonymization of health data. In: PRDC, pp 397–400, URL http://doi.ieeecomputersociety.org/10.1109/PRDC.2007.24

Ruotsalainen P, Manning B (2007) A notary archive model for secure preservation and distribution of electrically signed patient documents. International Journal of Medical Informatics 76(5-6):449–53, DOI S1386-5056(06)00216-4, pMID: 17118701

Sax U, Kohane I, Mandl KD (2005) Wireless technology infrastructures for authentication of patients: Pki that rings. Journal of the American Medical Informatics Association: JAMIA 12(3):263–8, DOI M1681, pMID: 15684133

Schütze B, Kämmerer M, Klos G, Mildenberger P (2006) The public-key-infrastructure of the radiological society of germany. European Journal of Radiology 57(3):323–8, DOI S0720-048X(05)00342-6, pMID: 16324813

Torres E, de Alfonso C, Blanquer I, Hernndez V (2006) Privacy protection in health-grid: distributing encryption management over the vo. Studies in Health Technology and Informatics 120:131–41, DOI 16823130, pMID: 16823130

Urien P, Pujolle G (2008) Security and privacy for the next wireless generation. Int J Netw Manag 18:129–145, URL http://portal.acm.org/citation.cfm?id=1362791.1362795

Warren SD, Brandeis LD (1890-91) Right to privacy. Harvard Law Review IV(5):193–220, URL http://www.lawrence.edu/fast/boardmaw/

Weaver AC, III SJD, Snyder AM, Dyke JV, Hu J, Chen X, Mulholland T, Marshall A (2003) Federated, secure trust networks for distributed healthcare it services. Industrial Informatics, 2003 INDIN 2003 Proceedings IEEE International Conference on pp 162–169

Weerasinghe D, Elmufti K, Rajarajan M, Rakocevic V (2007) Securing electronic health records with novel mobile encryption schemes. International Journal of Electronic Healthcare 3(4):395–416, DOI 83M62814353865H8, pMID: 18048274

Chapter 4
Secure e-Healthcare Information Systems

4.1 Introduction

The e-Healthcare information systems (e-HIS) are, by nature, network-based and internet-enabled. In the developed countries, e-HIS typically operate in regional networks and international health management organisations and trusts. Therefore, e-HIS must meet the requirements of new emerging paradigms and international organisational phenomenon. These requirements include the support for distribution, cooperation and communication. However, the success and acceptance of e-HIS may not be guaranteed in the absence of security and privacy service components, incorporation of standards-based interoperability that takes into account the legal, ethical and organisational policy provision. The typical e-HIS are e-Healthcare record systems (EHR systems) and electronic-personal healthcare record systems (EPHR systems). The EHR systems are created, maintained by clinicians and healthcare organisations, while EPHR systems are created, maintained and controlled, at least in theory, by the individual subject of the health information. The concept of the EHRs is fairly older than the concept of EPHR, which is emerging coupled with the patient-centred paradigm. Consequently, the EHR systems are fairly established as compared to EPHR systems which are starting to be introduced.

This chapter presents an overview of the security and privacy provisions in the EHR, PEHR systems, and clinical decision-support systems, which heavily rely on personal e-Healthcare information for their efficay in their use for assisting in disease management. These issues are summarised in Figure 4.1. The key elements of security and privacy are explored within the context of the evolution of e-Healthcare information systems. A selection of EHR and PEHR systems of significance are explored and compared with respect to their security and privacy provisions. The key security and privacy challenges in e-Healthcare information systems are identified. Finally, the revolutionising impact of the patient-centred paradigm on both the EHR and PEHR systems is identified and mapped to create a future evolutionary path for e-Healthcare information systems.

4.2 The elements of Security and Privacy in e-Healthcare Information Systems

The law, policy guidelines and professional ethical consensus are part of the high level elements of security and privacy of e-Healthcare information. Any changes in these three elements has the effect of complicating and triggering the evolution of security and privacy requirements for e-Healthcare information. Law, policy and ethical consensus could be specified, for purposes of computerisation, in security and privacy policies, which are generally computationally ambiguous and incomplete. Formal policy specifications could assist in solving the ambiguity and incompleteness. The elements of security and privacy in e-Healthcare information systems are predicated by the evolution of these systems in response to changing paradigms within the healthcare domain. The Figure 4.2 illustrates the evolution of e-HIS. Most current e-HIS are organisation-centred since this span a single organisation with offering external access mechanisms. These systems use information technologies within an organisation and do not exploit ICTs for external interaction with other entities such as persons or other systems. Security and privacy in organisation-centred HIS have the following key elements:

1. Locally defined access rights;
2. Security and privacy rights are based on either formal or informal policies that are usually locally agreed;
3. Outsider access to the HIS is generally via a human agent.

The organisation-centred HIS are increasingly being transformed into process-centred HIS in order to support patient care process that span many organisations. As patients move between different healthcare organisations, there is inter-system communication of e-Healthcare information within the context of the process of care. Process-centred e-HIS exploit inter-organisational ICTs and constitute the emerging backbone for e-Healthcare. The emergence of ubiquitous networked computing

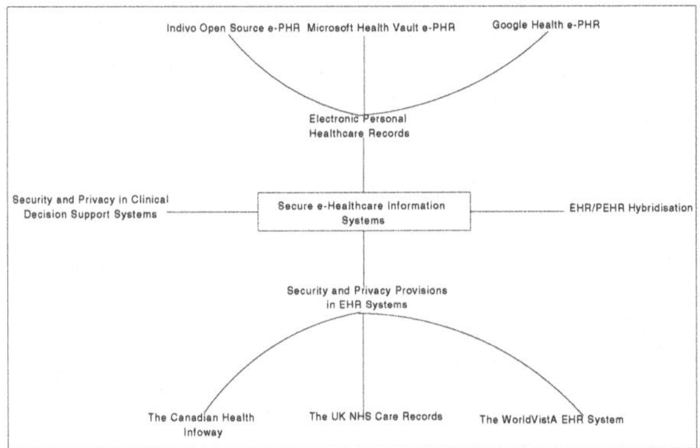

Figure 4.1 Current and future e-Healthcare Information Systems

devices is further enriching and enhancing the computing infrastructure for process-centred HIS. However, it is with Internet-based, process-centred HIS incorporating these networked ubiquitous devices that security and privacy of e-Healthcare information is posing major challenges. With process-centred HIS, access rights and control are no longer locally defined, external access is automated and security policies are no longer locally defined. The significance of data and privacy protection laws is a critical issue for process-centred systems.

It is now envisaged that process-centred HIS will continue to evolve to better support the paradigm changes within the healthcare domain, where increasing emphasis is now being placed on empowering the individual patient. The process-centred HIS are expected to be transformed into person or patient-centred HIS, which are characterised by the direct involvement of the patient in the ownership, creation, maintenance and control of the e-Healthcare record or information. A key aspect of person-centred HIS is the realisation of the virtual lifelong e-Healthcare record whose main characteristics are:

1. The logical integration of distributed EHR systems;
2. Availability and integration over the lifetime of the patient;
3. The support for shared e-Healthcare information among patient care providers.

In person-centred HIS, external access has new requirements especially relating to unlimited access by the patient. Disclosure of e-Healthcare information will now be mandatorily governed by patient consent.

An important aspect of person-centred HIS is that their adoption will largely depend on whether they can be trusted by individual patients whose main concerns relate to privacy and confidentiality. Since person-centred HIS are distributed, the question of technical trust will need to be addressed through a distributed trust man-

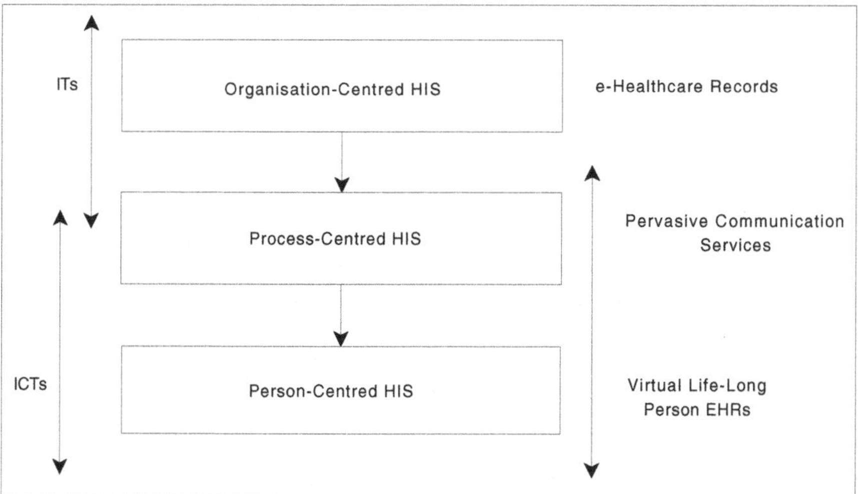

Figure 4.2 The evolution of e-healthcare information systems

agement framework that could also involve digital credentials capable of being used in trust establishment. However, the bulk of the user trust problem has more to do with perception rather than technical solutions.

At the international level, the core elements of security and privacy for e-HIS are generally agreed. These are formally spelt out and defined in the ISO standard ISO/TS 18308 and summarised here in Table 4.1. The elements presented in Table 4.1 constitute the core requirements for security and privacy of e-Healthcare information. In section 4.4, we investigate the security and privacy provision in selected major e-Healthcare information systems and e-personal healthcare record systems in accordance with the elements of security and privacy presented in this section.

Table 4.1 Elements of Privacy and Security in e-HIS based on ISO/TS 18308

ELEMENT CATEGORY	ELEMENT	DESCRIPTION
A. Security	1. Authentication	System or Person ID
	2. Authorisation	Granting rights
	3. Data integrity	Accuracy & consistency
	4. Non-repudiation	Confirmation of data integrity & origin
	5. Confidentiality	Extent of disclosure
	6. Consent	Informed consent of patient to access
B. Semantic Interoperability	Semantic integrity	Data sharing with understanding at conceptual level formal concept mapping
C. Author Responsibility	Accountability	Each contribution attributed to identified author
D. Audit Trail/Log	Traceability	Record activity in chronological order - allow reconstruction
E. Version Management/Control	Detection	Version at appropriate granularity & detect modification & updates
F. Patient Access	Transparency	Access to all information by patients
G. Data Archiving & Retention	1. Retention	Conforming to laws on data retention
	2. Archiving	EHR information moved to offline storage

4.3 Security and Privacy Provisions in EHR Systems

The information exchange between/across healthcare organisations is an important requirement in e-Healthcare. Ensuring the secure exchange of e-Healthcare information requires standards for security measures and privacy protection that span more than one organisation. Therefore, the EHR systems need to implement global security and privacy conceptualisations that include global standards for clinicians roles, patient consent, and semantically interoperable audit trails and logs. Security and privacy implementations in the EHR systems with need to incorporate the context, where e-Healthcare information resides in distributed sources where it would need to be pulled out and aggregated. Such an approach is futuristic, as e-Healthcare drives towards e-Personal Healthcare Records that empower patients to assemble their healthcare information from disparate EHR systems and make them shareable among caregivers.

Although the EHR systems are generally owned by healthcare organisations and maintained by clinicians, there are growing calls for empowering patients to participate, especially in deciding who has access to their information that is held in these systems. Such patient-centred features of controlling access and monitoring privacy and confidentiality may need to be implemented in the EHR systems in parallel to those required or already implemented by the health care organisations. Thus, standard data/information access protocols, mechanisms and policies to implement patient privacy and allow patients to automatically trace the flow of their e-Healthcare information are essential to the EHR systems. The success of the EHR systems integration into healthcare depends on these systems having the highest level of security and on enabling constant patient monitoring and maintenance of security and privacy measures.

4.3.1 The Canadian Health Infoway

Infoway is Canada's evolving robust and interoperable EHR solution that is planned for deployment and replication across the whole country. Canada Health Infoway Inc. is a not for profit corporation that was set up by Canada's first minister and mandated to establish and promote the deployment of an interoperable pan-Canadian EHR Health Infoway partiners with provincial and territorial governments in carrying out its mandate. Among the key challenges faced by Infoway is that of ensuring privacy and confidentiality of e-Healthcare information. Infoway's approach is to develop an interoperable national EHR system that evolves gradually from individual, local and regional solutions that are interoperable and interconnected. In doing so, Infoway provides blueprint technology neutral conceptual architecture. In 2003, Infoway released the conceptual architecture blueprint for the interoperable EHR system, which left a gap on how privacy and security requirements would be met within the interoperable EHR. This gap was filled in by Infoway's development of the Privacy and Security Conceptual Architecture (PSCA) in 2006. The PSCA is a synthesis of the privacy and security requirements drawn from regional, territorial and federal laws of Canada and international standards.

The PSCA seeks to ensure that personal e-Healthcare information in the EHR systems is placed at the strictest level of confidence while ensuring that the information enjoys a high degree of system availability. The PSCA consists of ten architectural component services that span the entire spectrum of the elements of privacy and security of personal e-Healthcare information. These privacy and security services can be summarised as follows:

1. User ID management services for accurately identifying users of the EHR system;
2. User authentication services for establishing the validity of the identity of the user;
3. Access control services for controlling access to e-Healthcare information based on user's role or association with a group or some discretionary criteria;
4. Consent directives management services for recording, management, application logging and overriding of an individual's consent directives;
5. ID protection services for the de-identification and re-identification of personal information during storage and use;
6. Anonymisation services for removing all personal identifiers from an EHR to facilitate secondary use of e-Healthcare information with violating personal privacy;
7. Encryption services for creating, renewing and revoking encryption keys and the use of cryptography to safeguard confidentiality of personal e-Healthcare information in the storage systems (e.g. databases, files) and during transmission and authentication processes;
8. Digital signature systems for the secure use of e-signatures;
9. Secure audit services for secure logging of access to and use of the EHR system; and
10. General security services for generic security activities that include virus scanning, secure backups, archiving data, destruction and restoration of data.

These privacy and security services (as illustrated in Table 4.2) together with the communication infrastructure constitute the backbone of the Canada Health Infoway's interoperable EHR system. Canada's evolutionary approach to security and privacy protection permeates both the legal and the technological frameworks for e-Healthcare information management. The federal privacy protection laws recognise the different regional and territorial laws which are expected to evolve towards a unified privacy protection legal framework under the guidelines of federal laws. Similarly, on the EHR system technology front, the Health Infoway's blueprint architectures for the EHR systems and privacy and security mechanisms recognises and calls of local and regional implementations that gradually become aligned with the blueprints at federal level. The Canada approach is in direct contrast with the American approach under HIPAA 1996, where the EHR system and privacy and security compliance measures are relatively immediately mandatory with no recognition for state-based local laws and approaches. HIPAA only set a legal framework which was progressively refined and specified through non-prescriptive and technology neutral rules that had force of law at federal level.

4.3.2 Security and Privacy Provisions in the UK NHS Care Records

The UK's National Healthcare Service (NHS) has introduced the Care Record Service (CRS) with the aim of improving patient care quality and service. The NHS

Table 4.2 Services within the Canadian Health Infoway Privacy and Security Conceptual Architecture (PSCA)

PSCA Service	Description of Service
User ID Management	A service for accurately identifying users of the EHR system.
User Authentication	A service for establishing validity of the identity of users.
Access Control	A service for access to the EHR based on user's role, association with a group, or based on some other criteria.
Consent Directives Management	A service for recording, management, application logging, and overriding of patient consent directives.
ID Protection	A service for de-identification and re-identification of person information for storage and during use.
Anonymisation	A service for removing all personal identifiers from an EHR to facilitate secondary use of the EHR information while preserving personal privacy.
Encryption	A service for creating and renewing and revoking encryption keys and use of cryptography in EHR storage and during transmission.
Digital Signature	A service for facilitating secure use of electronic/digital signature.
Secure Audit	A service for secure logging of access and use of EHR system.
General Security	A service for generic security tasks/activities, e.g., virus scans, secure backups, archiving data, destruction and restoration of data.

CRS is the responsibility of a government agency called NHS connecting for Health whose primary mission is to deliver the NHS National Programme for IT under the UK department of Health. The NHS connecting for Health was established in 2005 as part of the NHS review of its IT infrastructure and e-Healthcare information management. This review was triggered by public concerns which included concerns for security and privacy that led to erosion of trust for the NHS e-Healthcare information systems.

The NHS Care Record Service (NHS CRS) is composed of locally held detailed records and a nationally accessible Summary Care Record (SCR). The proposed NHS CRS promises to develop locally held detailed e-Healthcare records spanning all local care providers and linked for accessibility at local sites. Individual patients will be allowed the freedom to choose their degree of involvement in the NHS CRS. The NHS CRS is a national summary of the patient's locally held e-Healthcare information based initially on the GP's records but expected to incorporate other sources at later stages. Patients will be given an opportunity to contribute to decisions on confidential handling of their information in the NHS SCR. The NHS SCR will be viewable online by the patient through the HealthSpace service portal (www.nhs.uk/healthspace) where it will be possible for one to ensure accuracy and to add notes and comments.

The 1998 Data Protection Act protects the privacy of e-Healthcare information in the EHR systems within the NHS systems. The act does not require consent for the use of personal information in healthcare as long as the data controller can show that the specified purpose could not be undertaken without using the information.

4.3.3 Security and Privacy Provisions in the WorldVistA EHR System

For the past twenty years the US Department of Veterans Affairs (VA) has been developing an e-Healthcare information system called the Veterans Health Information Systems and Technology Architecture (VistA). The VA adopted an internal federal collaborative component-based development approach that was reminiscent of the open source model in covering VistA functions for patient registration, inpatient admission/discharge/transfer, outpatient clinic scheduling, pharmacy and laboratory information system and radiology system. VistA is now considered as one of the most advanced e-Healthcare information systems in the world. It is a massive US federal computerised patient record system that incorporates comprehensive medical imaging facilities and supports all types of clinicians across hospitals, clinics and residential care homes [1].

VistA source code is thus freely available under the US Freedom of Information Act (FOIA) [2]. Hence, it is a free open source software, which is licence-free, being developed under the US Federal Government. As a consequence, it has been adopted around the world including South America [3], Asia [4], Africa [5] and Europe [6]. One criticism of VistA is that it is written in a programming language, called MUMPS, that is fairly old and currently unfamiliar to most programmers. Furthermore, it is not considered to be interoperable with other systems, i.e., it is not standards-based.

In 2001, VistA was formalised as an open source community-based international project called WorldVistA [7] under the GNU General Public Licence (GPL) [8] and a not-for-profit foundation with the same name. The WorldVistA EHR now runs on the Linux operating system. It is interesting to note that a major planned future direction of the WorldVistA EHR system is its hybridisation with the PEHR module and present the final product throught the Internet using a web-based front-end.

---

[1] VistA Monograph:http://www.va.gov/vista_monograph

[2] Freedom Of Information Act: http://www.usdoj.gov/oip/introduc.htm

[3] Mexico: www.vistasoftware.org/why/sspdfs/VistA_Mexico_Status.doc

[4] Indian Health Service RPMS: http://www.ihs.gov/Cio/RPMS/index.cfm?module=home&option=index

[5] Nigeria: http://www.minphis.4t.com

[6] Finland:http://www.uku.fi/tike/his/english/musti.html

[7] WorldVistA: http://www.worldvista.org

[8] GNU General Public License: http://www.gnu.org/copyleft/gpl.html

In 2006, the Certification Commission for Healthcare Information Technology (CCHIT) [9] asserted that WorldVistA EHR VOE/1.0 met the comprehensive set of criteria for security [10], i.e., it satisfied the major requirements for ensuring healthcare data privacy and robustness to prevent data loss. CCHIT is a recognized certification body (RCB) for electronic health records and their networks, and an independent, voluntary, private-sector initiative. CCHIT's mission is to accelerate the adoption of health information technology by creating an efficient, credible and sustainable certification program. It has been argued that assigning certification of the EHR systems exclusively to CCHIT, an healthcare industry-based association, is a bit like allowing healthcare industries to regulate themselves.

The VistA software supports HIPAA standards, including role-based access for security controls, electronic signature required for approval of orders, and audit capability. Specifically, CCHIT in its certification confirmed that WorldVistA EHR VOE/ 1.0 has met access control, audit, authentication and technical services. WorldVistA EHR has been modified to allow users to use social security numbers or medical record numbers to identify patients, using these identifiers is major security issue, as they are being used in other scenarios, which means that once they are compromised in a different setting may pose security threat to medical records.

4.4 Security and Privacy Provisions in Electronic Personal Healthcare Records

The electronic personal healthcare records (e-PHRs) are online web-based healthcare records that are created, maintained and managed by the patient or individual who is the subject of these records. They have arisen as a result of the drive towards patient-centred care delivery that emphasise on the involvement of the patient in decision making and the control of privacy of their health information. The e-PHRs are emerging as free services that are provided by information technology companies, the most prominent of which include Microsoft and Google. The major motivations of these companies include their desire to capitalise on the modern trend of seeking health information on the Internet, to exploit the potential of online tools to empower the public to manage personal healthcare information and the potential for business given current IT investment in healthcare. At their onset, e-PHRs are challenged by security and privacy concerns of patients as well as trust concerns of clinicians. For e-PHRs to succeed, there is a need to address the issues of privacy and trust through the law, standards, policy and technology. This section presents an overview of some of the major e-PHR systems/services with a focus on their security and privacy provisions.

---

[9] Certification Commission for Healthcare Information Technology (CCHIT): http://www.cchit.org

[10] The CCHIT Security Criteria for 2006: http:www.cchit.orgfilesAmbulatory%20Domain Final%20Criteria%20-%20SECURITY-RELIABILITY%20-%20Ambulatory%20EHRs%20-%202006.pdf

4.4.1 Google Health e-PHR

The Google Health e-PHR allows users to create their online web-based health record as part of the Google application services. Authentication of the user is done using the Google e-mail, called Gmail, account profile. Users are enabled to pull information into Google Health from other systems, such as hospital health record systems, pharmacy systems etc.

Google Health's pre-launch two month trial at the Cleveland clinic showed that patients were eager to use Google Health e-PHRs. The trial participants were found to be unworried about privacy and confidentiality resulting from their health records being held by a large IT company, i.e., Google Inc.

Google Health consists of doctor's medical records, prescriptions, information on drug interactions and search for medical services, e.g. new doctors or health information. Users can push information from their Google Health e-PHRs to doctors or hospital medical records at their discretion. The user can also make profiles relating to aspects of their health in Google Health. The individual user controls and determines what information in their Google Health e-PHRs is shared with doctors, clinics or pharmacies. Hospitals and clinics may allow Google Health and other e-PHRs systems/services to connect to their e-Healthcare information systems.

The use of the Gmail account profile for Google Health authentication is a possible security and privacy concern. It could be seen to be easy for someone to discover one's universal Google Gmail login profile, which has a number of weaknesses from a security point of view. First, there is no minimum requirement for secure passwords for Gmail, although the user is advised as regards the degree of strength of the users chosen password. Second, once one gains access to Google services, this leads to access to a host of information in all of Google's web service applications such as email, documents, etc. Thus, Google's authentication profile could be a liability to the trust that can be given by uses to Google Health.

Like all other e-PHR service providers, Google Health's privacy policy is an attempt to gain users trust through outlining privacy issues/assurances and disclosure of how Google will use personal information and safeguard personal privacy. The privacy policy states, that user who agrees to use Google Health will grant to Google a license to use and distribute their information in connection with Google Health and other Google services. The privacy policy re-assures users that Google will not share identified or de-identified information without their consent except where the law mandates them to do so. In the case where Google is acquired or merges with a third party, transfer of information held in Google Health is done only after users have been notified. In other cases of transfer, only aggregated or statistical data or non-personal information are shared with third parties. For instance, Google may share the information that 40% of people with allergies use a particular anti-histamine medication/drug. Google Health security is implemented based on e-security measures that include secure socket layer (SSL), encryption and backup systems.

The legal and regulatory framework for Google Health and similar services is grossly lacking at the present moment. Many privacy protection laws do not take into consideration the protection of the privacy and confidentiality of e-Healthcare information in the PEHR systems offered by IT companies such as Google. For instance, both Google and Microsoft claim that Google Health and Health Vault are not covered under HIPAA 1996, since they are not covered entities as defined under this privacy protection law. The PEHRs are emerging systems whose regulation have not yet been legislated.

4.4.2 The Microsoft e-PHR service: The HealthVault

Microsoft's e-PHRs service is called the HealthVault, which was one of the pioneer e-PHRs to be offered by a large IT company. The HealthVault claims to be a secure service that enables users to centrally store e-Health information and aims to place users in control of assembling information from various healthcare providers while also able to control access to this information by whoever they decide. The benefits of HealthVault include enabling doctors to make more complete diagnosis by using extra information from other care providers, and the prevention of adverse drug-to-drug interactions.

The process of authentication in the HealthVault involves using a Windows Live ID together with a HealthVault account. The HealthVault account seems to be itself based on Windows Live ID. HealthVault allows an account holder to associate their accounts with other people as well. Thus, one person could manage all the health records for the family. The user can upload documents, enter data or pull and upload data from medical devices such as a glucometer used by diabetic patients.

Just as with all other e-PHR services, security and privacy concerns arise with putting one's personal health information online. Microsoft Live ID is similar to Google's Gmail account ID and, hence, suffers the same weaknesses as outlined for Google Health. The HealthVault provides basic security measures that include automatic logouts in case of expiry of a set period of inactivity. Microsoft offers the same assurances with respect to transfer of user's health information, which is ensured/promised to be based on user informed and explicit consent. However, unlike Google Health, Microsoft puts up advertisements on the HealthVault with the promise that the advertisements will not be contextually tailored to the user's health information.

The HealthVault uses encryption in all internal and external data transfers. Employee access users health information is controlled and subject to strict limits. Data backups are performed and encryption is applied to them as well. The HealthVault also claims to implement comprehensive audit trails and logs that capture incidents of creation, change, reading of health records, thus giving rise to a rich audit trail. HealthVault also claims to enforce a pretty complex password regime that requires the Live ID password to include numbers, letters and special characters and a minimum password length without which HealthVault will not allow access to the service.

4.4.3 The Indivo Open Source e-PHR system

Indivo (Mandl et al, 2007) is a personally controlled healthcare record that allows an individual patient to assemble, maintain and control a secure collection of her medical data. It is a project that is being led by the Harvard Medical School and the Children's Hospital in Boston, USA. The Indivo PEHR is being used by many organisations around the world with examples being Dossia [11] and the Norwegian PEHR (Jensen et al, 2006).

The key characteristics of Indivo is that it is open source, based on open and public standards, has open API, is Internet based, has a web-interface and claims to exceed HIPAA requirements in terms of its provision for security and privacy protection. The Indivo e-PHR claims to provide a ready integration of disparate sources of healthcare and medical information under the control of the patient. It recognises that e-PHRs are merely complements as opposed to replacements of e-Healthcare record systems maintained by clinics and hospitals. Indivo deployments are much older than those of Google Health and HealthVault as they stretch for a period since 2001.

When interacting with other systems, Indivo's security and privacy protection is centred on the principle that the root of trust is the patient-physician relationship (Mandl et al, 2007). Thus, Indivo's patient identification mechanism is based on patient-physician relationship, which leads to three authentication provisioning methods namely:

1. Authentication based on physical presence at the doctors office or surgery;
2. Authentication through physical presence at the registration desk;
3. Authentication through the well established ID management systems such as certificate based Kerberos system with username and password and second factor authentication (Sax et al, 2005).

Indivo also allows the use of institutional workflows for authentication which is applied prior to the issuing of what is termed an identity federation token (IDFT). The IDFT is an ID together with a signed version of that ID, i.e., it is a cryptographically secure ID of a patient at the institution that is the source of the medical data. The link between Indivo e-PHR and patient care organisation's records uses the issued IDFT.

4.4.4 Summary of Concerns and Issues with e-PHR systems and Services

While e-PHR systems and services such as Google Health, HealthVault and Indivo are beneficial in getting rid of the alienation of patients from participation in

[11] Dossia, http://www.dossia.org/, accessed: 20 October 2008

decision-making concerning their own health care, and in integrating data from disparate healthcare provides to facilitate healthcare information sharing, these systems and services brings concerns to both patients and clinicians. Patient's concerns mainly have to do with information privacy and security. The e-PHR systems and services are guaranteed to succeed if the following trust-building measures are undertaken to assure patients and individual members of the public:

1. Addressing privacy concerns;
2. Building privacy protection into laws, standards, policies, contracts and technologies;
3. Providing an assurance that sensitive information in digital form will be stored and shared safely and in a confidential manner;
4. Ensuring that long established fair information practices form the official basis of the national privacy framework.

Clinician's concerns relating to e-PHR have to do with their trust regarding basing medical decisions on the information that is controlled and maintained by the patient. Thus, patient entered information has limited trust being only as trustworthy as surveys that patients fill out when meeting a new physician. Patient's ability to add and delete data from their e-PHRs will only serve to make e-PHRs to suffer skepticism from clinicians, who are likely to restrict their trust to aspects of the e-PHR that are important and imported from other healthcare providers and only where the patient additions and deletions are disallowed. Some of the clinician's skepticism may arise from the following factors:

1. Patients may be poor at remembering everything that they are told by doctors;
2. Patients may not be in a position to enter everything that need to be held by their e-PHR on any aspect of their health;
3. Information in the e-PHR may be incomplete, inaccurate or even incorrect partly due to the above factors;
4. There may be some providers who may choose not to allow importation of health information into specific e-PHR services or systems leading to incomplete records.

The main concern of clinicians is that of trust. Hence, most of the above issues could be addressed by implementing a policy that disallows the patient to perform maintenance operations on all imported information and clearly de-lineating patient entered data from imported data. Google Health, HealthVault and Indivo projects are already aware of this strategy, and for them it is a question of making a choice between individual freedom and striking a balance between patient empowerment and clinician concerns.

It is important to point out here, that privacy protection laws are of fundamental significance in ensuring the success of e-PHRs. However, privacy protection laws such as HIPAA, have weaknesses in the form of gaps such as leaving many new and emerging players in e-Healthcare information management outside the scope of the legal frameworks. A typical example is that HIPAA does not apply to e-PHR services such as Google Health and HealthVault, due to their exclusion from the definition of a covered entity. The privacy and protection provision comparison of the e-PHRs are given in Table 4.3.

Table 4.3 Comparison of e-PHR systems

Privacy Protection Provision	Google Health (GH)	HealthVault (HV)	Indivo
1) Right of Access	Free, Immediate Web access Gmail account	Via Live ID & HealthVault ID with strong passwords	Indivo account based on user & password
2) Privacy a) Notice b) Enforcement	 Privacy policy Privacy laws excluding HIPAA	 Privacy policy Same as for GH	 Not based on large IT company & user in total control
3) Protected Information Third party use	Personal ID information is protected Third party subject to privacy laws	Same as for GH	
4) Disclosure a) Permitted b) Mandated by law	 Require notice and user authorisation Some laws mandate disclosure without consent e.g. court orders, subpoenas, Notice is given	 same as for GH Same as for GH	 Disclosure is completely on individual discretion May be mandated by law as well
5) Mechanism for authorisation of disclosure	User request & give Google permission to share info., sharing is revocable at any time	Same as for Google Health	User has total control over local disclosure & revocation subscription-based

4.5 Security and Privacy in Clinical Decision Support Systems

A clinical decision-support system (CDSS) is an active knowledge system that uses two or more items of patient data to generate patient-specific advice (Wyatt and Spiegelhalter, 1991). The CDSS needs to integrate an e-Healthcare record system, a medical knowledge base and a reasoning and inference engine in order for it to achieve the goal of patient specific advice. The major tasks/functions of CDSS are in the areas of administration, the management of clinical complexity and details (monitoring patients on clinical trials and protocols, tracking orders, referrals, follow-up and prevention care); cost control (avoiding duplicate and unnecessary test orders); and medical decision-support (diagnosis and treatment) (Perreault and Metzger, 1999). CDSS would fall into the category of e-Healthcare information systems that are sensitive and critical from a privacy and security perspective. Their potential for abuse in privacy breach would be the same as that for clinical data mining systems/approaches and techniques.

One of the major goals of Artificial Intelligence (AI) since its inception has been the development of clinical DSS (Shortliffe, 1986). The goal of Software Engineering has been the development of maintainable, secure and interoperable and distributed clinical DSS. The design of clinical DSS requires the consideration of Doctor's and patient's needs. The clinical or medical decision making processes may be Geographically distributed and involve information sharing and interaction among clinicians at different sites. The EHR is typically distributed or scattared across disparate EHR systems that are generally not integrated. This complicates access to e-Healthcare information by clinical DSS by bringing extra dimensions such as patient privacy protection. For DSS to be successful in e-Healthcare, it has to be a distributed DSS, undertaken in a secure and privacy preserving way.

A CDSS is designed to hold large amounts of sensitive e-Healthcare data and information. Healthcare information privacy and protection laws, organisational policies and professional ethics mandate CDSS to guarantee a high degree patient privacy and information protection. The acceptance and success of CDSS has been hampered by their lack of usability within the healthcare environment. Non-user friendly security measures and procedures could further exacerbate the traditional complains that hamper the adoption of CDSS in healthcare. Consequently, technical and appropriate security measures and procedures should be chosen for their effectiveness to mitigate security risks in CDSS without being disruptive to the patient care environment.

Evidence-based medicine (Eddy, 2005) in the form of clinical practice guidelines (CPG) (Field and Lohr, 1990) are a modern effort to integrate state-of-the-art research evidence into the daily routine used by clinicians in their decision-making process. CDSS are generally used as tools for supporting CPGs. It has been argued that data warehousing provides a useful appropriate platform for the generation of evidence-based CPGs as well as for supporting CPGs at the point of patient care. Thus, data pulled from different sources and systems is collected into a data warehouse on which data mining tools can be applied to identify patterns and trends and to discover best practice for clinical problem management. The combination of CPGS, data warehousing and mining renders evidence-based CDSS to be highly sensitive systems.

When considering security and privacy protection for e-Healthcare information in computerised CPGs, there is a need to focus on two major areas of CPG management, namely,

1. The development and/or generation of CPGs from medical evidence, and
2. The use of CPGs in the process of patient care.

Guidelines development could benefit from clinical data warehouses from which CDSS draws the data for the tasks of data mining and knowledge discovery. Guideline development does not require personally identifiable information since the resulting CPGs are not specific to the individual patient.

Figure 4.3 illustrates the security issues and aspects that need consideration in CPG management that is assisted by CDSS. As illustrated in the diagram, CPG development could involve clinical data warehousing and CDSS and requires no use of personally identifiable information. Hence, anonymisation and pseudonymisation constitute the key measure for the protection of patient privacy and confidentiality of healthcare information. Furthermore, CPG development results in generic clinical guidelines that apply to a generic category of clinical problems and hence requires no reversal of either anonymisation or pseudonymisation.

The use or application of CPGs for patient and disease management is the second key aspect of CPG management that needs security and privacy consideration. CDSS are also in widespread use in this area, whose key characteristic is being patient-specific and its consequent use of personally identifiable information. During CPG use in patient care, the role-base access control (RBAC) scheme as well as other authorisation and authentication schemes are important security and privacy protection measures.

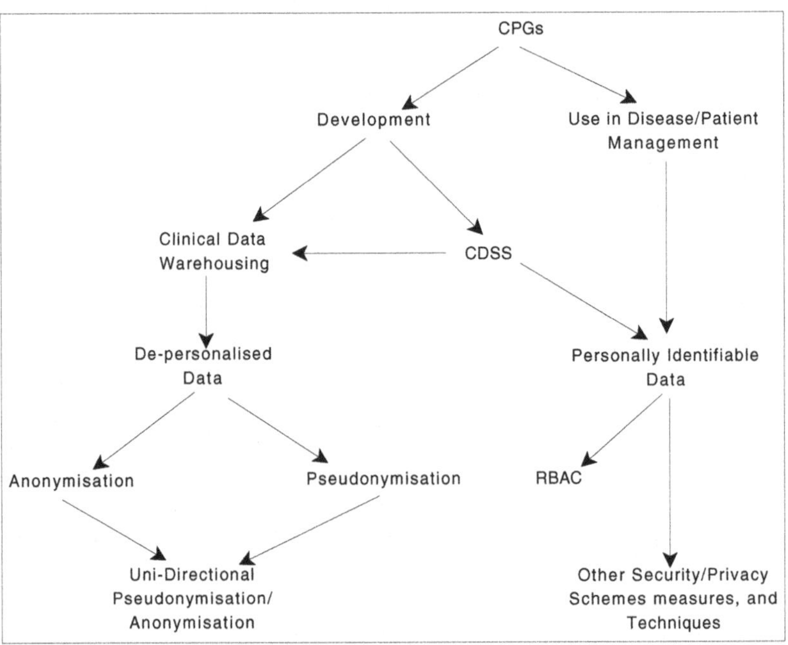

Figure 4.3 Security Issues in CPG Management

4.6 The Challenges from Security and Privacy for e-Healthcare Information Security

The e-Healthcare information security challenges persist as evidenced by the growing list of privacy breach stories (HPP, 2008) that seem to defy both security technology advances and introduction of stringent legal regimes such as HIPAA 1996. The elements of security that are summarised in Table 4.1 are all capable of being implemented with existing technologies, which are quite mature and well researched/established with the possible exception of patient consent. The modeling and security challenges that are associated with patient consent are still yet to be fully investigated as health management organisations such as the NHS in the UK move to introduce new consent models in efforts to appease public privacy concerns that threaten their e-Healthcare Information Systems such as the NHS. The crucial security challenges have continued to lie at the boundary of computer systems and human factors and agents where identity plays a crucial role and the aspects of authentication and authorisation continue to be the weakest points of security for e-Healthcare information. The physical theft of e-Healthcare information held in computers and storage media continue to pose challenges. The increased need for transmission of e-Healthcare information through communication channels based on the Internet continue to pose ever-present challenges that are shared by most Internet-based services. The expectation of biometric security technologies, especially those based on personal genomics, remains a challenge in providing a solution to identity theft and secure authentication for e-Healthcare information systems. Due to the multiplicity of players, who need to access and use e-Healthcare information, the confidentiality aspect of the security of personally identifiable e-Healthcare records continue to be mine-field of security breaches.

Table 4.4 Summary of Security Challenges facing modern e-HIS

Category	Nature of Challenge
Law, Policy and standards	1. Mandatory disclosures; 2. Mapping to formal technical specification; 3. Legal loopholes e.g. HIPAA exclusion of Google Health and HealthVault; 4. Compliance issues.
Human Factors	1. Trust building; 2. Patient consent technical modeling and implementations; 3. Identity theft ; 4. Contain in confidentiality breaches.
Transmission of e-Healthcare Information	1. Physical theft of storage media and computers; 2. Electronic interception of information; 3. Accidental disclosure; 4. Accidental dissemination.

Table 4.4 summarises the main challenges that are facing modern e-Healthcare information systems. The drive towards patient empowered has brought challenges in the form of mandatory requirements to implement system-level consent mechanism as well as unrestricted patient access to their own information. Further challenges arised in the form of authentication-based security breaches and identity theft. Patient empowerement has also been accompanied by legal requirements whose formalisation and modeling is a challenge to security engineering. Patient empowerment has also brought about a paradigm shift from organisation and process-centred healthcare information systems to person-centred e-Healthcare information systems that are supported by new generation Internet technology. The major challenge is for all e-Healthcare information systems to accommodate the person-centred paradigm in which the patient exercises a high degree of access and control over their own e-Healthcare information while at the same time ensuring the medical accuracy, reliability and trustworthiness of the e-Healthcare information.

The emergence of new and disruptive information and communication technologies, especially ubiquitous, mobile and wireless networked devices, bring the challenges of a computing infrastructure that is difficult to secure. A further challenge to e-Healthcare information is that deployed applications are not mature technologies that come prepared and built using software and security engineering methods that may be unprepared for the new and evolving domain of e-Healthcare. This domain is also plagued by the lack of comprehensive framework that synthesize the key elements and converges the privacy and confidentiality protection laws, the information and security standards and the enabling technologies into a coherent conceptual platform that can serve as a sound basis for providing the support for security and patient privacy and confidentiality required for e-Healthcare information.

The emergence of personal e-Healthcare record systems on the vehicle of the Internet and Web technologies is a major challenge to the privacy of e-Healthcare information. Privacy breaches such as the recent breaking into the Yahoo email account of the US Republican vice-presidential candidate, Alaska Governor Sarah Palin, by exploiting privacy preserving mechanism of Yahoo mail together with personal information obtained on the internet through search engines, has triggered major distrust for personal e-Healthcare records (BBC, 2008). Therefore, the acceptance of online personal e-Healthcare record services, such as Google Health and HealthVault, will face an uphill struggle unless more steps and measures are taken to change public perceptions as well as to actually eliminate legal, security and privacy loopholes in these systems.

4.7 Future e-Healthcare Information Management: Towards the EHR/PEHR Hybridisation

The emerging legal, policy and regulatory frameworks in countries around the world and the operational demands for e-Healthcare information management will render the viability of pure EHR and PEHR systems difficult, if not impossible, in the future. This can be observed from the emerging trend that is currently exemplified by the NHS Summary Care Record (SCR) and HealthSpace (Greenhalgh et al, 2008). It presents the NHS EHR system as consisting of the NHS Care Record, which is wholly controlled by NHS healthcare units and a limited PEHR presented through a web portal, which does not allow the patient to modify his e-Healthcare record while giving the patient control in deciding who can and cannot access his or her e-Healthcare information. It can, therefore, be postulated that the future of e-Healthcare information management will be characterised by the hybridisation of clinician or health organisation maintained EHRs and personally-controlled PEHRs with enhanced powers of control being given to the patient.

The PEHR systems will be required to provide mechanisms for allowing e-Healthcare information exchange between them, on one hand, and organisational EHR systems, on the other hand. Thus, import and export of e-Healthcare information between the PEHR and EHR systems will be supported, which gives rise to security and privacy threats that are associated with the transmission of information over the Internet.

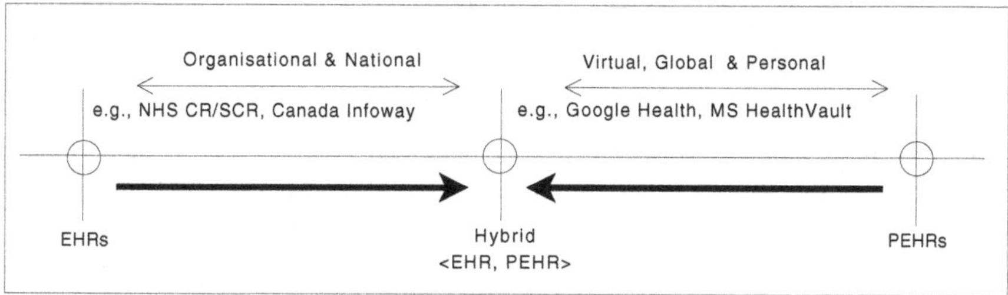

Figure 4.4 The move towards hybrid e-Healthcare information systems and away from pure EHR and PEHR systems

Figure 4.4 illustrates the emerging and future trend, where pure EHRs will need to incorporate aspects of the PEHR system in order to meet the legal requirement to grant access and control to individual patient's e-Healthcare information. Pure PEHRs will also seek to incorporate the EHR in order to be complete. Patients' control with respect to modifying e-Healthcare information may need to be curtailed by disallowing modification of the information imported from the EHR systems. This will be necessary in order for clinicians to rely on the EHR elements in the PEHR. Already Google Health and Microsoft's HealthVault allow the incorporation of EHR from various healthcare organisations.

The resulting hybrid systems will inherit the security and privacy challenges of both the EHR and PEHR systems. The resulting hybrid system will, however, be able to arrest the alienation of patients by allowing them to access their health information and empower them to decide who can access their records. These EHR/PEHR hybrid systems will also give rise to the need to review gaps in privacy protection laws such as HIPAA's exclusion of providers of the patient e-Healthcare information services such as Google and Microsoft. New comprehensive frameworks will need to be developed to wholistically address the security and privacy protection requirements of the new paradigm in e-Healthcare information management that is centred on the empowered individual patient.

4.8 Summary

Generally, e-Healthcare information systems are networked, distributed and usually Internet-based. This renders the e-Healthcare information that is held in these systems to be vulnerable to security and privacy threats. The organisational setting for these systems include regional networks of organisations, international health management organisations (HMOs) which places demands on these systems to support communication, distribution and cooperation. The evolutionary scale of e-Healthcare information systems has tended to be from organisation, to inter-organisational processes, to virtual online personal e-Healthcare records than span an individual's life-time and support mobility of the individual patient. This evolution is accompanied by complexities in provisioning of security and privacy of information held in these e-Healthcare systems. The complexity is further worsened by the ever increasing networked-enabled wireless mobile devices. The legal domain is challenged to produce gapless laws for protecting patient privacy and confidentiality. Standardisation efforts are challenged to ensure security and privacy protection interoperability across e-Healthcare information systems. Identity theft together with vulnerability in authentication mechanisms constitute challenges that could benefit from exploitation of emerging security technologies such as biometrics and personal genomics. The new paradigm shift based on patient empowerment as a way to gain public trust and combat privacy and confidentiality concerns brings in challenges of modeling and implementation of consent mechanisms and providing ways of access and control of e-Healthcare information by the patient.

Modern e-Healthcare information systems are of two general types. The first type is that controlled by clinicians or healthcare organisations and occurs in the form of e-Healthcare records (EHRs) systems. These systems are increasingly being governed by emerging legislation for patient protection under national frameworks of e-Healthcare information management. The second type of e-Healthcare information systems are the personally controlled e-Healthcare information systems, which are increasingly becoming popular with large IT companies who are seeking to exploit the potential lucrative business opportunities that accompany the systems. Typical examples of these EPHR systems include Google Health, Microsoft HealthVault and Indivo, which are Internet-based services offered for free to the public. These systems suffer the challenges generally associated with sensitive online-based systems. Clinician and hospital-controlled EHR systems and personally-controlled PEHR systems lie at the two ends of a bi-polar scenario, in which security and patient privacy concerns and clinicians trust on the realibility of the e-Healthcare information interplay. It is envisaged that e-Healthcare information systems of the future should be a hybrid of the EHR and PEHR systems, whose security challenges will be different but more complex the two independent systems.

Clinical decision-support systems (CDSS) are heavily dependent on e-Healthcare information systems and may not be functional in a useful way in the patient care set up. The major challenge for CDSS is to catch up with the paradigm shifts that are affecting e-Healthcare information systems while also adopting and complying with the security and privacy protection that govern the access and utilisation of personally identifiable information.

References

BBC (2008) Palin e-mail hack details emerge. BBC News (Online) Friday, 19 September 2008, URL http://news.bbc.co.uk/2/hi/technology/7624809.stm

Eddy DM (2005) Evidence-Based Medicine: A Unified Approach. Health Aff 24(1):9–17, DOI 10.1377/hlthaff.24.1.9, URL http://content.healthaffairs.org/cgi/content/abstract/24/1/9, http://content.healthaffairs.org/cgi/reprint/24/1/9.pdf

Field M, Lohr K (1990) Attributes of good practice guidelines. In: Field M, Lohr K (eds) Clinical Practice Guidelines: Directions for a New Program, National Academy Press, Washington, DC, pp 53–77

Greenhalgh T, Wood GW, Bratan T, Stramer K, Hinder S (2008) Patients' attitudes to the summary care record and healthspace: qualitative study. British Medical Journal 0:1–11, DOI http://doi:10.1136/bmj.a114, URL http://www.bmj.com/cgi/reprint/bmj.a114v1(accessed:19October2008)

HPP (2008) Health privacy stories. Health Privacy Project August 2008, URL http://www.healthprivacy.org/usr-doc/Privacystories.pdf

Jensen T, Larsen KH, Kofod-Petersen A (2006) Towards a norwegian implementation of electronic personal health records. In: Kofod-Petersen A, Brasethvik T (eds) Proceedings of the International Symposium on Electronic Personal Health Records 2006 (ISePHR 2006), Trondheim, Norway, September 28, 2006, pp 1–10

Mandl KD, Simons WW, Crawford WCR, Abbett JM (2007) Indivo: a personally controlled health record for health information exchange and communication. BMC Medical Informatics and Decision Making 7:25, DOI 1472-6947-7-25, pMID: 17850667

Perreault L, Metzger J (1999) A pragmatic framework for understanding clinical decision support. Journal of Healthcare Information Management 13(2):5 – 12

Sax U, Kohane I, Mandl KD (2005) Wireless technology infrastructures for authentication of patients: Pki that rings. Journal of the American Medical Informatics Association: JAMIA 12(3):263–8, DOI M1681, pMID: 15684133

Shortliffe E (1986) Medical expert systems knowledge tools for physicians. Western Journal of Medicine 145:830 – 839

Wyatt J, Spiegelhalter D (1991) Know-Based Systems in Medicine, Applications and Evaluation, Heidelberg: Springer Verlag, chap Evaluating medical expert systems: what to test, and how?, pp 274 –290

Chapter 5
Towards a Comprehensive Framework for Secure e-Healthcare Information

5.1 Introduction

The world is witnessing escalation in security and privacy breaches in e-Healthcare, despite advances in information security and privacy enhancing technologies. The international drive to introduce healthcare information privacy protection laws has not led to the abatement of security and privacy breaches. The emergence of a wide variety of standards has not brought e-Healthcare close to the securing of e-Healthcare information and protecting patient privacy. Escalating increase in pervasive computing devices in an increasingly wireless networked environment has created a conducive breeding infrastructure for security and privacy breach attacks in e-Healthcare. It would, therefore, seem to be necessary and worthwhile to seek for a comprehensive framework that allows for a more holistic provision of security and privacy protection. It would seem to be logical that such a framework would have based on a convergence of the key drivers to e-Healthcare information privacy and security. Such key drivers are crucial and determining factors in the protection of privacy and security of e-Healthcare information. Privacy protection laws, organisational policy, human factors, paradigmatic developments in the healthcare domain, governance and leadership, and advances in the IT security and computing technology are some of the key drivers to the provision of security and the protection of privacy.

This chapter addresses the problem of the search for a comprehensive conceptual approach and framework that allows for the convergence of the key drivers to the security and privacy protection of e-Healthcare information in both the construction method, process and the resulting architecture for privacy protection and securing of the e-Healthcare information. The constant theme of the chapter is centred on the convergence of these drivers. The chapter first identifies and characterises the problem of securing e-Healthcare information and then sets the context and key concepts for securing e-Healthcare information. Second, the chapter characterises the current paradigmatic changes in the control of e-Healthcare information, the future directions in the evolution of the management of e-Healthcare information and the role of security metrics before outlining the future-enabled requirements for the security and protection of privacy of e-Healthcare. Third, the chapter presents the conceptual approach adopted here to the problem of securing e-Healthcare information by following the theme of convergence of the drivers to privacy and security of e-Healthcare information. Forth, the chapter presents the elements of the proposed conceptual framework by first discussing the key drivers to privacy and security of information. A model of the evolution of the control of e-Healthcare information and security and privacy risks is presented as a way to set the context for the conceptual framework. Finally, the conceptual framework itself is presented in terms of first the conceptual process of crafting the security and privacy protection for e-healthcare information, and then the generic conceptual security and privacy framework that underlie that process. The chapter concludes with a discussion and summary of the issues raised in the earlier sections of the chapter.

5.2 The Problem of Securing e-Healthcare Information

The e-Healthcare information is private and sensitive information of a personal nature. The preservation of patient privacy is crucial to the treatment of the patient in that it builds patient trust in the healthcare system.

Cumulative e-Healthcare information is useful to clinicians in the patient care process. Clinicians create records of this healthcare information for future use in disease management and as a legal record of what they decide and do in treating the patient. The clinicians are creators, users and custodians of private and sensitive personal health information for their patients. Fair procedures now mandates that patients should be allowed access to their own healthcare information. Furthermore, a legal duty of protecting the confidentiality of patient information is placed on the clinicians. The disclosure of information requires patient consent. Hence, patient access and consent are now emerging as a key ingredients of the security and privacy mechanisms for e-Healthcare information.

Patient mobility, involvement of many players in the disease management process, the need for management information for healthcare planning and medical research for the public good, all necessitate the sharing of e-Healthcare information and hence access to it by a large spectrum of individuals. The sharing of healthcare information and access to it by a large spectrum of individuals threatens the privacy of the patient and yet is necessary for the benefit of both the patient and the public. Therefore, patient privacy needs to be preserved, while sharing needs to be facilitated.

The legal empowerment of the patient through mandating the involvement of the patient in the control and access to e-Healthcare in formation is being widely adopted around the world. Requirements from the privacy protection laws that are emerging from this empowerment drive will need to be flexibly incorporated into the e-Healthcare information security and privacy infrastructure. Flexible incorporation of the laws means that future changes in laws will be easy to incorporate into the security and privacy mechanisms.

The healthcare care environment is constantly undergoing changes that impact on the security and privacy of e-Healthcare information. The managed care paradigm has seen the emergence of health management and financing organisations that have a regional, national, federal and even continental span causing radical changes in way patients are treated, and how e-Healthcare information is managed and secured. The patient-centred paradigm shift now places the patient at the centre of the decision-making process in the management of diseases while empowering the patient with the ability to monitor the privacy and confidentiality of their e-Healthcare information. Therefore, e-Healthcare information disclosure and access need to be governed by both the law and patient consent, which must be informed. Furthermore, e-Healthcare information management now needs to be technically brought under the control of the patient.

Advances in computer information technologies (ITs) continue to bring both benefits to e-Healthcare information management and threats to security and the protection of privacy of e-Healthcare information. On one hand, the managed care paradigm is supported by the organisation-controlled EHR systems, which are made possible by ITs. On the other hand, the privacy and security breaches of centralised organisation-controlled patient databases that affect large patient populations have been made possible by ITs. Again, on one hand, the patient-centred care paradigm will be facilitated by advances in computer information and communication technologies (ICTs) based on the Internet and the Web. On the other hand, ICTs are already wrecking havoc by facilitating widespread security and privacy breach attacks on the EHR and PEHR systems.

The problem of securing e-Healthcare information is, therefore, a complex challenge that constitutes balancing acts of: facilitating sharing and disclosure while preserving patient privacy and confidentiality; supporting paradigmatic changes in healthcare environment while not compromising patient privacy and care quality; exploiting technological advances for e-Healthcare information management while eliminating technology-facilitated security and privacy threats; meeting legal privacy protection requirements while facilitating access to e-Healthcare information for the public good.

5.3 The Context and Concepts for Securing e-Healthcare Information

The healthcare environment makes up the context for the security and privacy protection for e-Healthcare information privacy. A comprehensive characterisation of the healthcare environment is indispensable for the accurate determination of the requirements for securing e-Healthcare information and protecting its privacy. This permits the identification of key areas of the healthcare domain that are critical to the security and privacy of e-Healthcare information. Figure 5.1 illustrates a contextual framework incorporating the relevant issues and areas upon which a conceptual foundation of the security and privacy of e-Healthcare information can be laid.

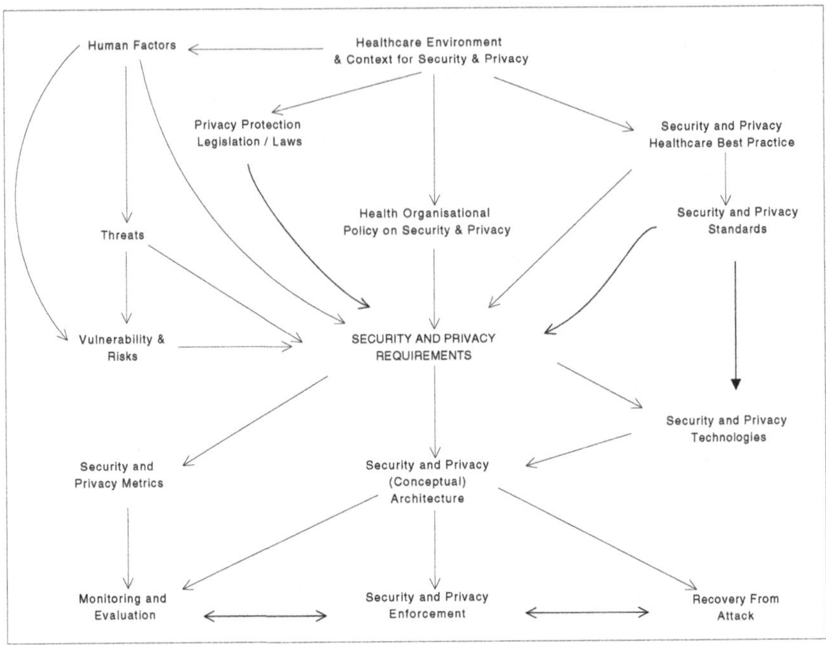

Figure 5.1 The Contextual Framework for e-Healthcare Information Security and Privacy

The major aspects of the e-Healthcare environment, that impact on security and privacy, include: human factors, privacy protection laws, healthcare organisational policies and best practice for the healthcare domain. A careful analysis of these aspects of the healthcare domain would allow the development of a comprehensive set of security and privacy requirements for e-Healthcare information, which should then be employed in the determination of the appropriate security and privacy implementation technologies.

Human factors are increasingly receiving attention in information security and privacy research. The impact of social and psychological aspects of people on security and privacy of information is increasingly becoming recognised to be significant. Many aspects of computer security are now considered to be mature and capable of helping in attaining adequate security and privacy levels for e-Healthcare information, and yet they are hardly enough given the escalating privacy breaches. Hence, human factors are emerging as the missing piece that prominent security experts believe may still require to be thoroughly investigated. Threats, vulnerability and risks may be either technical or human factor based or a combination of these two. Security and privacy approaches and frameworks for e-Healthcare information security have tended to emphasise more on technical aspects of threats, vulnerabilities and risks than on human factors.

The governance and leadership in the domain of security and privacy within healthcare organisations have been relegated to lower-level personnel with minute budgets and little influence. It is clear, that governance and leadership at high organisational level are crucial factors in security education, awareness and the effective implementation, execution, monitoring and recovery from security failures and privacy breaches.

Privacy protection laws are seeking mandatory enforcement of the patient-centred healthcare paradigm through e-Healthcare information privacy, individual person's access to information concerning their own healthcare and the individual involvement in deciding who can access his or her e-Healthcare information. At the same time, privacy protection law also mandates the availability of the person's e-Healthcare information for the public benefit especially for planning and medical research purposes.

The legal concept of patient consent emerges as a new concept in information management, which requires modelling and native support within the computational mechanism. The model of consent required needs to incorporate the degree of knowledge of the person who is giving consent and, hence, to distinguish between informed and uninformed consent.

Health organisational policy on security and privacy of e-Healthcare information is increasingly getting aligned to the requirements of the privacy protection law and healthcare best practice on patient privacy. Associated with organisational policy, the subject of security and privacy, leadership and governance within healthcare organisations is increasingly emerging as a determinant prerequisite for the success of security and privacy policies.

Healthcare best practice in e-Healthcare information security and privacy is grounded on professional ethics, which are based on the Hippocratic Oath and have continued to evolve through paradigmatic changes in Healthcare such as managed healthcare coupled with its emphasis on cost reduction and care quality improvement through evidence-based healthcare practice as well as the current drive towards patient-centred healthcare practice that seek to empower the patient throughout the process of care.

The Secure e-Healthcare Record (SecEHR) is a critical requirement for the success of modern e-Healthcare information management within healthcare organisations. The SecEHR has both adequate security and the protection of privacy to the extent required by privacy laws, standards and best practice guidelines. The question of the criteria to be achieved by an e-Healthcare record in order for it to be considered to be secure is difficult to resolve, since security is not an absolute and often involves trade-offs and compromises.

The secure Personal e-Healthcare Record (SecPEHR) would require that adequate security measures, which also incorporate all the privacy protection requirements required by the law, are in place in order to gain public trust and attain regulatory compliance.

Security and privacy protection standards for e-Healthcare information management are important in ensuring the interoperability of security and privacy protection measures across e-Healthcare environments. As e-Healthcare information is accessed and shared among care-givers and secondary users, it is a desirable requirement that information source and recipient systems and environments have uniform security and protection measures.

Security and privacy requirements for e-Healthcare information need to be drawn from a robust consideration of human factors, privacy protection laws, healthcare organisational policy, security technologies and healthcare best practice, which all must be drawn from the healthcare environment and context that is increasingly involving the individual patient in decision-making processes as well as in the controlling position.

Security and privacy technologies for e-Healthcare information management must be selected for their capacity to meet the comprehensive set of privacy requirements and their compliance with security and privacy standards.

The monitoring, evaluation and adjustments of operational security and privacy mechanisms are important aspects of any security and privacy protection framework, since security and privacy protection are moving targets. The reason for the latter is because new threats, vulnerabilities and risks are constantly emerging and triggered by the dynamic nature of the e-Healthcare environment, especially the accelerating move towards a pervasive computing environment.

The enforcement of security and privacy laws, policies, standards and measures is a significant factor that has distinguished and set apart the HIPAA 1996 from other legal and regulatory frameworks for securing e-Healthcare information. Enforcement occurs at all levels of the system, department, organisation to national level, and can be technical, organisational or legal. Without the various forms of enforcement, there is not much security and privacy protection to talk about, as organisations will find no reason to devote resources towards this area of information management.

5.4 Towards Future-Enabled Requirements for Securing e-Healthcare Information

In the future patient-centred healthcare service delivery will place patient privacy and confidentiality concerns at the centre of e-Healthcare information management. In order to realise and protect the public and individual benefits that will arise from the widespread adoption of e-Healthcare, attention is turning to legally regulated privacy and confidentiality protection of e-Healthcare information as well as standards-based information security measures. It is here contended that future-enabled requirements for e-Healthcare information security must be drawn from and with the guidance of a comprehensive framework that represents a convergence of privacy protection laws, the healthcare domain context, organisational policy and governance, human factors, best practice and information security standards.

The fundamental changes brought about by the patient-centred healthcare paradigm will shift e-Healthcare information access and usage control to patients and broaden maintenance participation for e-Healthcare information to incorporate both patients and clinicians. These revolutionary changes will also heavily depend on unprecedented exploitation of the Internet, which will expose e-Healthcare information to security and privacy threats, vulnerability and risks on an unprecedented scale.

This section sets the context for the requirements for security and privacy of the emerging and constantly evolving scenario in e-Healthcare information management.

5.4.1 The Security and Privacy Impact of the Evolution of the Control of e-Healthcare Information in Context of the Patient-Centred Paradigm

In general, e-Healthcare information occurs in the form of e-Healthcare records (EHRs). Ever since their inception, EHRs have been created, maintained and controlled by clinicians and healthcare organisations. The key characteristics of EHRs have been fragmentation, organisation-centred, hardly sharable among clinicians and inaccessible to the individual patient. Growing discomfort with the limitations of these EHRs have led to research during the past decade that focused on mainly middleware-based virtual integration and interoperability among disparate sources of the e-Healthcare information. Figure 5.2 illustrates a high-level trace of the evolution into the future of e-Healthcare information management in the form of the EHRs and PEHRs.

In Figure 5.2, the key milestones are labelled A through E. It should be pointed out here that, in reality, the periods and milestones do not occur at specific points in time nor do they occur one after another as the timeline shows. Instead, the periods and milestones are not accurately durative and could be without strict start and end points. They actually do overlap and also run concurrently.

Progress within e-Healthcare information management has passed points A and B, and has just approached point C in 2007-8 as a result of the introduction of Microsoft HealthVault, Google Health and the UK NHS Care Record and Summary Care Record. There is now clearly a rapid move towards point D, which incorporates the hybrid the EHR/PEHR as a solution to the legal and operational or functional limitations of pure EHRs and/or pure PEHRs. Point E is a possible state of progress in the future, where cloud computing may have been successful, and e-Healthcare exploits the cloud and healthcare organisations would have deemed it cheaper and beneficial to move all e-Healthcare information management into the computing cloud. All these points of progress or evolution have security and privacy challenges with the introduction of the Internet and networking bringing in further security and privacy complications.

The points A, B and C characterise the present scenario for e-Healthcare. In this scenario, e-Healthcare information, in the form of e-Healthcare records (EHRs), is generally controlled by clinicians and healthcare organisations with no patient participation of any form. Patient access occurs only during the discovery process of court procedures during litigation and under the Freedom of Information Acts.

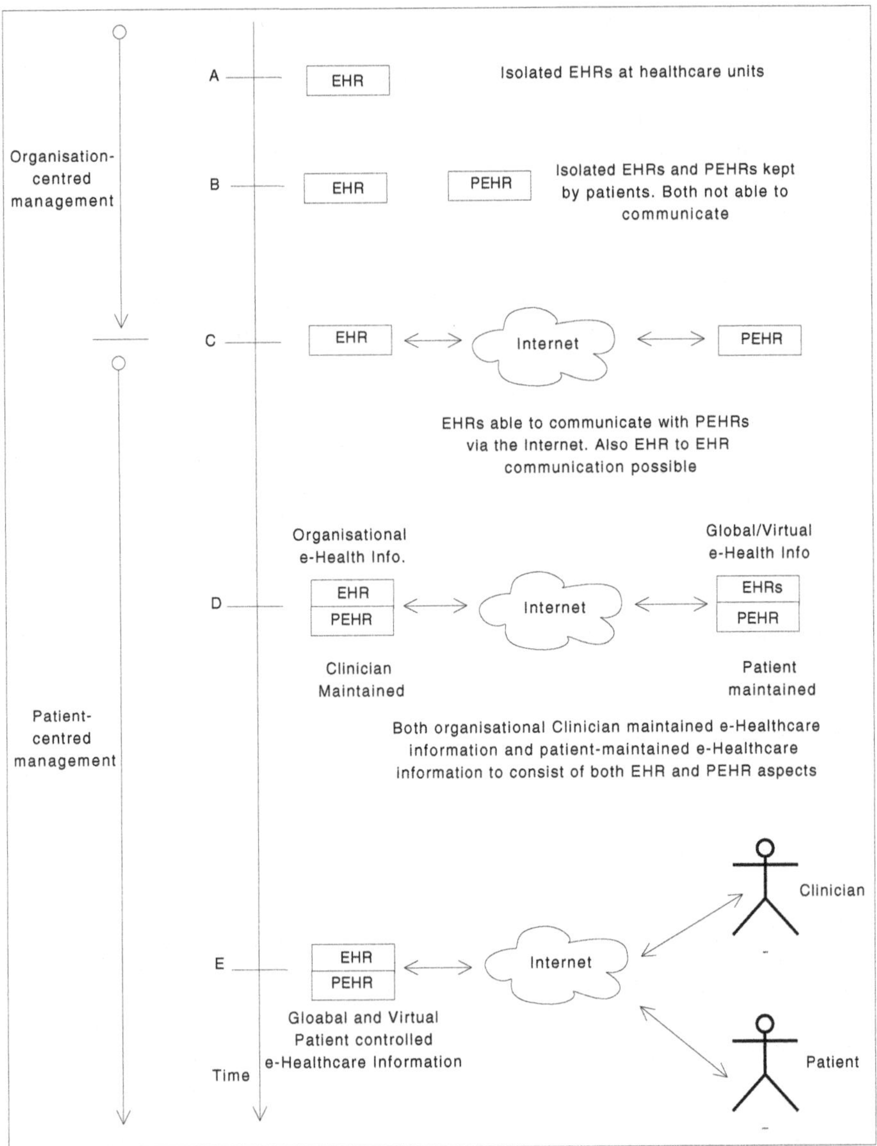

Figure 5.2 The Evolution of e-Healthcare Information Management and Future of EHR/PEHR

Patient privacy and confidentiality is an obligation that is borne by clinicians and healthcare organisations who are in control of e-Healthcare information. The general environment for EHR systems at A and B is based on organisational LANs that are accessible only internally. Hence, the balance of security and privacy threats, vulnerabilities and risks weighs heavily against those that are inside the healthcare organisation as opposed to those that are external. Human factor-based privacy and security breaches, such as identity theft, remain issues of concern regardless of the underlying network infrastructure although open networks, such as the Internet, would further jeopardise security and privacy protection. At B, early personally controlled EHRs (PEHRs) begin to be introduced with the main focus being to support chronic disease management, which is a domain where clinicians rely on PEHRs maintained by the patient on a daily basis. These PEHRs rarely exchange information with clinician-maintained EHRS and where this occurs, it is done during doctor-patient encounters and, hence, within the healthcare organisational LANs with little or not use of the Internet. Hence, at A and B, e-Healthcare information was shielded from the overwhelming security challenges that are inherent on the Internet.

At point C, we note the emergence of Internet-enabled EHRs that were triggered by the need for e-Healthcare information sharing between clinicians and between organisation-controlled/clinician-maintained EHRs and patient controlled and maintained PEHRs. The security and privacy challenges, experienced generally by Internet-enabled applications, are now brought to bear on e-Healthcare information. At this point, the patient-centred paradigm shift begins to take root and places demands on e-Healthcare information management to empower patients from two major perspectives: first, patients are to be enabled to access their e-Healthcare information, i.e. EHRs, on demand; and second, patients are to be either directly involved in access control decisions affecting secondary use of their own e-Healthcare information or they are to assume absolute and total control of the disclosure of their e-Healthcare information to anyone including clinicians. Thus, from point C onwards, electronic identity, patient access and patient consent to access and disclosure are to play a central role in e-Healthcare information management and usage.

The upcoming period of the development of e-Healthcare information management is represented by points D and E. This period is characterised by the widespread adoption of PEHRs that are closely linked through information exchange to organisational EHRs. Furthermore, pure EHRs and pure PEHRs will be deemed to be inadequate to support the patient-centred paradigm and legal requirements for patient access and consent, while at the same time maintaining clinicians' trust on the e-Healthcare information that is maintained and controlled by the patient. Hence, organisation/clinician-controlled EHR systems will incorporate PEHR views or components while PEHRs systems PEHRs will incorporate EHRs. This scenario is already evident in the recognition that Google Health and Microsoft HealthVault alone will not be useful, unless support for import and export of e-Healthcare information from and to EHR system is incorporated. The scenario is also evident in the recognition by the UK National Health Service that EHRs within its healthcare units also need to be exposed to access and control by the patient, thus, effectively presenting the EHRs as PEHRs. Therefore, both the patient and the clinician must be accommodated in either the EHR and PEHR systems.

Point E illustrates a future scenario, where cloud computing as well as web-based services such as Microsoft HealthVault and Google Health would have taken root in e-Healthcare to the extent that healthcare organisations, clinicians and patients take the hybrid EHR and PEHR into the cloud computing infrastructure for management. Cloud computing is the IT environment that includes all elements of the IT stack and network products and supporting services, that enable the development, delivery and consumption of cloud services, which are essentially consumer and Business products, services and solutions that are delivered and consumed in real-time over the Internet. Some of the major challenges to cloud computing are concerns as well as real risks, threats and vulnerabilities that jeopardise the security, privacy and confidentiality protection for e-Healthcare information held in the clouding computing infrastructure.

5.4.2 The nature, security and privacy implications of the EHR/PEHR hybrid

The e-Healthcare information management is evolving towards the convergence of the EHRs and PEHRs into a hybrid that will have the characteristics of each and, hence, will inherit the security and privacy risks, threats and vulnerabilities that are associated with each of the original principals. This convergence is driven by the paradigm shift that places the patient at the centre of the management of disease and its prevention, as well as the realisation that extreme patient control is untenable as it may hamper professional practice, healthcare management planning and clinical or medical research that will benefit the public good. The EHRs will move towards incorporating elements of the PEHRs as in the case with the NHS Summary Care Records. The PEHRs will also attempt to incorporate the EHRs in order to gain clinician trust in the resulting e-Healthcare information, which has been outlined in the case for Microsoft HealthVault and Google Health's move to incorporate EHRs from various hospitals in the US.

Figure 5.3 illustrates the hybridisation of the EHRs and PEHRs so that each will have two components: one, that is maintained by the clinician and the other by the patient. The control of access and usage will be concentrated on the patient in line with the patient centred paradigm shift as supported by security, privacy and confidentiality protection laws and policies.

It should be noted that the EHRs and PEHRs may conceptually continue to exist as separate units of e-Healthcare information in the hybrid scenarios. However, each may incorporate an aspect that has features of the other. In other words, hospitals and clinics may continue to have their own EHRs, but these will have to be a hybrid that also incorporates either an PEHR (may be an actual implementation of a PEHR or a view of the existing EHR) or a provision to allow the information to be pushed to the patient's existing PEHR, i.e., import and export tools. In any of these cases, control will remain with the patient.

In the same way, personally controlled PEHRs may also conceptually exist but they will have to be a hybrid that incorporates an EHR, which will be maintained by the clinician and/or the health care organisation.

Table 5.1 presents a comparison of the PEHR-EHR hybrid to each of the PEHR and EHR forms of e-Healthcare in formation. The PEHRs are controlled by the

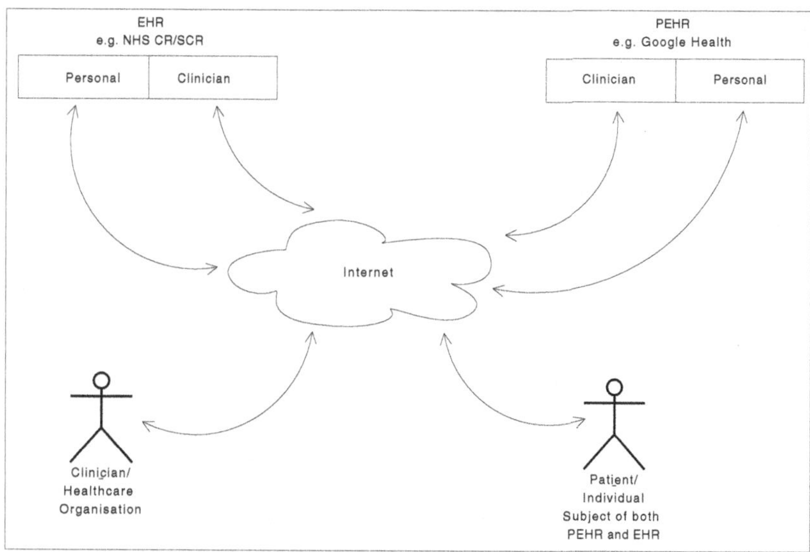

Figure 5.3 Characteristics of the PEHR/EHR Hybrid

individual patient, while EHRs are controlled by the clinician or the health service organisation. The hybrid is controlled by the individual patient, since it arose out of the need to support the patient-centred paradigm, which seeks to empower patients.

The hybrid holds e-Health information that is jointly maintained by the patient and clinicians. It should be noted, that clinicians may require the patient's consent to access and perform maintenance of the information. EHRs are generally maintained by the clinician, while the PEHRs are maintained by the patient. However, the PEHRs are generally recognised to be global or virtual and to incorporate EHRs from various types of care-givers. Where such information is drawn from the healthcare providers' information systems, the patient may be restricted in manipulating the EHR in order to increase the doctor's trust and confidence in the reliability of the information. Therefore, some portions of the hybrid e-Health information are modifiable by the clinician only, while others are modifiable by the patient.

It has been noted that the hybrid e-Health record is universal and virtual. It is process-centred with ability to span organisations that are involved in the patient care process as opposed to being organisation-centred. Thus, the hybrid e-Health record is capable of supporting the e-Health information requirements of each health service organisation. The EHR is highly organisation-centred so that each healthcare provider organisation maintains its own EHR. The hybrid record collects these EHRs into a centralised virtual e-Health information record. The PEHR is virtual and hence accessible globally through the Internet. It can support the information needs of more than a single healthcare provider organisation.

The EHR is generally fragmented across departmental and organisational units. The PEHR is theoretically complete as it collects and aggregates all EHRs and other e-Healthcare information from all healthcare provider organisations. The hybrid e-

Table 5.1 Characteristics of the EHR/PEHR Hybrid

	EHR	PEHR	HYBRID
Control:			
Personal	×	√	√
Clinician	√	×	×
Maintenance:			
Personal	×	√	√
Clinician	√	×	√
Span/Scope:			
Organisational	√	×	√
Process-centred	·	·	√
Global/Universal	×	√	√
Lifelong (Theoretical)	·	√	√
Nature and Content:			
Theoretically complete	×	√	√
Fragmented	√	×	×
Virtual	×	√	√

Healthcare record attempts to be both a PEHR and an EHR. Thus, the hybrid e-Healthcare record gets the advantages of both. However, it also inherits the security and privacy problems suffered by both. The compounded security and privacy problems erodes patients' trust in e-Healthcare information systems, which may threaten the widespread adoption of e-Healthcare.

5.4.3 The Role of Security Metrics

Security metrics facilitate quantitative measurements of various aspects of e-Healthcare information security and privacy provisions. There is a growing significance of the individual patient's rights. This also increases the seriousness of the implications of privacy protection within the context of the patient-centred paradigm. The measurement of various provisions, particularly the security and privacy protection of e-Healthcare information, becomes critical. Security metrics offer an important solution in measuring the effectiveness, or lack of it, of the existing security and privacy provisioning for e-Healthcare information. The need to consider metrics to be of fundamental significance in e-Healthcare information management is necessitated. The relevance of established security and privacy metrics is an interesting question given the unique complexity of the healthcare domain and e-Healthcare information. The introduction of new metrics for measuring aspects that are unique or that take into account the complex nature of the healthcare domain is also an interesting question.

5.4.4 Summary of Security and Privacy Requirements for Future-Enabled e-Healthcare Information

The patient-centred paradigm mandates the involvement of the patient in all aspects of the management of e-Healthcare information. The e-Healthcare advances are based on harnessing the Internet as the enabling platform for the EHR/PEHR hybrid. Both, the patient-centred paradigm and e-Healthcare are as revolutionary in healthcare as they are challenging to the domain of security and privacy protection. The EHR/PEHR hybrid extends the span and the terrain of security and privacy beyond a single healthcare organisation. Furthermore, the hybrid e-Healthcare record involves the principal, i.e., the patient or individual member of the public, with a diverse nature and characteristics that are difficult to manage and provide for in terms of security and privacy practices.

The current fragmented islands of e-Healthcare information makes it difficult to provide for a unified set of security measures and common framework. The EHR/PEHR hybrid will require a unified security and privacy framework that is flexible enough to accommodate security and privacy requirements that would be unique to particular locations and legal jurisdictions.

Due to the sensitive nature of e-Healthcare information, legislation is often required for certain essential developments in e-Healthcare information management, e.g., the introduction of the unique healthcare identifier (UHI). Therefore, strong legislative intervention and compliance is a key requirement in the security and privacy protection landscape for the hybrid e-Healthcare record.

The importance of facilitating the use of the information within the EHR/PEHR hybrid to benefit everyone, especially in terms of better patient care and safety, requires a thorough analysis of stakeholders and their role-based access entitlements to e-Healthcare information.

Placing e-Healthcare information under the control of the individual means that such information may not always be readily available for a host of secondary purposes. There is a need to ensure that e-Healthcare information is available for health research and planning purposes. Robust mechanisms for de-identification of information, that allow individual owners to participate and gain trust, will be important requirements.

5.5 The Approach to Securing e-Healthcare Information

In general, information security's generic focus is on protecting information and information systems from unauthorized access, use, disclosure, disruption, modification, or destruction and is particularly concerned with the confidentiality, integrity and availability of data in any domain. This generic focus for information security is also relevant for e-Healthcare information security. However, the securing of e-Healthcare information has distinguished itself from securing information in other domains such as business where financial and commercial information is handled. The multiple stakeholders, purposes and uses to which e-Healthcare information can be put is a complicating factor in the efforts to secure it.

Since considerable amounts of sensitive e-Healthcare information is generated everyday in relation to individuals throughout the system, the e-Healthcare record is one of the most sensitive collections of personal information as well as a major prime target for attacks of a security and privacy nature. The sensitivity of e-Healthcare information could even span several individuals and generations. Patient privacy focuses on the ability of an individual patient or group to seclude themselves or their e-Healthcare information about themselves and thereby reveal themselves selectively with preference to care givers. Unlike in the business domain, there is a lack of clarity on how e-Healthcare information may be used, which has a negative impact on the determination of how the information could be secured and its sensitivity preserved through privacy protection. Medical privacy allows a person to keep their medical records from being revealed to others. A fundamental aspect of e-Healthcare information privacy is Internet privacy. In e-Healthcare, patients should have the ability to control what health information one reveals about oneself through the Internet-based e-Health record, and to control who can access that health information.

The approach presented in Figure 5.4 is based on a generic, high-level and holistic characterisation of the nature of security and privacy protection for e-Healthcare information. Figure 5.4 illustrates an approach that uses the pyramidal structure for handling security and privacy for e-Healthcare information.

The generic security and privacy protection methods and mechanisms are found at the bottom of the pyramid. These methods and mechanisms are numerous and applicable across domains. The typical examples of the generic security and privacy protection methods are those that deal with the fairly established aspects of security and privacy protection that include: authentication, authorisation, integrity, non-repudiation, confidentiality, anonymisation and pseudonymisation.

In the middle of the pyramid, we have domain-specific security and privacy protection methods and mechanisms. These methods could also employ the generic methods at the base of the pyramid as building blocks to attain their objectives. The main focus of this level of security and privacy provisions are aspects that are specific to the healthcare domain in general and to e-Healthcare information in particular. For instance, the patient-centred approach to healthcare delivery requires that the various forms of the patient's legal consent be incorporated within the access control mechanisms for e-Healthcare information.

Privacy protection laws, policies and best practices are important enabling frameworks for creating a secure environment for e-Healthcare information. These are located at the top of the pyramid, which allows the conceptual and technological formalisms and techniques for ensuring secure e-Healthcare information to be formulated within legal and organisational contexts. Security and privacy protection laws and organisational policies could be realised though domain-specific as well as generic methods and mechanisms.

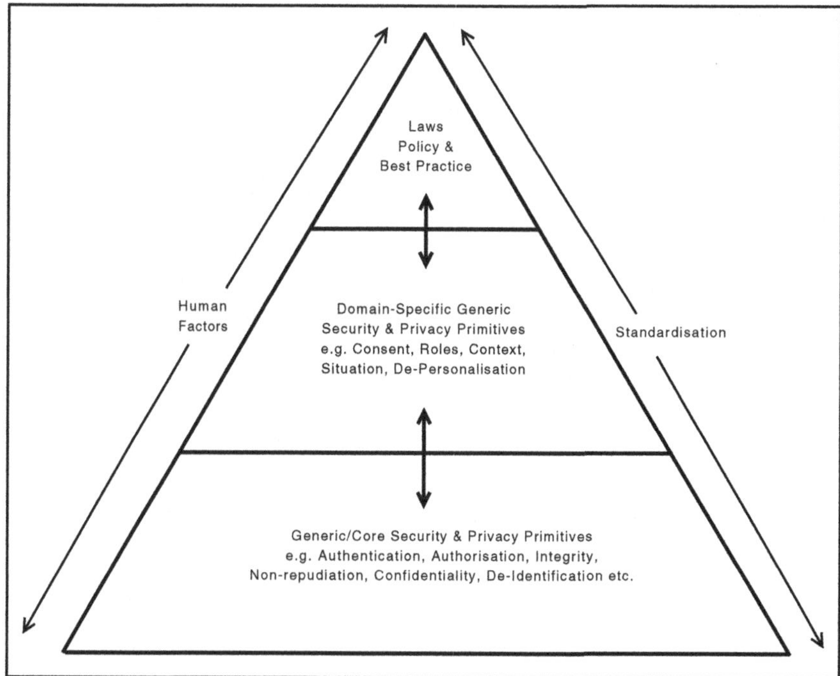

Figure 5.4 The Pyramid of Security and Privacy for e-Healthcare Information

5.6 The Framework for Securing e-Healthcare Information Security and Privacy

The framework presents a set of canonical categories of the elements of security and privacy aspects that needs to be incorporated into the infrastructure for securing e-Healthcare information. The complexity of the healthcare information management domain and the extreme sensitiveness and personal nature of health information demands for a comprehensive security and privacy protection framework that draws from all the dimensions that impact security and privacy of information. In this section, we identify the key drivers to the security and privacy of e-Healthcare information and characterise the evolutionary path of the control and security risk-level. These will enhance the conceptual framework, which we propose for securing e-Healthcare information.

5.6.1 The Key Drivers to the Security and Privacy of e-Healthcare Information Security

Security and privacy of e-Healthcare information is characterised by the key underlying drivers which are: the public concerns about privacy, the regulatory and legal frameworks, the need for healthcare information sharing, security and privacy standards, the technological frameworks and threats and vulnerabilities. The presence of overhanging threats and vulnerabilities is evidenced by the escalating reports of security and privacy violations. The interplay among these key drivers is crucial in development of a dynamic framework that is comprehensive in searing e-Healthcare information. These drivers are always in dynamic interaction with each other as illustrated in Figure 5.5, which presents these key drives and some of the major interactions among them.

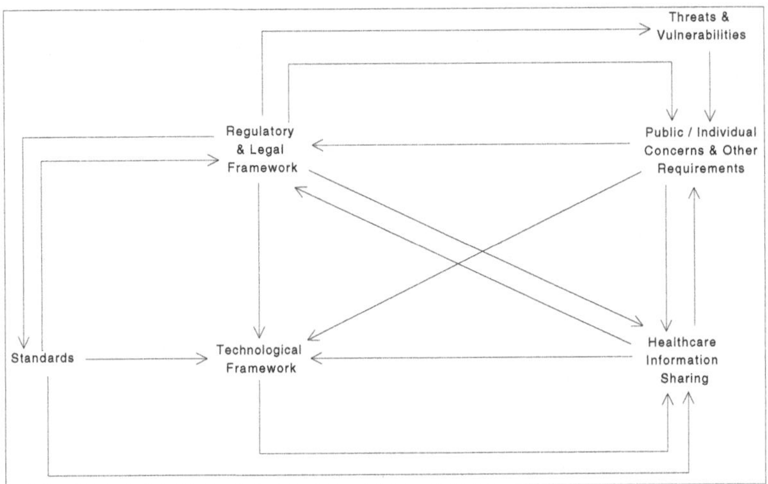

Figure 5.5 The drivers to e-Healthcare information security and privacy

As shown in the Figure, security and privacy threats interacts with public concerns, the legal and regulatory framework and security standards. There is overhanging threats and vulnerabilities to security and privacy in systems for managing e-Healthcare information. Perceived threats and known vulnerabilities are the main causes for public and individual concerns that diminishes trust in e-Healthcare information systems. They also have a direct influence on security and privacy standards, regulatory and legal frameworks, whose major goal would be to mitigate the impact of threats, vulnerabilities and actual attacks.

As illustrated in Figure 5.5, public concerns are affected by security and privacy breaches, threats and vulnerabilities and, in turn, drives regulatory and technological frameworks and security standards while also impacting on how e-Health information is shared. Public concerns about the privacy of e-Healthcare information has been a major obstacle to the adoption of e-Healthcare systems. These concerns are made worse by escalating incidents of privacy breaches, violations and security attacks as well as exposures of security and security vulnerabilities in e-Health information systems. Public concerns in the area of patient care are also a driver to the patient-centred paradigm in healthcare. The major impact of public concerns for the security and protection of privacy of e-Healthcare information is the legislative response in the form of the setting up of legal frameworks for regulating the security and protection of privacy of e-Healthcare information.

The need for e-Healthcare information sharing is a core aspect of healthcare and disease management. The Figure 5.5, shows the sharing of e-Health information that interacts with privacy laws, standards and public concerns. Sharing e-Healthcare information is fundamentally impacted by insecurity and lack of patient information privacy. Sharing information is also affected by diminished public trust in e-Healthcare information security and privacy solutions. Legal and regulatory frameworks seek to ensure that information sharing for the purpose of enhancing the quality of care remain unhindered. The privacy laws outlaw privacy and confidentiality breaches. The regulations is used to enforce the lawful secondary uses of e-Health information. The existence of security and privacy laws and regulation also help to enhance public confidence and trust in e-Health information systems. Many standards address the problem of the lack of interoperability between e-Health information systems and, thus, make the sharing of e-Health information possible. Privacy and security standards ensure the uniformity of the protection of e-Health information across systems and jurisdictions that share e-Health information.

The standards for providing the security and privacy of e-Healthcare information take into consideration the suppression of security and privacy risks, threats and vulnerabilities while allowing the sharing to occur in conformance to privacy laws and regulations. Standards may sometimes be used to put into effect existing regulations and laws governing security and privacy of e-Health information.

Security and privacy enhancing technologies are at the core of secure e-Health information. Security and privacy technologies are the means to implement standards, laws and regulatory frameworks and, ultimately, the secure sharing of e-Health information that impacts public trust. It is also the case that security and privacy technologies may address risks, threats and vulnerabilities that may not be perceived through standards and security and privacy laws.

Privacy laws and standards may be both complementary and supplementary in facilitating the secure sharing of e-Health information and arresting public mistrust and lack of confidence in e-Health information systems. Security and privacy technologies realise many aspects of the privacy laws and standards in e-Health information systems. The technologies also reduce the impact of security and privacy risks, threats and vulnerabilities. Secure e-Health information is not easy to attain unless we have a systematic convergence of risk, threat and vulnerability assessments; privacy laws and standards; security technologies; an assessment of public concerns and fears; and finally the information sharing requirements of healthcare.

5.6.2 The Model for the e-Healthcare Information Control and Security and Privacy Risk Level Over Time

The drive to protect patient privacy and ensure the security of e-Healthcare information has been accompanied by the question of control over access, usage and disclosure of this information. Patient-centred care seeks to involve the patients in decision-making that will affect their own health as a way to foster personal involvement in disease management, home-based care and preventive care, all of which are recognised as capable of reducing the cost of healthcare. A key enabling aspect of this patient-centred paradigm is the empowerment of the patients through giving them control over their own e-Healthcare information. The patterns of control of e-Healthcare information are evolving and changing impacting the security and privacy of the information.

Figure 5.6 is a graphical illustration of the evolution of the control of clinician and patient control of e-Healthcare information and the level of security risk, threat and vulnerability over time. The time period covered includes the immediate past (region 1), the present (region 2 and 3A) and the immediate future (region 3B and 4). Therefore, the graph is also predictive. Periods 1 and 2 are characterised by e-Healthcare information in the form of EHRs. Period 3, i.e., 3A and 3B, are characterised by e-Healthcare information in the form of the PEHRs. Period 4 is the period of the hybrid EHR/PEHR systems.

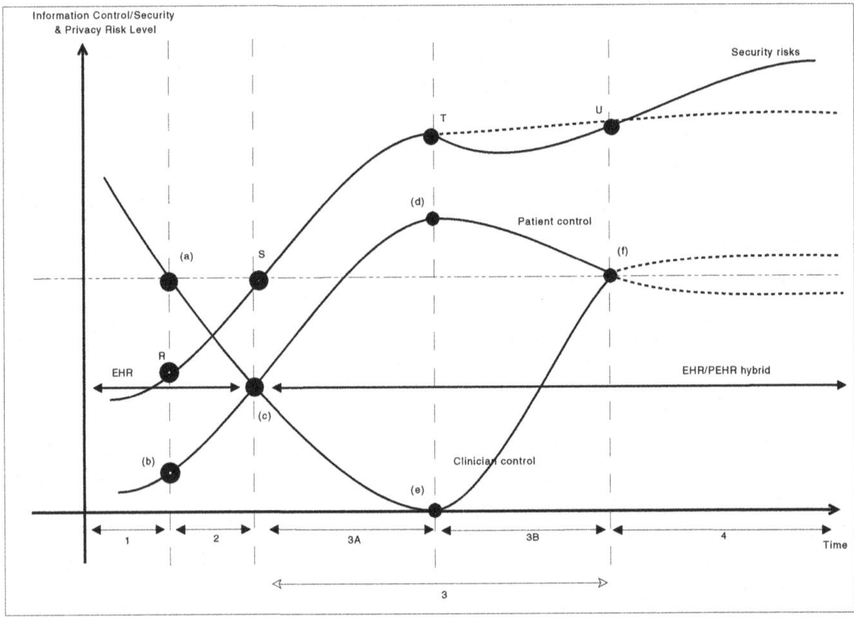

Figure 5.6 The Graph of "e-Healthcare Information control" or "Security and Privacy Risk Level" over time

It should be pointed out here that there is, effectively and in practice, no clear-cut separation between these time periods. The characterisation of control and security and privacy may actually persist into other periods in the same way that technologies, old and new, may co-exist in various time periods. The following subsections (5.6.2.1, 5.6.2.2, 5.6.2.3) describe the characteristics and security implications of the various stages in the evolution and changes in the control of e-Healthcare information. The next sections are based on the e-Healthcare information (EHRs and PEHRs).

5.6.2.1 Period 1: The immediate past - absolute control by the clinician or healthcare organisation

Period 1 occurs from the inception of e-Healthcare information systems. Typically, e-Healthcare records were or are created, maintained and controlled by the clinician or the healthcare organisation. The patient had no access to this information except later in the period where the courts have ordered patient access through the discovery procedure under the involvement of expert witnesses. EHRs are organisation-centred but are not internet-enabled although later they become intranet-enabled for organisation-wide access. Security and patient privacy protection for e-Healthcare information is the responsibility of the clinician and the healthcare organisation. The EU Directive characterises the key stakeholders to e-Healthcare during this epoch using the terms: *controller, processor* and *subject*, but avoids the contentious question of the *owner* of e-Healthcare information. According to this scheme, the patient is the e-Healthcare information subject whom the EU law envisage not to have control but whose privacy rights needs to be protected while allowing personal, consent-based and legally mandated access to e-Healthcare information. Thus, this period has not seen the use of personally controlled PEHRs but research works that had foreseen PEHRs had began to emerge. However, the concept of an PEHR had not been generally accepted and hence the PEHRs are excluded within privacy protection laws and regulations. The major threats to security and privacy are limited to those that associated with internal organisational factors, which could also be exploited by external threats.

5.6.2.2 Period 2 and 3A: The present - transition to patient control

The transition from purely organisational and clinician controlled e-Healthcare information to patient involvement in the control of their own e-Healthcare information occurs in Period 2 and 3A. In this epoch, healthcare organisations and clinicians still control e- Healthcare information but there is growing awareness and concrete moves towards patient empowerment in the form of legislative and regulatory frameworks based on clearer advocacy than before. The growing widespread use of the Internet in the management and dissemination of e-Healthcare information has become a key characteristic of this period. However, increased security and privacy risks as evidenced by a large number of reported actual breaches and the consequent exposure of a large number of individual patients to privacy violations spur the drive towards patient empowerment. This period is characterised by an accelerated momentum towards giving access and control of EHRs to patients while placing clinicians and healthcare organisations that collect, process and utilise sensitive e-Health care in formation under regulatory frameworks and legal regimes for privacy protection. Accompanying the introduction of security and primary protection laws, is the introduction of e-Healthcare information specific security and privacy standards as well as the emergence and growing attention towards personally controlled PEHR systems such as Google Health and Microsoft HealthVault.

In period 2, which would seem to be the current moment, patient control of e-Healthcare is expected to surpass the clinicians and healthcare organisations, at least from perspectives such as the privacy protection law, which seem to be already on the verge of this realisation. In Period 3A, patient control would be expected to increase as more and more people embrace and adopt Stealthier information services such as the web-based PEHR e.g. Google Health and Microsoft HealthVault. In this scenario, security breaches are compounded as more and more e-Healthcare information becomes accessible via an increasingly Internet and web-based environment with advanced computational tools and techniques for effecting security and privacy breaches. As it is illustrated in Figure 5.6, the level of security risks, threats and vulnerability are soaring reaching the peak when individual patients theoretically attain total control of their own healthcare information.

5.6.2.3 Periods 3B and 4: The immediate future- Balancing professional requirements with patient privacy

Periods 3B and 4 would appear to be the immediate future where the patients have theoretically gained total control of their own e-Healthcare information with such control being exercised with the support of the privacy protection laws and organisational policies. Period 3B begins with the peak of patient control over their health information, which is accompanied by a high level of security risks due to the extensive use of the Internet. This assumes that viable PEHR systems will be typically represented by online web-based series such as Microsoft HealthVault and Google Health. It is envisaged that patient control declines from its peak due to the need to accommodate clinician trust over e-Healthcare information. Therefore, the PEHR will not be useful if clinicians cannot trust the information held in it. Consequently, patient control needs to be diminished to a point were it balances with professional requirements for establishing clinician's trust over e-Healthcare information. Thus, total control of a-healthcare information will be found untenable due to factors that include:

1. Clinician's lack of trust in e-Healthcare information that is personally controlled and maintained by the individual patient;

2. Total patient control of e-Healthcare information operating to wide the secondary use of the information for purposes of the public good such as clinical research and planning for healthcare resources;
3. Litigation concerns may drive healthcare organisations and clinicians to demand retaining some form of control over aspects of the PEHRs;
4. The need to protect patients from the danger of emotionally depressing and psychologically damaging information about their own health may necessitates that some information within the PEHR be restricted from the access of the subject patient;
5. The lack of uniformity in expertise and medical knowledge among patients and the different levels of completeness, accuracy and quality assurance in the PEHRs and associated systems would drive clinicians and healthcare units towards demanding some of the traditional control over e-Healthcare information on the basis of patient safety and quality of care.

The healthcare units and clinicians would exploit their powerful role in lobbying against the total loss of control of e-Healthcare information in either EHRs or PEHRs. However, this will not allow them to return to the traditional scenario where they had total control. Eventually, a balance is reached where both the patient and the clinician enjoy the control that is necessary for privacy and confidentiality protection and for the exercise of professional role respectively.

Clinician's trust and privacy breaches would be some of the key factors that militate against individually controlled PEHRs. It is envisaged that Period 3 may be skipped as a result of foresight based on the overwhelming disadvantages of purely personally controlled PEHRs. This is evidenced by the current inclusion of clinician controlled e-Healthcare information in Microsoft HealthVault and NHS Summary Care Record. The coupling of EHR systems with PEHR systems and PEHR to PEHR creates a hybrid e-Healthcare record system. If Period 3 is skipped, then the immediate future will be Period 4, which is characterised by e-Healthcare information in the form of a hybrid of the EHR and the PEHR under a single system. Within the hybrid, the EHR will continue to be fragmented, distributed, domain-specific, organisational and process-oriented while the PEHR will be a virtual and even global e-Healthcare information that is delivered through the medium of the Internet and the Web. The PEHR will also present information from the EHR. This hybridisation of PEHRs and EHRs will serve to compound the security and privacy problems that continue to escalate and plague e -Healthcare information especially as a result of the harnessing of the Internet and Web 2.0 technologies. Security and privacy threats, risks and vulnerabilities in this period will rise partly due to increasing interest in using personal healthcare information and the advances in technologies that increase risks while at the same time enabling or empowering attackers with a variety of better technological tools and computing power.

5.6.3 The Conceptual Framework for Secure e-Health Information

The problem of ensuring the security and privacy of e-Healthcare information is critical to the building of trust among patients and members of the public. The adoption of e-Healthcare information systems is critical in supporting the major paradigm shift in healthcare, especially the patient-centred paradigm, and in realising the goals of improving healthcare quality and optimising healthcare service delivery, on one hand, while reducing care costs, on the other.

A framework for secure e-Healthcare information should engender security and privacy policies that are risk optimised. Such a framework needs to be made relevant to increasingly converged environments that are characterised by the need to address the security and privacy aspects of clinical processes as well as technical issues. The framework also needs to incorporate legal and regulatory mandates to protect e-Health information privacy, integrity and confidentiality. The Figure 5.7 illustrates some characteristic aspects of the security and privacy framework.

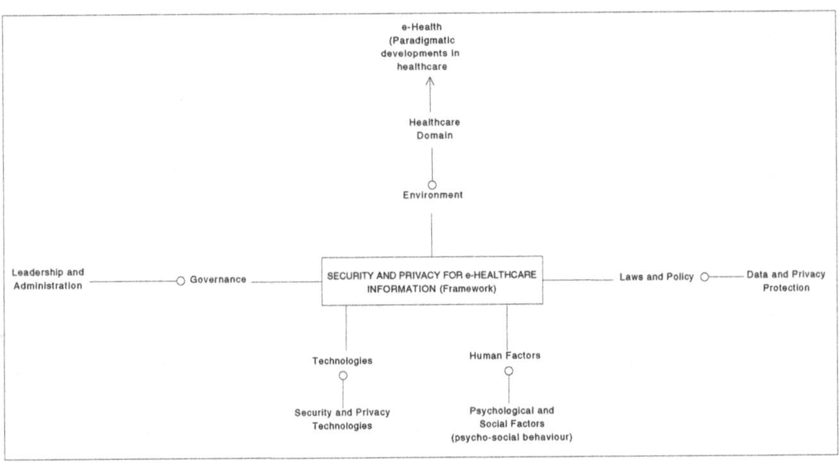

Figure 5.7 Security and Privacy Characterisation Framework

The security and privacy framework needs to be sensitive to the e-Healthcare environment and the paradigm shifts under which it operates. As illustrated in Figure 5.7, the e-Healthcare Environment is the healthcare domain. Associated with the healthcare domain are paradigmatic changes particularly the move to managed care, patient-centred care, the emphasis on evidence-based best practice and on preventive and/or home-based care. The key aspect of the healthcare environment is that it hosts the patient care setting. The characteristics of the patient care setting that are significant to security and privacy of e-Health information are mobility and multiple healthcare providers. The need to share e-Health information sharing is essential within the e-Healthcare environment. Such sharing of e-Health information needs to happen in a privacy and confidentiality preserving way. The security and privacy framework needs to layout the conditions and circumstances for appropriate e-Healthcare information sharing.

Privacy law and policy as illustrated in Figure 5.7 are important aspects of modern security and privacy framework for e-Health information. Privacy protection laws and policies generally encapsulate and reflect the public's concerns as well as the organisation's projection of these and its own concerns. Information security provides ways of implementing privacy requirements as may be stipulated in privacy laws. Within the e-Healthcare systems, high level and organisational privacy policies are implemented as low-level computable information security policies that set out the appropriate clinical care context that is deemed to be appropriately matched to the identities of key stakeholders and their credentials, i.e, the roles and privileges for these identities. The call to involve the patient in the care process, especially in decision-making, inspires the patient-centred paradigm and privacy laws. As part of this paradigm and the emerging privacy law regime, patient consent and patient access are key new aspects that need to be considered and provided for within the framework for securing e-Health information.

Governance and leadership are essential to the realisation of secure e-Healthcare information. Security and privacy governance relates to decisions that define expectations, grant power, or verify performance of the security and privacy provisions for securing e-Healthcare information. As illustrated in Figure 5.7, governance needs to be part of the security and privacy framework for secure e-Healthcare information.

Security and Privacy Standards and Technologies are essential aspects of the security and privacy of e-Healthcare information. The quality and adequacy of measures for ensuring privacy and security appropriate for e-Healthcare information require compliance and adherence to privacy and security standards. Standards-based security technologies provide a firm and sound basis for the implementation and enhancement of privacy requirements.

Most, if not all, e-Healthcare information systems are about people and involve people. Consequently, a wide range of human factors have a fundamental impact on the effectiveness of privacy protection measures and on the real or perceived security or insecurity of e-Healthcare in formation that they hold. Bruce Schneier has singled out *behavioral finance* as impacting economic decisions that deal with risks, the *psychology of decision-making* as impacting how decisions having to do with security risks are made; the *psychology of risks* as impacting risk perception and ultimately the extent of the exaggeration and down-play of risks; and, finally, the *human neuroscientific factors* as impacting how the brain and other human bodily mechanisms deal with threats (Schneier, 2008). While these human factor aspects are pathological and would seem not to be easy to formalise for incorporation into a practical privacy and security framework, it is essential that e-Healthcare information privacy and security frameworks should be premised on exploiting positive advantages that are derivable from these factors. The most practical, immediately manifestable, recognisable and actionable human factors of direct relevance to privacy protection and security of e-Healthcare are awareness and ethical considerations.

Privacy and security awareness among e-Healthcare information stakeholders is attained through formal and informal training programs. Such raising of privacy and security awareness among stakeholders should be essential components of national e-health frameworks while the lack of the relevant privacy and security awareness would have a negative impact on public trust in e-Healthcare information systems practice and in the introduction of unified e-health records at national levels (Fernando and Dawson, 2008). A key aspect of privacy and security of e-Healthcare information is that it necessarily needs to be segmented and multidimensional due to the heterogeneity of stakeholders, their complex roles and the context under consideration. The major challenge is to this stakeholder awareness of the privacy and security of e-Healthcare information it to keep it on-going and undiminished.

Ethical considerations deal with the e-Healthcare information privacy and security implications of the various actions undertaken by stakeholder with respect to others. Thus, stakeholders within the healthcare domain must bear the responsibility to preserve and protect the privacy of the subjects of e Health information in all their actions.

5.7 The Conceptual Architecture

Creating a secure e-Healthcare infrastructure based on the approach and framework presented in this chapter requires the adoption of a conceptual process that permits the convergence of privacy protection laws, privacy and security standards, organisational policy that is informed by healthcare domain practices the consideration of human factors and, finally, governance and leadership at higher levels of health organisations. The Figure 5.8 illustrates the conceptual process.

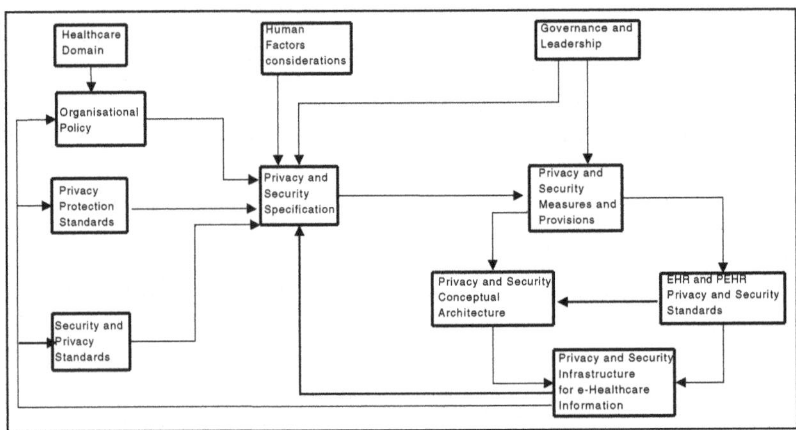

Figure 5.8 The process of establishing a secure e-Healthcare information infrastructure

The convergence of these key privacy and security areas should give rise to a comprehensive and wholistic privacy and security requirement specification or conceptual framework for the desired infrastructure. Such a conceptual specification of required privacy and security provisions should lead to the development of a set of privacy and security measures and provisions that adequately provide for the areas or domains that converged within the specification.

The privacy and security measures and provision developed will allow two key tasks to be undertaken. The first task involves the assessment of the applicable EHR and PEHR privacy and security standards that may be relevant to the measures and provisions developed. Such an assessment will enable the relevant privacy and security standards that are specific to the e-Healthcare information management domain to be applied in augumenting the generic security and privacy measures and in catering for the unique requirements of the e-Healthcare information domain. The second task involves the development of the privacy and security conceptual architecture, measures and provisions as well as to comply with the PEHR and EHR privacy and security standards that have been selected in the above task. Such a conceptual architecture would then be used as a basis for the construction or implementation of a particular instance of the privacy and security infrastructure for secure e-Healthcare information.

It is important to note the relevance of privacy and security governance and leadership, which is crucial in supporting the adopted security measures through:

1. monitoring,
2. provision of resources,
3. granting authority to implement the measures.

Once a security and privacy protection infrastructure has been established and becomes operational, it begins to provide important feedback. Such feedback is useful in evolving and improving the organisational policies, privacy protection, laws, and security and privacy laws. This feedback arises in the form of the experiences and insights gained from operating the infrastructure for protecting patient privacy and ensuring the security of the e-Healthcare information. Therefore, the process of establishing a secure e-Healthcare information infrastructure is never static, it is neither terminal, nor finite; instead its iterative or cyclical process must be adaptive to the changing environment and new threats.

The key advantage of the process described in Figure 5.8 is the convergence of privacy law, standards, policies, human factors and governance. Its cyclical nature that allows feedback and evolution is another key advantage.

The process outlined in the previous section eventually leads to a specific implementation of a security and privacy infrastructure for e-Healthcare information. However, the conceptual architecture could be conceptualised at a more generic level. Figure 5.9 illustrates a conceptual architecture that would underlie the process presented in the preceding section.

As illistrated in the figure, e-Healthcare information would exist in the form of the EHRs or/and PEHRs, which would be expected to be compliant with relevant standards. In the generic architecture security aspects consist of generic part and the e-Healthcare specific aspects. The Healthcare information security allows and domain-specific aspects of security to augment and/or enhance the core generic

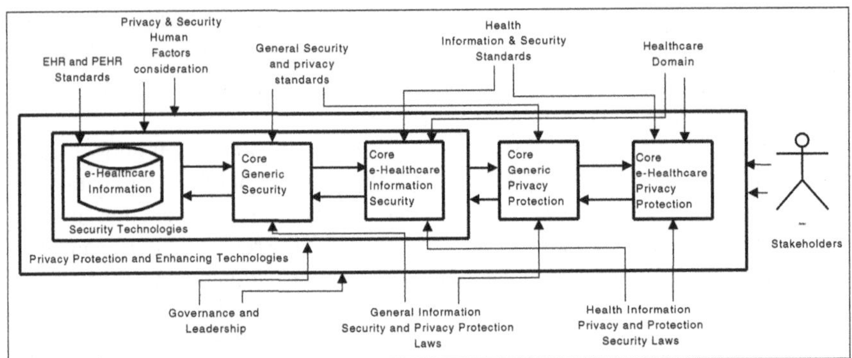

Figure 5.9 The e-Healthcare Information Privacy and Security Conceptual Architecture

security aspects. Furthermore, security and privacy protection laws would also be applied both at a general as well as at the healthcare domain-specific level.

Privacy protection would be at a higher-level than security, allowing aspects of privacy to be implemented using security technologies. It is important to note that the generic privacy protection shows distinctive features from healthcare domain. This allows privacy protection laws and standards to be applied both from a generic perspective and from e-Healthcare specific perspective.

The e-Healthcare stakeholders include patients clinicians and secondary users of e-Healthcare information. The conceptual architecture presents a unified e-Healthcare privacy protection interface to all stakeholders. It would be important to note that human factors consideration should be applied to both their security aspects and the privacy aspects. The same would apply to the issues of governance and leadership.

A key advantage of such a conceptual architecture is the 2-step incremental approach to both security security and privacy. First, the more generic aspects of security are applied and later the domain-specific e-Healthcare security are implemented allowing the comprehensive treatment that unique aspects of e-Healthcare domain require.

5.8 Discussion and Summary

The problem of securing e-Healthcare information is a complex challenge that also manifest as a multi-dimensional trade-off problem where sharing information needs to be balanced with privacy and the use of technological advances need to be balanced with technology facilitated privacy and security threats. The healthcare environment defines the context for e-Healthcare information privacy and therefore largely dictates the key privacy and security requirements within e-Healthcare. The patient-centred paradigm in healthcare has triggered a revolution that has huge impact on the privacy and security requirements in e-Healthcare information management framework. The protection of privacy and security of e-Healthcare information, patient consent and patient control and access to e-Healthcare information system core and fundamental aspects. The hybridisation of the EHRs and PEHRs would seem to be the future scenario for e-Healthcare information management. The EHR-PEHR hybrid is besotted by compounded privacy and security challenges that need to be mitigated to levels that can be balanced with the benefits of the hybrid.

The approach to privacy and security presented in this chapter forges a convergence of the key drivers to e-Healthcare information privacy. These drivers include privacy protection laws, privacy and security standards and essential aspects that include security technology, human factors and organisation policies. The convergence of these drivers are used here in order to create a holistic and comprehensive conceptualisation and a robust conceptual framework for secure e-Healthcare information. This approach needs to strive for the formalisation of the linkages or interfaces and inter-dependecies among the key security and privacy drivers such as privacy laws, standards, human factors, technologies and governance or leadership. This chapter has presented a pyramidal structural view that places privacy protection laws at the apex and generic security measures and primitives at the base. The unique aspects of the e-Healthcare information management domain occur in the middle of the pyramidal conceptualisation while standardisation of privacy protection and security will spread through the level of the pyramid.

The high-level conceptual framework proposed in this chapter exploits the conceptualisation in the approach that has just been outlined by first identifying and characterising the key drivers to e-Healthcare information. These key drivers are then placed into the context of the evolution of the control of e-Healthcare information under the influence of one of the most revolutionising paradigm shifts within the healthcare domain, especially the patient-centred or community-centered paradigm. The control of e-Healthcare information is seen to have moved from healthcare organisations to the individual patient who, in turn, is expected to participate in the healthcare process and the decision-making therein. The privacy and security challenges gets compounded by the ubiquitous harnessing of the Internet and wirelessly networked devices as well as the heterogeneity of e-Healthcare information users and the apportionment of the legal control of the e-Healthcare information. Ultimately, this chapter has observed, effective control will rest with the individual patient while clinicians will, for professional and patient safety reasons, demand jurisdictions to maintain and prevent modification of their own portions of the overall body of e-Healthcare information about an individual. This will lead to what has been termed in this chapter as *the EHR/PEHR hybrid.* This hybrid will have privacy and security challenges that are inherited from both EHRs and PEHR. Thus, this hybrid will be more insecure than the EHR and the PEHR individually. This will be so unless the advances in privacy and security techniques and technologies start to mitigate the privacy and security challenges.

This chapter has also presented the high-level conceptual process of establishing a privacy protection and security infrastructure that embodies the key concepts of the framework. The process creates a security and privacy specification for e-

Healthcare information from the results of formalising the relevant considerations of the key drivers to e-Healthcare information privacy and security. The specification itself represents a convergence of these key drivers. The resulting specification becomes the blueprint for setting out the security measures and provisions required to secure the e-Healthcare information. The conceptual architecture for privacy protection and security for e-Healthcare information incorporates the privacy and security measures and provisions together with results of and assessment of the security and privacy standards EHRs and PEHRs, which is specific to the PEHR or EHR frameworks that is used to implement e-Healthcare records. The advantage of the process proposed in this chapter is its incorporation of feeback to earlier sub-processes, which allows for the short and long-term evolution of the privacy protection and security specification and architecture within the context of the overall convergence of the key drivers for privacy and security of e-Healthcare information. The chapter has presented a generic conceptual architecture for the security and privacy protection of e-Healthcare information that would underlie the process described here. The conceptual architecture mirrors the pyramidal conceptualisation of the key privacy and security drivers as well as relationship and inter-play of the of these drivers. The generic security practices are ensured for e-Healthcare information and then e-Healthcare-specific security requirements are applied to augment them. Similarly, generic privacy protection practices are ensured for e-Healthcare information and augmented or enhanced with e-Healthcare specific privacy stipulations. It is important to note that certain security practices can be harnessed to attain privacy protection. Through the aspects of the conceptual architecture, the key drivers of privacy laws, standards, policies, technologies, human factors, governance and healthcare domain best practices mirrored the convergence of these drivers.

A concrete privacy protection and security infrastructure for e-Healthcare information that follows this conceptual approach, framework and architecture as well as that builds in flexibility wouldl be able to supprt the EHR and PEHR hybrid and to withstand other future paradigmatic changes that take place within e-Healthcare. A demonstration of this claim is a core part of our on-going work.

References

Fernando J, Dawson L (2008) Clinician assessments of workplace security training-an informatics perspective. Electronic Journal of Health Informatics 3(1)

Schneier B (2008) The psychology of security. Tech. rep., BT

Chapter 6
Towards a Unified Security Evaluation Framework for e-Healthcare Information Systems

6.1 Introduction

The domain of security engineering has developed some agreed core concepts but it lacks comprehensive framework. This could be seen to be particularly the case for e-Healthcare information systems. *Evaluation* deals with how other people can be convinced that security and privacy protection measures that have been put in place will work. Anderson has defined evaluation of systems as *the process of assembling evidence that a system meets, or fails to meet, a prescribed assurance target* and identifies two main purposes, which are: to convince one's superiors that work has been done and completed in compliance with standards and laws and to reassure people who will rely on a product or system. Evaluation is a function of the question of whether the system will actually work, which is termed assurance (Anderson and Cardell, 2008). Thus, the lower the likelihood, the higher the assurance there can be and the higher the likelihood, the less the assurance there can be. This chapter explores the solutions and technologies currently available for evaluating security and privacy problems in e-Healthcare information systems.

6.2 Evaluating Privacy and Security in e-Healthcare

The e-Healthcare information privacy laws and regulations covered in Chapter 3 (Health Insurance Portability and Accountability Act (HIPAA)) require that health-care organizations exercise due diligence in an effort to ensure the security and privacy of e-health information. Given the *subjective nature of most of these laws and regulations,* healthcare organizations may find it difficult to determine if they are meeting the health information privacy and security standard set therein. The problem is addressed by undertaking e-health information privacy and security in which risk assessment is also an important dimension. Consequently, risk assessment is often done by human experts. Human reasoning and perception processes are generally not easily expressed precisely.

Without doubt, health information exchange (HIE) implementations are not yet fully established. For this reason, formative evaluation has been recommended so that what is learned through evaluation can be immediately applied to assist in HIE development efforts (Ash and Guappone, 2007). The qualitative methods can be useful for formative evaluation because they can guide ongoing HIE growth while taking context into consideration.

It has been noted that it is *hard for security practitioners and decision-makers to know what level of protection they are getting* from their investments in security and privacy. This is particularly common when organisations have invested in a number of technologies and processes that interact and manage e-Healthcare information. Beres et al (Beres et al., 2009) contends that it is even harder to estimate how well these investments can be expected to protect organisations (including those that manage e-health information) in the future as security and privacy policies, regulations and the threat environment are constantly changing.

Nichols and Peterson's (Nichols and Peterson, 2007) approach to web functionality and user base have evolved with the threat landscape, *although technology-based security and privacy controls are essential, they are wholly insufficient for providing overall system security.* Technology-based security and privacy controls do little to aid the application to resist attack against the system's implementation or design processes and activities.

The evaluation of e-Healthcare information security and privacy has encountered *consistency and repeatability* problem. For instance, in smart card security, the deeply specialised technologies, large parameter spaces for attacks, and the evolving attack types and countermeasures mean that *the scope for variation in evaluation practice, and hence in evaluation conclusions, is potentially huge* (Boswell, 2009). This scenario is also found in e-Healthcare information privacy and security. Boswell et al (Boswell, 2009) also point out that the situation is further complicated by the fact that countermeasures against some types of attacks depend on both hardware and software and yet there is also a need to evaluate hardware without specific software or present at the time of evaluation. In e-healthcare information privacy and security, the scenario is further complicated since counter-measures against some attack types further dictated by the nature of healthcare work as well as the patient care environmental set-up and organisational context.

The simulation of attacks can be quite useful in the task of evaluating e-Healthcare information privacy and security within networked environments. In security and privacy evaluation, it is often necessary to generate a realistic synthetic traffic that keeps all the characteristics of the real traffic for purposes of simulation in evaluation. The latter has proved to be difficult, security and privacy testers often use real traffic traces in their test or evaluation. Gaelrab et al (Gadelrab et al., 2009) oberserved the available traces are often limited in number or size necessitating merging and manipulating traffic traces to create a test environment that would be representative of the operational environment, and to inject synthetic attacks into the traffic. A variety of tools for recording, replaying as well as forging packets can be obtained easily. Gaelrab et al (Gadelrab et al., 2009) suggested few tools for manipulating traces that modify the traffic composition, at least from the networking viewpoint. Therefore, there is no tool for manipulating traces without destructing their security-relevant characteristics.

6.3 Approaches to Evaluation of e-Healthcare Information Security and Privacy

6.3.1 Standards-Based Security and Privacy Evaluation

In 1994, von Solms *et al* (von Solms et al., 1994) noted the lack of either internationally recognized or accepted information security standards and criteria, which prevented their information security model to be implemented in its totality at that time. The international security or privacy criteria or international security or privacy standards play a crucial role in enabling information security evaluation according to internationally accepted criteria.

It would be beneficial for e-Healthcare information security and privacy if a standards-based evaluation criteria were formed on a community basis to address the problem of inconsistency and repeatability and to achieve international mutual recognition of evaluation results. Lessons could be drawn from stakeholders in the smart card security area who have formed a Community that has successfully created and applied interpretation of Common Criteria (ISO 15408) to achieve the same goal (Boswell, 2009).

6.3.2 Privacy Policy Evaluation

Organisational privacy can ensure adherence to privacy promises and regulations. The privacy technologies have not yet been fully investigated in securing e-Healthcare information and yet they have emerged as a way to implement enterprise privacy policy enforcement by formalising privacy policies. Privacy evaluation mechanisms incorporated into these technologies are used to automatically determine if a user is authorised to access specific data for a specific purpose. Typical examples of privacy evaluation mechanisms are privacy policy evaluation engines, which enable queries on whether a specific user is allowed to access specific data for a specific purpose. Backes et al (Backes et al., 2004) noted that while tools for authoring, maintaining, and auditing privacy policies may be available, tools to deal with *unification* within such policies, e.g., to enable queries about data that might be modified by a given user, or how many user entries satisfy a certain constraint are not generally available (Baader and Snyder, 2001). The solution to the latter problem were achieved by embedding enterprise privacy policies into Prolog using IBM's Enterprise Privacy Authorization Language (EPAL) (Ashley et al., 2003).

6.3.3 Ontology-Based Privacy Evaluation

The *user perceived privacy* and how *data subjects* can be empowered to control their own data consistently within their own interests, are of particular relevance to electronic personal healthcare records (PHRs). The privacy ontology expresses both generic and perceived concepts of privacy. Laws and regulations spell out empowerment matters as well as privacy principles.

To support building and evaluation of privacy-aware applications, Hecker and Dillon proposed a privacy ontology, which they related to privacy principles (Hecker and Dillon, 2007). The privacy ontology consists of core concepts and domain specific extensions. *The domain-specific part of the ontology includes concepts such as abstract security and consent mechanisms, privacy policies and support for legislative systems.* Hecker and Dillon mapped out how the privacy principles are influenced by the core concepts in the ontology as well as by each other. The privacy principles were derived from OECD Guidelines on the Protection of Privacy and Transborder Flows of Personal Data as well as EU Directive 95/46/EC. The influence of the privacy principles were used by Hecker and Dillon to evaluate the level of privacy for a particular transaction, when applying and extending the core concepts for an application domain.

6.3.4 Security and Privacy Metrics

A metric is a system of measures that permits some well-defined characteristic to be quantified. According to Frankland, meaningful and well-designed metrics and measurements for a business or organisation are created by carefully defining their scope and purpose (Frankland, 2008). The purpose of a security metric is to measure or assess the extent to which a system meets its security objectives (Pamula et al., 2006). A security metric allows the quantification of the degree of security. The degree of security is the degree of freedom from the possibility of suffering damage or loss that result from malicious attack. The mathematical metric properties rely on some assumptions of the nature of the domain. Metrics can be used to address a wide range of IT security and privacy management issues. These include the satisfaction of legislative and regulatory requirements, adherence to internal procedures, measurement of progress in achieving goals and objectives, justification of budgets and investment, and promotion of the effectiveness of training and awareness programmes. The nature of security in e-Healthcare varies widely over time. This variation renders the metrics for privacy and security to be unstable and of limited scope. Users or stakeholder of e-Healthcare information systems need to understand the privacy and security risks. To gain this understanding, there is a need for security metrics as well as tools and techniques for security and privacy evaluation as stated in previous chapters.

6.3.4.1 Policy-Based Security Metrics

A security/privacy policy is a document that states what is and what is not permissible in a system during routine operation. A security/privacy policy consists of a set of rules that could be expressed in formal, semi-formal or very informal language. Generally, a system can be considered secure and trustworthy if the policy enforced by its security administrator is trustworthy too. From this standpoint, it has been argued that it is possible to evaluate the system security by evaluating its policy (Casola et al., 2007).

Casola et al (Casola et al., 2007) further developed a policy-based methodology to formalize and compare policies and Security Metric which evaluates the security level that a system is able to grant.

6.3.4.2 Risk Security Metrics

Risk security metrics have been used mainly in the area of network security. The use of these types of security metrics is based on the argument that the effective means to evaluate network security level is to identify those metrics that measure the quality of security configuration objectively and dynamically (Al-Shaer et al., 2009).

Alshaer et al proposed a comprehensive security metric framework that identified and quantified objectively the most significant [network] security risk factors (Al-Shaer et al., 2009). The security metric framework focused on existing and future vulnerabilities based on historical trends, security configuration immunity to attack occurrence and propagation, and traffic trends that reflect the insider and outsider user behaviour.

6.3.4.3 Attack Graph-Based Security Metrics

Generally speaking, to quantify the likelihood of potential multi-step attacks that combine multiple vulnerabilities is now feasible due to a model of causal relationships between vulnerabilities, namely, the attack graph (Lufeng et al., 2009; Sheyner et al., 2002; Wing, 2006). According to Lufeng et al. the common way by which an attacker can break into a network is through a series of exploits, where each exploit in the series satisfies the precondition for subsequent exploits and makes a causal relationship among them. Lufeng et al. refer to such a series of exploits as an attack path and the set of all possible attack paths as an attack graph. Attack graphs are important tools for analysing security vulnerabilities in enterprise networks and could be a useful evaluation tool in the formal evaluation of e-Healthcare information security and privacy.

Lingyu et al. proposed an attack graph-based probabilistic metric for network security and studied its efficient computation (Wang et al., 2008). The attack graph formalism has been used mainly in the evaluation of network security. Pamula et al. introduced a novel quantitative metric for the security of computer networks that is based on an analysis of attack graphs (Pamula et al., 2006). Their metric measures the security strength of a network in terms of the strength of the weakest adversary who can successfully penetrate the network. The inputs to their algorithm are: a specific network configuration, a set of known exploits, a specific goal state, and an attacker class (represented by a set of all initial attacker attributes) (Pamula et al., 2006).

Lufeng et al. proposed a network security analysis method by the generation of network attack graph (Lufeng et al., 2009). After analyzing network vulnerabilities, linking relation between devices and the characteristic of attack, a model of network security states was implemented to generate the algorithm of attack graph.

Beres et al. placed most emphasis on process-based metrics in measuring the effectiveness of security processes in large organizations (Beres et al., 2009). The process-based metrics demonstrated how the process-based metrics can be combined with executable, predictive models, based on a sound mathematical foundation. The latter were used to assess organizations' security processes under current conditions and to predict how well they are likely to perform in potential future scenarios. This approach to privacy and security evaluation metrics may benefit the evaluation of privacy provisions in patient-centred, inter-organisational and collaborative care process that is increasingly being driven by clinical practice guidelines.

6.3.4.4 Arguments Against Security and Privacy Metrics

Most of the security metrics currently in use represent the past history of the state of the system. These security metrics are hard to obtain as information systems which are the source of data, may not have or support appropriate tools for collecting relevant data. Over time research efforts have been taking place to design and implement tools for collecting required data from these systems. It is difficult to obtain security metrics in real time. This is made even worse by the level of automation which is required to obtain data and analyse it to come up with security metrics that are objective, i.e., metrics that do not depend on the background and experience of the evaluator. Metrics are hard to use for decision making especially when comparing several organisations' security posture because systems that are being used change continuously. For example, the configuration of the systems drifts away from the original setup configuration. Therefore, this parameter alone may make comparison among organisations difficult to achieve.

Without doubt security metrics are expected to result in systems improvement. However, once the system is improved in any way it is practically impossible to measure objectively what might have happened if we had not improved our information security controls. The validity and usefulness of security metrics depend wholly on the accuracy and relevancy of data collected, in most cases it is difficult to collect clean and appropriate data. Guidelines and standards (for example, NIST SP 800-128 DRAFT Guide for Security Configuration Management of Information Systems) for security metrics stipulate that more data should be collected, making the cost of collecting data from the long list provided by these standards to be prohibitive expensive.

Bellovin concluded that current software architectures are not amenable to metrics of the sort he wanted, because any piece of software can be buggy, including security software (Bellovin, 2006). He noted that even layering of protection will not address the problem since once a layer is broken, the next layer is exposed and can potentially suffer the same problem.

6.3.4.5 The Qualities of a Good Security or Privacy Metric

The purpose of a security metric is to measure or assess the extent to which a system meets its security objectives (Pamula et al., 2006), the security of complex infrastructures, such as those found in healthcare, depends on many technical and organisational issues that need to be properly addressed by a security policy (Casola et al., 2007). Network security level depends on a number of dynamically changing factors including emerging of new vulnerabilities and threats, policy updates and network traffic (Al-Shaer et al., 2009). While calling for a panel discussion, Saydjari outlined the qualities of a good metric as follows (Saydjari, 2006):

- A metric must support the decision that needs to be made, i.e., it must measure the right thing.
- A metric should be quantitatively and accurately measurable. A metric should be capable of being validated against ground truth.
- A metric should be inexpensive, both in time and cost, to execute.
- A metric should be able to be referred independently. A metric should be repeatable so that the results are independent of the analyst performing the measuring.
- A metric should be scalable from small systems to large enterprise networks.

Since meaningful quantitative security metrics are largely unavailable, the security community primarily uses *qualitative metrics* for security (Pamula et al., 2006). However, in order to protect critical resources in today's networked environments, it is desirable to quantify the likelihood of potential multi-step attacks that combine multiple vulnerabilities (Wang et al., 2008).

Saydjari et al. further identified five types or categories of security metrics (Saydjari, 2006):

1. The risk metric allow the assessment of security benefit by examining the size of the expected loss that can be avoided and the probabilities of the range of possible attacks succeeding.

2. Criteria-compliance is a security metric that gives a prescription of design processes and independent system checking by evaluators while not directly addressing what security is.
3. Intrusion detection-based metrics generally measure the performance of security mechanisms that detect intrusions such as intrusions that were not detected and went on to cause damage; and the number of viruses detected per day.
4. Policy-based metrics measure quantities that are usually the subject of control insecurity policies. Thus, these metrics may measure the minor of failed login attempts, file accesses or attempts to execute unauthorised operations.
5. Incident-based metrics quantify actual successful attacks that take places, their frequency and the real damage caused.

According to Wayne (Johnson, 2009) the main uses of metrics fall into three broad classes.

- *Strategic support*: Assessments of security properties can be used to aid different kinds of decision making, such as program planning, resource allocation, and product and service selection.
- *Quality assurance*: Security metrics can be used during the software development life-cycle to eliminate vulnerabilities, particularly during code production, by performing functions such as measuring adherence to secure coding standards, identifying likely vulnerabilities that may exist, and tracking and analysing security flaws that are eventually discovered.
- *Tactical oversight*: Monitoring and reporting of the security status or posture of an IT system can be carried out to determine compliance with security requirements (e.g., policy, procedures, and regulations), gauge the effectiveness of security controls and manage risk, provide a basis for trend analysis, and identify specific areas for improvement.

There are few reported security metrics applications which have proven to be useful in practice. However, in other areas such as finance, metrics have been used in decision making for a long time. Therefore, for security metrics to be used as standardized measurements and decision making tools the information system security would require realistic assumptions and inputs to attain reliable results.

The security metrics are difficult to establish, as it is difficult to establish the baseline. This baseline must be based on agreed set of criteria. Until now there are no agreed set of criteria among security professionals which may be used to establish a baseline. It is also important to define the security goals such as operational, data and process integrity. There are a number of studies which suggest that we are measuring the wrong thing and that our understanding of what we must measure is wrong as well. This tally with Lord Kelvin's observation[1] that measurement is vital to deep knowledge and understanding, unless we can measure security and privacy our understanding is superficial, or its converse, which states that it must be possible to improve security as a result of measuring, because we understand it.

---

[1] PLA, vol. 1, "Electrical Units of Measurement", 1883-05-03

Rice (Rice, 2008) argues that most of the software we are currently using is insecure. The software buyers do not have a way of differentiating between insecure and secure software. The situation is made even worse by the lack of strong, clear and pro-active legislative environment. Therefore, the current security metrics research and practice efforts are done under the back drop of insecure software. This means that unless there is a paradigm change where we will be able to write secure software, metrics as cornerstone of security is doom to fail because security metrics research and practice efforts are being frustrated by software vendors (Rice, 2008). It is in their best interest not to have robust and reliable measures by which different software products or systems can be objectively compared. The argument given by software vendors is that software is still an immature area. This has allowed software vendors to continue writing insecure software that impact many critical systems.

As discussed earlier security metrics are important factor in making informed decisions about various aspects of security, ranging from the design of security architectures and controls to the effectiveness and efficiency of security operations. Security metrics can help people change their behaviour in a way that cannot be accomplished using complex information obtained in other ways. Security metrics strive to offer a quantitative and objective basis for security assurance and trust.

According to NIST (Johnson, 2009), security metrics must involve the application of a method of measurement to one or more entities of a system that possess an assessable security property to obtain a measured value. The difficulty involved in identifying and measuring these assessable security properties can be enormous, as in most cases they depend on the knowledge and experience of the assessor. From an organizational perspective, security measures and metrics should enable an organization to gauge how well it is meeting its security objectives.

The repeatability of information security metrics when done by two evaluators or the same evaluator at different times is important. Achieving this property in security metrics is hard. For example, results in penetration testing or other methods of assessment that involve specialized skills are sometimes not repeatable, since they rely on the knowledge, talent, and experience of an individual evaluator, which can differ from other evaluators with respect to a property being measured.

It is important to acknowledge that nearly all major efforts to measure or assess security such as Trusted Computer System Evaluation Criteria (TCSEC), Information Technology Security Evaluation Criteria (ITSEC), Systems Security Engineering Capability Maturity Model (SSE-CMM), and Common Criteria, had limited success. There are several reasons for this poor show of security metrics. For example, the characteristics of security attributes which require to be measured, the subjective nature of the measure depending on the knowledge of the evaluator.

Metricon is a working group that meets at least yearly during the Usenix conference to discuss the latest development in security metrics. The main contributions of Metricon are the usefulness of Security Metrics and advancing the theory and practical applications of metrics. It has been argued by Jaquith that measuring an individual is difficult and most do not like such measurements (Jaquith, 2007). Therefore, a way forward is to obtain team measurements. These team measurements must be based on the team goals.

Security metrics as a process must be automated as much as possible for a number of reasons. First, by automating the measurement process as much as possible the cost of getting the measurements is reduced significantly. Secondly, automating measurement can reduce the dependence on human factors such as experience. Thirdly, automating ensure that metrics are consistent, repeatable, and reproducible.

6.3.5 Model-Based Approach to Security and Privacy Evaluation

The model-based security evaluation approaches are mainly based on Markov models whose advantage is the simplicity in the analysis aimed at deriving quantitative measures, that is, *security metrics.* Fujimoto et al. singles out discrete- and continuous-time Markov chains (DTMC and CTMC) without general distributions as being popular in the development of the security models and went on to propose MRSPN (Markov regenerative stochastic Petri net) based model for evaluating security of an intrusion tolerant system. Fujimoto et al. believe that, in general, since the security evaluation must deal with *rare probabilistic events* on security threats, (e.g., DoS attack, intrusions and compromises), the *model-based evaluation* is essentially needed to estimate quantitative security measures (Fujimoto et al., 2009). The MRSPN based model consists of four modules: system module, vulnerability module, intrusion tolerance module and maintenance module, each of which is modelled using the Petri net.

6.4 Frameworks for e-Healthcare Information Privacy and Security Evaluation

Geiger and Cranor's privacy tool evaluation study raised the question of how much privacy protection we can realistically expect (Geiger and Cranor, 2006). This section gives an overview of frameworks for evaluating security and privacy of information.

6.4.1 Information Security Management Model-Based Evaluation Frameworks

According to Solms et al. (von Solms et al., 1994), Information Security Management consists of various facets, which include: Information Security Policy, Risk Analysis, Risk Management, Contingency Planning and Disaster Recovery. Solms et al. also recognised these facets to be all interrelated in some way and believed them to often cause uncertainty and confusion among top management. Solms et al. (von Solms et al., 1994) proposed a model for Information Security Management, called an Information Security Management Model (ISM2), which puts all the various facets of InfoSec Management in context and consists of five different levels, defined on a security axis.

Farn et al. (Farn et al., 2004) analyzed and studied the evaluation knowledge and skills required for auditing the certification procedures in terms of what they reckoned to be the three aspects of Information Security Management System (ISMS), namely, asset, threat, and vulnerability. Therefore, in the literature, risk analysis has been modelled using a framework which elements are: threat levels, vulnerability and asset value .

6.4.2 Security Metric-Based Evaluation Frameworks

Ahmed et al. proposed a *security metric framework* that identifies and quantifies objectively the most significant security risk factors (Ahmed et al., 2008). These factors included:

1. Existing vulnerabilities,
2. Historical trend of vulnerability of the remotely accessible services,
3. Prediction of potential vulnerabilities for any general network service,
4. Estimated severity of the predicted potential vulnerabilities, and finally
5. Policy resistance to attack propagation within the network.

Al-Shaer et al. also proposed a comprehensive *security metric framework,* which they named *Risk based prOactive seCurity cOnfiguration maNAger* (ROCONA) (Al-Shaer et al., 2008). ROCONA identifies and quantifies objectively the most significant security risk factors. These risk factors include existing and future vulnerabilities based on historical trends, security configuration immunity to attack occurrence and propagation, and traffic trends that reflect the insider and outsider user behavior. Nichols and Peterson (Nichols and Peterson, 2007) presented a metrics framework that could help to quantify the security impact that process changes in one development life-cycle phase have on other phases.

6.4.3 Security and Privacy Policy-Based Evaluation Frameworks

A system could be considered secure and trustworthy if the policy enforced by its security administrator is trust-worthy as well. Amato et al. concluded that within its context it is possible to evaluate the system's security by policy. Casola et al. proposed a policy-based methodology, the *reference evaluation methodology* (REM), to define and evaluate the security level that a system is able to provide (Casola et al., 2007). Amato et al. went further to illustrate the implementation of the *REM framework* to automatically evaluate the security level provided by a system and applied it to a real case study on the evaluation of the Certificate Authorities involved in the EUGridPMA project (Amato et al., 2008).

6.5 Towards a Unified Privacy and Security Evaluation Framework for e-Healthcare Information

The e-Healthcare information systems are too sensitive for privacy and security support approaches and mechanisms to take an *ad hoc* approach in their evaluation. The highly coupled relationship and inter-dependence between privacy and security for e-Healthcare information means that any evaluation of one must necessarily take a holistic approach that includes the evaluation of the other. The complex nature of e-Healthcare information and the complicating factors that directly impact on its security and privacy calls for an evaluation framework that unifies evaluation approaches as well as the various component dimensions that need to be evaluated. This section proposes the evaluation framework for the privacy and security of e-Healthcare information.

6.5.1 The Security and Privacy Evaluation Challenges for e-Healthcare Information

The compliance and assurance are the key goals of security and privacy evaluation. Evaluation therefore seeks to establish whether or not there is compliance with laid out privacy and security measures and stipulations. The evaluation seeks to quantitatively and qualitatively re-assure patients and the public that organisational and technical systems are in place to provide security and privacy. The personal nature and high-level of sensitivity of e-Healthcare information sets a unique context that demands a radically different approach to privacy and security evaluation from that of information in other domains.

The unique context for privacy and security of e-Healthcare information has given rise to separate laws, policies and standards that sometimes cascade onto those that already exist for general or ordinary information. A complicating dimension results from the long-lasting nature of e-Healthcare information, especially an indivual's e-Healthcare Record, which is, theoretically, a cradle-to-grave longitudinal record of information about an individual's health. Such information ideally remain valid for some time beyond the lifespan of an individual, which could potentially be eighty or more years. Furthermore, e-Healthcare information is of a multimedia nature that is distributed across disparate systems, organisations and even regions within and across national borders. The dimensions of security and privacy within such a complex scenario are many and their interactions are also complicated.

The paradigm shift in healthcare from fragmented care to managed care and patient-centred, evidence-based healthcare brings further complicating dimensions to security and privacy of e-Healthcare information and, hence, their evaluation. Information is no longer localised into isolated islands within specific healthcare units. Transactions that involve e-Healthcare information now span several organisations, regions and national borders. Security and privacy of e-Healthcare information within this context become even more difficult to attain and the effectiveness of any measures are difficult to evaluate.

The paradigm shifts in healthcare have also been accompanied by the shift to e-Healthcare information management from paper-based health records, and from organisational e-Healthcare records to the globally accessible personally maintained e-Healthcare records (e.g., GoogleHealth and Microsoft HealthVault). The e-Healthcare information will ultimately have an additional new environment that is owned and controlled by the individual patient while being kept by a vendor IT organisation offering a distributed, globally accessible and web-based information management infrastructure, provided by Google and Microsoft.

The e-Healthcare information domain could be seen as presenting unique privacy and security requirements that challenge conventional evaluation approaches and frameworks. The security and privacy standards, policy and legal frameworks are lagging behind the healthcare domain and e-Healthcare information management paradigm shifts. The drive to align standards, policy and legal frameworks to healthcare domain shifts have led to ad hoc approaches that further complicate the task of ascertaining compliance aspects of the evaluation of e-Healthcare information security.

6.5.2 Towards a Unified Framework for Evaluating Privacy and Security of e-Healthcare Information

The security and privacy evaluation for e-Healthcare information reguires a unified framework that meets the challenges. Traditional approach to the information security evaluation process has focused on risk analysis to establish assets and threats to these assets, certification to assess design characteristics and security mechanisms and measures of intrusion into the system. This classical approach may not be adequate for e-Healthcare information due to its little emphasis on privacy-related assurance, legal provisions and assessment of handling of patient concerns, preferences and health professional ethics. For the evaluation of privacy and security for e-Healthcare information, the aim for an evaluation framework is to enhance the classical evaluation approaches by providing for the unique security and privacy requirements for e-Healthcare information. We propose a framework that takes a holistic view and support compliance and assurance within both the infrastructure that implements and support privacy and security for e-Healthcare information and the healthcare domain represented by the organisation.We summarise the core requirements for such an evaluation framework as follows:

- Compliance should be a key dimension to assess both the IT infrastructure and organisation environment for security and privacy of e-Healthcare information with respect to existing laws, policies and standards
- Due to the sensitivity of health information and the special position of the subjects of the information, assurance should be a key dimension in the evaluation of security and privacy within the IT infrastructure and organisation environment for e-Healthcare information;
- Laws, standards and policies should be key elements in the determination of compliance and assurance in the evaluation of security and privacy of e-Healthcare information;
- Health professional requirements and ethics as well as patient concerns and/or preferences should be some of the key elements in the assessment of compliance in the evaluation of security and privacy of e-Healthcare information;
- Technologies employed in realising security and privacy for e-Healthcare information should be special target for both compliance and assurance aspects of the evaluation

The ACIO framework presents evaluation as consisting of a fixed plane composed of four interacting dimensions that create a field of activity for dynamic elements in the evaluation process. The Figure 6.1 illustrates the ACIO framework that addresses the unique challenges that are found in providing security and privacy for e-Healthcare information. The first dimension is that of compliance, which interacts with two further dimensions that focus on the technical infrastructure as well as to the higher level organisational aspects. Compliance is viewed as conformance to security and privacy standards, laws and policies. The ACIO framework imposes the categorisation of compliance into compliance within the technical infrastructure, for example, as spelt out in standards and laws, and compliance within the organisation's processes and procedures, for example, as spelt out in its privacy and security policies and laws.

The second dimension is that of assurance, which must be established for the technical infrastructure as well as for the organisation's processes and practices. In assurance, the evaluation seeks to establish a declaration tending to inspire full confidence in security and privacy provisions that are associated with e-Healthcare information. The ACIO framework also imposes interactions between security and privacy assurance and the infrastructural and organisational dimensions. Thus, we have four dimensions that interact in the evaluation process, namely, compliance and assurance, on one hand, and infrastructural and organisational aspects, which are the third and forth dimensions, on the other hand.

In the Figure 6.1, the dimensions, compliance and assurance make up the rows, and the dimensions, infrastructure and organisation make up the columns within the evaluation plane. These dimensions create four regions in the plane which represent the interactions between these dimensions with the centre of the region representing the intersection of the four regions. The region denoted by (C_1, I_1) in the Figure 6.1 represents evaluation of security and privacy compliance within the information technology (IT) infrastructure for e-Healthcare information while the region denoted by (C_2, O_1) represents evaluation of security and privacy compliance within

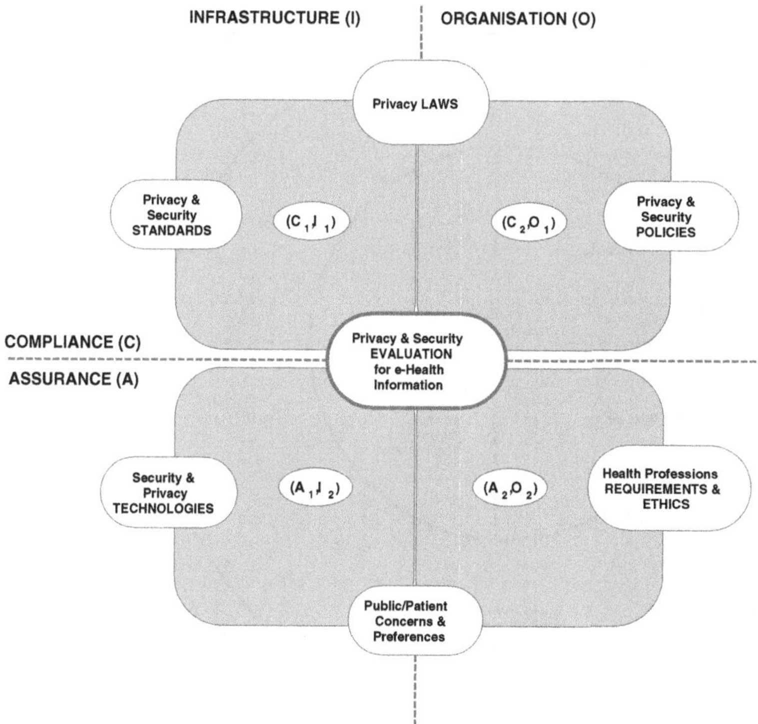

Figure 6.1 The ACIO Framework for the evaluation of security and privacy for e-Healthcare Information

organisational environment for e-Healthcare information that lie outside the IT infrastructure. The region denoted by (A_1, I_2) evaluation of security and privacy assurance within the IT infrastructure environment for e-Healthcare information while that denoted by (A_2, O_2) represents the evaluation of assurance within the organisational environment for e-Healthcare information. These regions are the fixed aspects of the ACIO framework on which we have the key elements illustrated by the shaded region and the ellipse that rotate within these denoted regions along the two lines of symmetry indicated in by dotted lines. Therefore, security and privacy laws and patient concerns and preferences are interchangeable and can be considered in combination as a result of rotational dynamics of the framework and so are the following combinations:

- Standards and policies
- Technologies and health profession requirements and ethics
- Standards and technologies
- Policies and health profession requirements and ethics

The dynamic view of these elements within the framework is best conceptualised and presented in the form of two spinning disks as illustrated in the Figure 6.2.

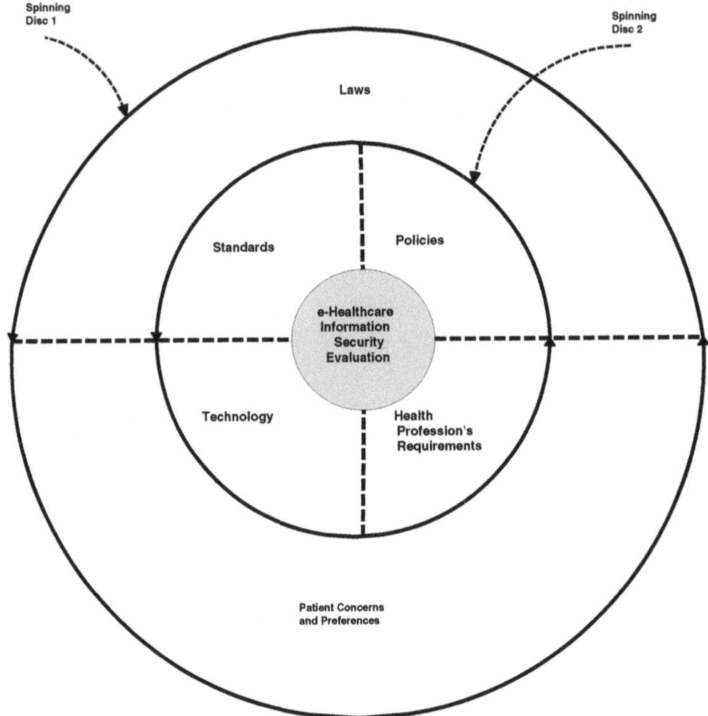

Figure 6.2 The spinning discs illustrating the dynamics of the ACIO framework

By rotating any of the discs while holding the other fixed will allow the evaluation process to consider aspects of the evaluation on the smaller disc, namely, standards, policies, professional requirements and ethics and technology, to be considered for evaluation within the context of security and privacy laws and patient concerns and preferences. Furthermore, if the outer disc is split into two halfs, then it will then be possible to consider patient concerns together with associated legal provisions as a context for the evaluation of security and privacy

The Common Criteria (CCITSE) and its accompanying methodology (CMITSE) focus on evaluation of information technology, especially IT products or systems, as the primary means of assurance and assumes that most of the required information in the evaluation must relate specifically to the system that is being targeted for evaluation and specifies in detail how the evaluation is to be conducted. For example, incorporating standard guidelines and criteria relating to:

- Health professional practice and ethics;
- Patient privacy, safety, concerns and preferences;
- Information security and privacy laws;
- Organisational policies that enhance or augment technical security and privacy;

• The long-lasting and sensitive nature of e-Healthcare information with implication spanning more than one individual across generations within families.

The ACIO framework is a higher level framework, which mainly focuses on placing the general security and privacy evaluation practices into the e-Healthcare context by emphasising the unique and sensitive aspects of e-Healthcare information. The unique and sensitive aspects are encapsulated in the above factors, which distinguish e-Healthcare information from information in other domains. The framework recognises the role of evaluation approach such as the Common Criteria and guides the evaluation of security and privacy for e-Healthcare information. The growing advocacy for security and privacy metrics has continued despite that some of the above factors are difficult to measure or to get any metrics for use in evaluations. Indeed, one of the criticisms of security metrics is the difficulty in either identifying relevant and useful security metrics or getting reliable data for computing those security metrics that have been identified. Furthermore, the on-going research in computer-based formalisation of laws, policies, guidelines and rules of professional practice and ethics that permit the capture and translation of knowledge into computational formalisms and software patterns will support the ACIO framework.

6.6 Human Factors in Evaluating e-Healthcare Information Security and Privacy

The impact of human factors in evaluation is both positive and negative. For the evaluation to be successful the human bias must be reduced or if possible eliminated. This can be achieved by increasing the level of automation in whole process of evaluation. However, we still need the human involvement especially when it comes to evaluating policies, laws, regulation and compliance in general.

6.6.1 Impact of Technological Human Factors

Generally speaking, the technological human factors are an integral part of evaluating the impact of technological human factors. Therefore, human biases and experience have a significant part, which strongly implies that the security and privacy metrics do not have the repeatability characteristic. It has been noted, in many cases, that the same evaluator cannot get the same results if he repeats the experiment.

Human factors in security are kind of a new phenomenon. The emphasis in security research and practice all along has been on the technical issues such as encryption, key management and public key encryption. These were perceived that they will be able to eliminate or at least mitigate security problems. When it became apparent that security and privacy issues cannot be solved by using technical solutions that is when the soft issues (human factors, user awareness, ethics, compliance etc) in security started being important.

Schneier argues that human factors are more difficult to solve than technical issues. Humans will do what they want to try and make their life easier and they are the weakest link in the security chain. The efforts to make systems usable are in direct conflict with the aims of security and privacy. The more usable the system is, the less secure it becomes. Lately, Schneier is advocating that we need a holistic solution to security and privacy that takes into account both technical and soft issues.

Schneier emphasizes that security is a process. Therefore, decision makers should be made aware of this fact and stop thinking that investment in security is a once-off activity where, once done, you wait until you get bad news or bad publicity to invest in security again. Sadly, the political agenda in security seems to strongly support the idea of security being a product, which may seem to be driven by commercial interests.

The political agenda in e-Healthcare security is taking the same approach and is likely to do so for some time to come. This is particularly so given that investment is dictated by political pressure, public opinion and fear of bad pressure. The reputation of healthcare organisation always takes precedence over the real security concerns. Schneier refers to this as security theatre, but in reality, has little real effect in the overall scheme. The main issue he talks about is just misguided security investment which makes us feel secure where in reality we are not. Scheneir further points out that the feeling of security is very different from the reality of security (psychology of security). In essence what comes out very clearly from Schneier is that the political agenda in security is there to protect government and organisations' officials from criticism, should an attack take place or IT systems compromised.

Another political angle is that some regulations and laws have a negative effect in the vision of the EHR and PEHR. For example, the EU data protection law prohibits data from EU countries from being shared or send for processing in other countries outside EU, unless there is a guarantee that data will be accorded the same protection as in EU. The e-Healthcare security has to acknowledge and put provisions of mitigating the insider threat, where users of the system conspire to sabotage it. Some of the efforts to mitigate the insider threats have made IT systems nearly unusable or have led to low morale among users. One popular solution has been to invest in user awareness programs, but these programs are hard to quantify and evaluate their success.

6.7 Summary

The metrics in Information Systems Security is a comparatively new area, which has been receiving a lot of attention lately due to proliferation of security attacks and the society increasing dependence on critical information systems. Metrics have the capability to make people take actions in ways that complex arguments or threats may not. However, security metrics are difficult to establish because for metrics to be useful a baseline must be established. This baseline must be based on agreed set of criteria. Until now there are no agreed set of criteria among security professionals which may be used to establish a baseline. The assurance which is provided by using the evaluation metrics in e-Healthcare information systems allows the e-Healthcare data to be used in different areas of research, i.e. technical and non-technical medical research. This is because the security and privacy concerns, especially those related to e-Healthcare information systems will have been given some guarantee, therefore, paving way for this e-Healthcare data to be shared among researchers.

In this chapter we proposed a higher level evaluation framework, which addresses specific security and privacy concerns in e-Healthcare. The ACIO framework main focus is to place in the e-Healthcare context the general security and privacy evaluation practices by emphasising the unique and sensitive aspects of e-Healthcare information as encapsulated in the following factors:

- Health professional practice and ethics;
- Patient privacy, safety, concerns and preferences;
- Information security and privacy laws;
- Organisational policies that enhance or augment technical security and privacy and;
- The long-lasting and sensitive nature of e-Healthcare information with implication spanning more than one individual across generations within families.

The above factors distinguish e-Healthcare information from information in other domains. The ACIO framework recognises the role of the evaluation approach and guides the evaluation of security and privacy for e-Healthcare information.

References

Mohammad Salim Ahmed, Ehab Al-Shaer, and Latifur Khan. A novel quantitative approach for measuring network security. In *INFOCOM*, pages 1957–1965, 2008. doi: 10.1109/INFOCOM.2008.260.

Ehab Al-Shaer, Latifur Khan, and Mohammad Salim Ahmed. A comprehensive objective network security metric framework for proactive security configuration. In *CSIIRW '08: Proceedings of the 4th annual workshop on Cyber security and information intelligence research*, pages 1–3, New York, NY, USA, 2008. ACM. ISBN 978-1-60558-098-2. doi: http://doi.acm.org/10.1145/1413140.1413189.

Ehab Al-Shaer, Albert G. Greenberg, Charles R. Kalmanek, David A. Maltz, T. S. Eugene Ng, and Geoffrey G. Xie. New frontiers in internet network management. *Computer Communication Review*, 39(5):37–39, 2009. doi: http://doi.acm.org/10.1145/1629607.1629615.

Flora Amato, Valentina Casola, Antonino Mazzeo, and Valeria Vittorini. The rem framework for security evaluation. In *ARES*, pages 1097–1103, 2008. doi: 10.1109/ARES.2008.95.

C. Lindsay Anderson and Judith B. Cardell. Reducing the variability of wind power generation for participation in day ahead electricity markets. *hicss*, 0:178, 2008.

ISSN 1530-1605. doi: http://doi.ieeecomputersociety.org/10.1109/HICSS.2008.368.

Joan S. Ash and Kenneth P. Guappone. Qualitative evaluation of health information exchange efforts. *Journal of Biomedical Informatics*, 40(6, Supplement 1):S33 – S39, 2007. ISSN 1532-0464. doi: DOI:10.1016/j.jbi.2007.08.001. URL http://www.sciencedirect.com/science/article/B6WHD-4PJ6GKF-2/2/172c507b314b262b1e40a68006426c41. Developing Common Methods for Evaluating Health Information Exchange.

Paul Ashley, Satoshi Hada, Gnter Karjoth, Calvin Powers, and Matthias Schunter. Enterprise privacy authorization language (epal 1.2). Technical report, IBM, 2003. URL http://www.zurich.ibm.com/security/enterprise-privacy/epal/Specification/index.html.

F. Baader and W. Snyder. Unification theory. In J.A. Robinson and A. Voronkov, editors, *Handbook of Automated Reasoning*, volume Vol. I, chapter Chapter 8, pages 447 – 533. Elsevier Science Publishers, 2001. URL http://lat.inf.tu-dresden.de/research/papers/2001/BaaderSnyderHandbook.ps.gz.

M. Backes, M. Durmuth, and G. Karjot. Unification in privacy policy evaluation - translating epal into prolog. In *Policies for Distributed Systems and Networks, 2004. POLICY 2004. Proceedings. Fifth IEEE International Workshop on*, pages 185–188, June 2004. doi: 10.1109/POLICY.2004.1309165.

S.M. Bellovin. On the brittleness of software and the infeasibility of security metrics. *Security & Privacy, IEEE*, 4(4):96–96, July-Aug. 2006. ISSN 1540-7993. doi: 10.1109/MSP.2006.101.

Y. Beres, M.C. Mont, J. Griffin, and S. Shiu. Using security metrics coupled with predictive modeling and simulation to assess security processes. In *Empirical Software Engineering and Measurement, 2009. ESEM 2009. 3rd International Symposium on*, pages 564–573, Oct. 2009. doi: 10.1109/ESEM.2009.5314213.

Tony Boswell. Smart card security evaluation: Community solutions to intractable problems. *Information Security Technical Report*, 14(2): 57 – 69, 2009. ISSN 1363-4127. doi: DOI:10.1016/j.istr.2009.06.002. URL http://www.sciencedirect.com/science/article/B6VJC-4WRD6D1-1/2/d597ad103edca1eb284099b28e6df2c8. Smart Card Applications and Security.

Valentina Casola, Antonino Mazzeo, Nicola Mazzocca, and Valeria Vittorini. A policy-based methodology for security evaluation: A security metric for public key infrastructures. *Journal of Computer Security*, 15(2):197–229, 2007. ISSN 0926-227X. URL http://iospress.metapress.com/content/drey94ehayv332m8/.

Kwo-Jean Farn, Shu-Kuo Lin, and Andrew Ren-Wei Fung. A study on information security management system evaluation–assets, threat and vulnerability. *Computer Standards & Interfaces*, 26(6):501 – 513, 2004. ISSN 0920-5489. doi: DOI:10.1016/j.csi.2004.03.012. URL http://www.sciencedirect.com/science/article/B6TYV-4C8DCR8-1/2/0dacb11345b748201337279240ef9768.

Jane Frankland. It security metrics: implementation and standards compliance. *Network Security*, 2008(6):6 – 9, 2008. ISSN 1353-4858. doi: DOI:10.1016/S1353-4858(08)70075-8. URL http://www.sciencedirect.com/science/article/B6VJG-4SR10FV-6/2/98d4172be9102ce41def47fb4e2ca77c.

Ryutaro Fujimoto, Hiroyuki Okamura, and Tadashi Dohi. Security evaluation of an intrusion tolerant system with mrspns. *Availability, Reliability and Security, International Conference on*, 0:427–432, 2009. doi: http://doi.ieeecomputersociety.org/10.1109/ARES.2009.143.

Mohamed Gadelrab, Anas Abou El Kalam, and Yves Deswarte. Manipulation of network traffic traces for security evaluation. *Advanced Information Networking and Applications Workshops, International Conference on*, 0:1124–1129, 2009. doi: http://doi.ieeecomputersociety.org/10.1109/WAINA.2009.36.

M. Geiger and L.F. Cranor. Scrubbing stubborn data: An evaluation of counter-forensic privacy tools. *Security & Privacy, IEEE*, 4(5):16–25, Sept.-Oct. 2006. ISSN 1540-7993. doi: 10.1109/MSP.2006.132.

M. Hecker and T. Dillon. Privacy support and evaluation on an ontological basis. In *Data Engineering Workshop, 2007 IEEE 23rd International Conference on*, pages 221–227, April 2007. doi: 10.1109/ICDEW.2007.4400995.

Andrew Jaquith. *Security Metrics: Replacing Fear, Uncertainty and Doubt*. Addison-Wesley, 2007.

Wayne Johnson. Directions in security metrics research, 2009. URL http://csrc.nist.gov/publications/nistir/ir7564/nistir-7564_metrics-research.pdf.

Zhang Lufeng, Tang Hong, Cui YiMing, and Zhang JianBo. Network security evaluation through attack graph generation. *World Academy of Science, Engineering and Technology*, 54:412 – 415, 2009. URL http://www.waset.org/journals/waset/v54/v54-73.pdf.

E.A. Nichols and G. Peterson. A metrics framework to drive application security improvement. *Security & Privacy, IEEE*, 5(2):88–91, March-April 2007. ISSN 1540-7993. doi: 10.1109/MSP.2007.26.

Joseph Pamula, Sushil Jajodia, Paul Ammann, and Vipin Swarup. A weakest-adversary security metric for network configuration security analysis. In *QoP*, pages 31–38, 2006.

David Rice. *Geekonomics: The Real Cost of Insecure Software*. Addison Wesley, 2008.

O. Sami Saydjari. Is risk a good security metric? In *QoP*, pages 59–60, 2006.

Oleg Sheyner, Joshua Haines, Somesh Jha, Richard Lippmann, and Jeannette M. Wing. Automated generation and analysis of attack graphs. In *SP '02: Proceedings of the 2002 IEEE Symposium on Security and Privacy*, page 273, Washington, DC, USA, 2002. IEEE Computer Society. ISBN 0-7695-1543-6.

R. von Solms, H. van der Haar, S. H. von Solms, and W. J. Caelli. A framework for information security evaluation. *Information & Management*, 26(3):143 – 153, 1994. ISSN 0378-7206. doi: DOI:10.1016/0378-7206(94)90038-8. URL http://www.sciencedirect.com/science/article/B6VD0-45P0BVW-7F/2/c14399af664c5a1749e8fad3806ea719.

Lingyu Wang, Tania Islam, Tao Long, Anoop Singhal, and Sushil Jajodia. An attack graph-based probabilistic security metric. In *DBSec*, pages 283–296, 2008. doi: http://dx.doi.org/10.1007/978-3-540-70567-3_22.

Jeannette M. Wing. Attack graph generation and analysis. In *ASIACCS '06: Proceedings of the 2006 ACM Symposium on Information, computer and communi-*

cations security, pages 14–14, New York, NY, USA, 2006. ACM. ISBN 1-59593-272-0. doi: http://doi.acm.org/10.1145/1128817.1128822.

Chapter 7
Discussions

7.1 Introduction

The essential functions of e-Healthcare information systems are to facilitate health information and data processing, diagnostic test result management, order entry management, treatment decisions, electronic communications and connectivity, patient education and monitoring, scheduling and billing, and clinical data collection. The e-Healthcare information systems will bridge the gap between the discovery of new treatments and medical practice.

Generally speaking, e-Healthcare information systems are vulnerable to security and privacy threats. The organisational setting for these systems include regional networks of organisations, international health management organisations (HMOs) which place demands on these systems to support communication, distribution and cooperation. The evolutionary scale of e-Healthcare information systems has tended to be from organisation, to inter-organisational processes, to virtual online personal e-Healthcare records that span an individual's life-time and support mobility of the individual patient. This evolution is accompanied by complexities in provisioning of security and privacy of information held in these e-Healthcare systems. The complexity is further worsened by the ever increasing networked-enabled wireless mobile devices. Identity theft together with vulnerability in authentication mechanisms constitute challenges that could benefit from exploitation of emerging security technologies such as biometrics and personal genomics.

The e-Healthcare information offers unique security, privacy and confidentiality challenges that require a fresh examination of the mainstream concepts and approaches to information security. The significance of security for e-Healthcare information is that issues of individual consent, privacy and confidentiality are the main determinants to the adoption and successful utilisation of e-Healthcare information. Current trends in the domain of e-Healthcare information management point to the need for comprehensive incorporation of security, privacy and confidentiality safeguards within the review of e-Healthcare information management frameworks and approaches. This raises major challenges that demand holistic approaches spanning a legal, ethical, pyschological, information and security engineering. For example, the legal domain is challenged to produce gapless laws for protecting patient privacy and confidentiality. Standardisation efforts are challenged to ensure security and privacy protection interoperability across e-Healthcare information systems. These challenges are further amplified by the lack of investment in healthcare, and even when the investment is available there is limited expertise to implement e-Healthcare information systems. This book has explored challenges facing e-Healthcare information systems and proposed solutions to mitigate its security risks.

7.2 Securing Personal e-Healthcare

Securing personal e-Healthcare information aims mainly at protecting the privacy and confidentiality of the individual who receives healthcare services that are delivered through e-Healthcare information systems. Advances in security technologies have so far not eliminated the challenge posed by the need to secure e-Healthcare information. The rate of privacy and confidentiality breaches continue to increase unabated. These breaches pose challenges to all domains that converge on the task of securing information and building trust in e-Healthcare information management. Only a holistic approach that positions itself at the point of convergence of the domains of law, organisational policy, professional ethics and IT security could offer the promise to mitigate, if not eliminate, the major challenges to securing e-Healthcare information. The e-Healthcare information systems use security mechanisms and services found in Operating Systems, Networks and protocols, together with e-Healthcare specific security requirements to achieve trust of users. The e-Healthcare specific requirements include consent (informed or uninformed), anonymisation, notice and disclosure.

The EHR is a record of electronically maintained information about individual's lifetime health status and health care, that serve multiple legitimate uses. These records are usually held and maintained by health providers and public or private health professionals. Due to the restrictive access nature of the EHR, we are now witnessing the emergence of the PEHR, which are internet based that empower healthcare users to maintain their own records. The PEHRs offer an integrated and comprehensive view of health information, including information that the people generate, information from doctors and test results, and information from their pharmacies and insurance companies. The latter conflicts with health professionals who are not happy in letting patients maintain their records.

The EHR and the PEHR are facilitating efficient and cost effective access to healthcare services. Their use has lead to improved quality of patient care and lowering of the running cost for healthcare. Patient safety has been improved and medical errors have been minimised. The increased productivity in healthcare provision may in some cases lead to fewer health professionals being used to deliver patient care. It must be noted that the EHR and PEHR are the most sensitive of all personal information, therefore, their protection in the e-Healthcare information systems setting is one of the most challenging problems. Despite all the benefits of the use of e-Healthcare Information Systems, they have significant risks, which can negatively impact patient care and public trust. For example, the ever growing capabilities of e-Healthcare Information Systems require increasingly complex software, this heightens the danger of software failures that may harm patients. The complexity of software used in e-Healthcare information systems increases their security and privacy concerns. Further, the functional or mission creep can in the future be a major problem of the EHR/PEHR when they are used for other purposes apart from which they were designed. For example, data collected in healthcare related issues being used for immigration purposes or for matching the EHR data with other personal information databases.

The boundary issue of transmitting personal data remains questionable. The fundamental right to the protection of personal data in Europe is based on Article 8 of the European Convention for the Protection of Human Rights and Fundamental Freedoms and on Article 8 of the EU Charter of Fundamental Rights. More precise rules are in particular laid down in the EC Data Protection Directive 95/46/EC and in Directive 2002/58/EC on privacy and electronic communications, and in the national laws of the Member States implementing these Directives ((Directive-95/46/EC, 1995), (Directive-2002/58/EC, 2002)). The e-Health by definition requires the sharing of patient identifiable data when and where it is necessary. Users of e-Health applications therefore have to ensure that they respect the fundamentals rights of the individuals concerned, and comply with the legal obligations for the protection of personal data of the patients. When the processing of such personal data relates to a person's health, processing is particularly sensitive and therefore requires special protection. In the e-Health context, the processing of personal data in health systems across Member States may vary due to their national specifics and the diverse transposition and implementation of the Directive.

It is therefore important to consider whether the EU should adopt special interpretative guidelines to the provisions of Directive 95/46/EC, or other actions to promote proper implementation and improved enforcement of the Directive so that e-Health-related stakeholders will be more aware of the rules for personal data processing in the field of e-Health. In particular, the Article 29 Working Party, that brings together national data protection supervisory authorities, alongside the Member States representatives in the i2010 sub-group on e-Health, could provide a key element for insight into these aspects of data protection in the health area, in particular in seeking greater EU-wide enforcement. The European Commission will also pursue proper implementation of the provisions of Directive 95/46/EC at national and international levels.

Liability for the quality and safety of e-Health goods is covered reasonably well by the general legislation in Europe on product safety and consumer protection. However, e-Healthcare products are still rather new and the uncertainty that exists about who is liable for what and how liability is split among different service providers in the e-Health continuum, especially when this uncertainty relates to cross border healthcare beyond that already provided by international private law. In this context, based on the Directive 374/1985/EEC of 25 July 1985 on liability for defective products, efficient protection for civil liability against defective goods and services must meet the objectives of spreading fairly the risks inherent in a modern high-technology society, protecting consumers' health, stimulating innovation, securing undistorted competition, and facilitating trade. Connection to the law of the place where the person sustaining the damage has his or her habitual residence, together with a 'foreseeability clause', is a balanced solution in regard to these objectives. To ensure consumer rights, national surveillance authorities have been established to monitor product safety and to take appropriate measures. The European information system (RAPEX) was put in place to impose collaboration between distributors, producers and the national authorities but also between Member States and the European Commission. Accordingly, the Commission's permanent task remains to enhance better enforcement of consumer protection by the Member States and information dissemination for citizens to use the existing institutional framework also for e-Health products, for example, also through ECC-NET and SOLVIT (European-Communities, 2007).

7.3 Proliferation of New Technologies

It has been noted that the biggest threat to successful implementation of e-Healthcare information systems is user adoption, which relies on their willingness to overcome their fear of security and privacy invasion in relation to their sensitive health information. The proliferation of new technologies and the ever growing mountain of bad news in terms of security breaches does little to instil users with the confidence needed to use the e-Healthcare information systems. However, users must be made aware that they cannot stop the march of technology, as a society we have no choice but to embrace it and find ways of mitigating its security and privacy risks. The new paradigm shift based on patient empowerment as a way to gain public trust and combat privacy and confidentiality concerns brings in challenges of modeling and implementation of consent mechanisms and providing ways of access and control of e-Healthcare information by the patient.

In the future we believe that only the EHR and PEHR will co-exist and health professionals will add information to the PEHR which is controlled and maintained by the patient. These records will follow the patient wherever he/she goes. It is clear from the onset that health professionals will resist this scenario on professional grounds. However, if lessons from history are to be of any help, there will be one winner in this battle who is the patient. The patients must be assured that the systems are trustworthy and he/she is empowered and in control of his/her medical records.

The regulations and laws in e-Healthcare have number of common elements. First, they are designed to protect an individual against misappropriation and misuse of personal information. Second, the data privacy laws are complex, making compliance difficult and often require changes to organisational policies and operating procedures as well as the adoption of new technologies. Finally, although enforcement may focus on education and remediation, the laws in existance generally impose substantial penalties for non-compliance. The fear of having these penalties imposed have forced healthcare organisations to comply, but the cost of compliance has been high, however, the cost reduces in the long term. This has been demonstrated in the case of the Sarbanes-Oxley Law in Business.

Generally speaking, most of the countries are just starting to enact their Healthcare information bills. Lack of international laws, and slow moving standardisation affect efforts on ensuring interoperability and sharing. Further, this lack of global consensus affects innovation, design and implementation of secure e-Healthcare Information Systems. The current state of play makes the dream of getting a secure e-Healthcare Information System difficult. This comes from corporate greed, national interests that fail to realise the changing nature of the society (mobile society). Most security experts believe that future e-Healthcare Information systems if successful will be highly integrated, shareable and communicative.

Incidents of data breaches are on increase, especially those involving the EHR data which is rich and multimedia. Compromised EHR data is very attractive to hackers and there is anecdotal evidence that it fetches more money than other personal data in the underground economy. To make matters worse, it is not possible to create another EHR to replace the compromised one. For example, the records will include at some stage birth and death information, which if stolen is hard to detect and restore because it involves victims (minors and the deceased) who are not likely to have any prevention measures in place. Prevention and accurate reporting of incidence of identity theft is made difficult by the vague language used in many regulatory laws.

The current research and literature on security and privacy in e-Healthcare Information Systems is more commentary rather than based on any primary research data. This state of affairs will not change soon due to access, security and privacy problems in most healthcare facilities. The hope is if these facilities can be accessed remotely without affecting the offering of care and preservation of the privacy of patients. Even when secure access is provided to e-Healthcare information systems, healthcare professionals are not confident to see this information being accessed and available to the general public or patients.

Evaluation criteria are useful in providing a benchmark for users to assess the degree of confidence and trust they can place in e-Healthcare information systems. In this book we have proposed metrics that can be adopted in e-Healthcare Information Systems.

It is important that before deciding which applications to purchase, users analyse healthcare systems in terms of their security provisions, not on their track record in another software applications market segment. The issues of support and maintenance may be the achiles heel for the open source paradigm in its quest for widespread usage in healthcare.

The interoperability is essential element in order to fully realise the potential benefits of e-Healthcare information systems for both clinical operations and medical research. However, the rate of progress in getting different e-Healthcare information systems to communicate, exchange information and share data is slow. For example, it is hard to achieve semantic interoperability between e-Healthcare information system because the medical terminology is complex, variable, specialised, and evolving. The terminology varies between medical specialities, locales, and health care facilities, and it also varies with clinical context. Another barrier to achieving semantic interoperability is the fact that existing e-Healthcare information system produced by different vendors employ proprietary internal representations (models) of medical information that are generally incompatible with one another. Other factors making interoperability difficult to achieve include the complex, confused and reactive regislative environment, fragmented technological developments required, huge investment of e-Healthcare without certain return on investment and uniformed users. Financial disincentives between health providers, vendors and clinicians constitute a further impediment to interoperability.

7.4 Health Identifier

Unique health identifier for individuals in the health system would have many benefits, including improved quality of care, reduced administrative costs, continuity of care, accurate record keeping, effective follow-up and preventive care, and detection of fraud. Typically, identifiers differ across healthcare providers. The major challenges to unique health identifiers are increased mobility and aging population which create pressure for patient records that can manage large amounts of information to be available in different locations and at the same time may need to be easily transferrable among a variety of healthcare providers.

In order for the e-Healthcare information systems to have the trust of all users, they must protect security and privacy. However, in the process of protecting security and privacy there should be a balance as stringent security measures in e-Healthcare may end up affecting the patient care delivery. A number of security measures are in conflict with the spirit of healthcare delivery. Progress towards better security and safer patient data environment will start with a paradigm shift in the approach to patient data security, treating it as an ongoing operational and behavioural change that guards against both malicious theft of patient data records for fraudulent purposes as well as inappropriate access during treatment.

Achieving secure e-Healthcare systems is a monumental task due to the complex and fragmented technical, regulatory (state, territory, federal) and standardisation process involved. The vendors and Government have their own agenda, making even harder to achieve security. The ever increasing number of projects that fail in e-Healthcare is a manifestation of how big the problem is. For example, the projects involved are UK National for IT (NPfIT) and Australia HealthConnect. The funding options between the public and private sectors increase the complexity of e-Healthcare information systems because of the diferrent emphasis on the return on investment and profit motives.

Patient privacy and the sharing of healthcare information may lead to conflict. The law seeks to protect patient's privacy. The standards, with the exception of privacy and security standards, seek to facilitate interoperability for healthcare information sharing. Consequently, the law and standards have disparate perspectives. The two sometimes conflict with each other. However, they also cooperate and complement each other in privacy protection. Since it is mandatory and can be punitive, the law has an upper hand. The law could be an effective formal basis for adoption and compliance to these standards due its capability for punitive enforcement. A typical example of this is HIPAA 1996. The standards could also be a formal basis for the law in a persuasive and discretionary manner of influence on law-makers. The formal convergence of the law, standards and technology is significant to secure e-Healthcare information and warrants serious investigation. An example of the continued friction between patients and health professionals on who should access their medical record is a case in point in UK. The UK government introduced the requirement that doctors need permission to access patients' records. This has been a result of the uncertainty on the GPs not being happy in using the EHR and patients not trusting that their privacy and confidentiality will be preserved. The requirement that doctors get permission to access medical records is another setback in the effort of using EHR. As a compromise deal a free web space has been provided (Healthspace), where patients will be able to see their Summary Care Records and record their wishes on how their care should be managed.

7.5 Problem of Securing e-Healthcare Information

The problem of securing e-Healthcare information is a complex challenge that also manifest as a multi-dimensional trade-off problem where sharing information needs to be balanced with privacy, and the use of technological advances needs to be balanced with technology facilitated privacy and security threats. The healthcare environment defines the context for e-Healthcare information privacy and therefore largely dictates the key privacy and security requirements within e-Healthcare. The patient-centred paradigm in healthcare has triggered a revolution that has huge impact on the privacy and security requirements in e-Healthcare information management framework. In order to protect privacy and the security of e-Healthcare information, patient consent, control and access to e-Healthcare information must be the core and fundamental aspects. The hybridisation of the EHRs and PEHRs would seem to be the future scenario for e-Healthcare information management. The EHR-PEHR hybrid is besotted by compounded privacy and security challenges that need to be mitigated to levels that can be balanced with the benefits of the hybrid.

The approaches to privacy and security presented in this book forge a convergence of the key drivers to e-Healthcare information privacy. The pyramidal structure presented in chapter 5 shows the privacy protection laws at the apex and generic security measures and primitives at the base. The unique aspects of the e-Healthcare information management domain then occur in the middle of the pyramidal conceptualisation while standardisation of privacy protection and security will be permeating through the level of the pyramid.

The high-level conceptual framework proposed in chapter 5 exploits the conceptualisation in the approach that has just been outlined by first identifying and characterising the key drivers to e-Healthcare information and the interaction among themselves. These key drivers are then placed into the context of the evolution of the control of e-Healthcare information under the influence of one of the most revolutionising paradigm shifts within the healthcare domain, especially the patient-centred or community-centered paradigm. The control of e-Healthcare information is seen to have moved from healthcare organisations to the individual patient who, in turn, is expected to participate in the healthcare process and the decision-making therein. The privacy and security challenges get compounded by the ubiquitous harnessing of the Internet and wirelessly networked devices as well as the heterogeneity of e-Healthcare information users and the apportionment of the legal control of the e-Healthcare information. Ultimately, the effective control will rest with the individual patient for professional and patient safety reasons and the demand for jurisdictions to maintain and prevent modification of their own portions of the overall body of e-Healthcare information. This will lead to what has been termed in this book as *the EHR/PEHR hybrid*. The hybrid will have privacy and security challenges that has been inherited from both the EHR and PEHR.

A high-level conceptual process of crafting a privacy protection and security infrastructure that embodies the key concepts of the framework is presented in chapter 5. The process creates a security and privacy specification for e-Healthcare information from the results of formalising the relevant considerations of the key drivers to e-Healthcare information privacy and security. The specification itself represents a convergence of these key drivers. The resulting specification becomes the blueprint for setting out the security measures and provisions required to secure the e-Healthcare information. The conceptual architecture for privacy protection and security for e-Healthcare information incorporates privacy and security measures that include assessment of EHRs and PEHRs standards. The advantage of the process proposed in chapter 5 is the incorporation of feeback to earlier sub-processes, which allows for the short and long-term evolution of the privacy protection and security specification and architecture within the context of the overall convergence of the key drivers for privacy and security of e-Healthcare information. The Chapter 5 has presented a generic conceptual architecture for privacy and the security protection of e-Healthcare information that would underlie the process. The conceptual architecture mirrors the pyramidal conceptualisation of the key privacy and security drivers as well as relationship and inter-play of these drivers. The generic security practices are ensured for e-Healthcare information and then e-Healthcare-specific security requirements are applied to augment them. Similarly, generic privacy protection practices are ensured for e-Healthcare information and augmented or enhanced with e-Healthcare specific privacy stipulations. It is important to then note that certain security practices can be harnessed to attain privacy protection.

The security framework for e-Healthcare proposed in this book addresses existing and emerging security risks by taking into account legal, organisational, technical issues and all stakeholders. These frameworks provide protection to sensitive healthcare information and allows the systems to interoperate and secure the information required to deliver service. The frameworks embrace the influence of ever-increasing technological advacement encroching e-Healthcare at an unprecendented rate. Therefore, the nature of e-Healthcare results in large volumes of data and information being stored for a long time in order to provide continuous and improved quality of care to patients and law.

7.6 Contribution to Knowledge

The high-level conceptual framework proposed in this book exploits the conceptualisation by identifying and characterising the key drivers to e-Healthcare information systems. We have also presented the high-level conceptual process of crafting a privacy protection and security infrastructure that embodies the key concepts of our proposed framework. We have proposed an evaluation approach to e-Healthcare information systems.

Initial trends suggest that the regulatory environment in order to address to future security and privacy risks may need to have a global consensus. This can be in the form of international laws and directives. Laws and regulations will be changing frequently to reflect the ever changing needs of the society. In the process flimsy laws may be enacted lacking the knowledge and comprehensiveness to respond to the needs of the dynamic e-Healthcare. Key security and privacy concerns for e-Healthcare information systems include:

1. Hacking incidents on e-Healthcare information systems that lead to altering of patient data or destruction of clinical systems.
2. Misuse of health information records by authorized users of e-Healthcare information systems.
3. Long term data management concerns surrounding e-Healthcare information systems.
4. Government or corporate intrusion into private health care matters.

There is growing acceptance, whether we like it or not, e-Healthcare records will play a more important role in healthcare service delivery. With huge investment being made, we can be sure that the EHRs and PEHRs will be implemented in some fashion. For example, President Obama adminstration proposed to invest up to 20 Billion dollars in federal funds to achieve widespread deployment of e-Healthcare records. The security of e-Healthcare information systems depends on how best we protect either the EHR or PEHR. The e-Healthcare information security is a vehicle that will lead to achieving personalised e-Healthcare in the future.

7.7 Conclusion

The main objective of this work was to investigate and propose ways of securing e-Healthcare information systems which use sensitive personal data in the form of the EHR or PEHR in delivering healthcare. We are aware that software and hardware which are the main components of the infrastructure in the provision of e-Healthcare are riddled with flaws. The reasons for this sad state of affairs is the way the software market operates and the speed at which software must be delivered in order to meet the time to market. It is possible for better software to be produced in the future if governments and other private companies being the main customers can demand secure software. Governments should come up with regislation and policies which gives incentives to vendors who produce secure software.

At the current rate of technological development, society awareness and acceptance of new ways of using technology in everyday life, it is apparent that the dream of having e-Healthcare information systems is going to be realised. This will mean that e-Healthcare information systems will embrace technologies and utilise them in all aspects to patient-centred treatment plan. While this will have a positive effect in terms of improved quality of care and lowering costs among other things, these benefits will come at a much higher cost of security and privacy challenges. For example, in e-Healthcare software vendors main agenda is to sell their products even when they do not meet the requirements or they are not required in that particular situation, while on the other hand health professional will resist the use of software even if it may lead to improved quality of care or lower cost of healthcare provision. It is becoming crystal clear that the implementation of the e-Healthcare information systems is going to be expensive. The return on investment (ROI) equation does not paint a good picture, since it is difficult to quantify the ROI in e-Healthcare.

7.8 Future Work and Research Directions

The sensitive nature of the data in e-Healthcare makes it hard to share without violationg the security and privacy. In order to increase the sharearability of e-Healthcare information techniques to de-sensitize, it must be developed and used. Currently available techniques, while useful in cases where is the data is not sensitive, must be redesigned in order to provide the necessary privacy that is required. The e-Healthcare data can be used for research, drug and policy development and training of doctors. The de-anonymisation techniques which are going to be developed for sensitive data and information which is available in e-Healthcare, will pave a way to establishing of data banks that can be used testing and developing of algorithms, software and even special medical devices.

As security metrics become widely used, it will enable organisations to compare how secure they are with other organisations in the same market segment or industry. Security metrics may enable organisations to quantify their security posture and justify the investment made in security and security products. One of the most important issues which must be addressed by security metrics is how best can we evaluate complex e-Healthcare information systems, as we strugle to meet then demands from regulators, insurers, purchasers, providers and patients for evidence of effectiveness and efficacy in order to meet the standards of evidence based medicine.

Advances in medicine, treatments and monitoring devices are going to have a profound effect on e-Healthcare security and privacy. If this trend is to continue then soon or later most of the data and information in healthcare will be digital. That means more digital data will be generated, processed, shared, stored, and moved around at a much faster rate. The major challenge will be how to process, store, share, and communicate the e-Healthcare information and data securely. Digital chip implants which may be used to link the patient with his EHR will require robust measures to protect patients.

The dominance of the PEHR over EHR will be more pronounced in the future as the role of the Google, Microsoft and other vendors in e-Healthcare information systems increase. The healthcare professionals will resist the wide use of PEHR, but their resistance will diminish over time. The e-Healthcare information systems will result in more data and information being stored than ever before, because storage devices will be cheap and the data and information will be a key component in continued, quality healthcare.

References

Directive-2002/58/EC. of the european parliament and of the council of 12 july 2002 concerning the processing of personal data and the protection of privacy in the electronic communications sector, oj l 201, 31.7.2002, 2002.

Directive-95/46/EC. of the european parliament and of the council of 24 october 1995 on the protection of individuals with regard to the processing of personal data and on the free movement of such data, oj l 281, 23.11.1995, 1995.

European-Communities. e-health taskforce report 2007, accelerating the development of the e-health market in europe, composed in preparation for the lead market initiative, european commission information society and media, 2007.

Appendix A
International Standards Organisational Technical Committee (ISO/TX) 215 Healthcare Informatics Standardisation

The ISO/TC 215 is the Technical Committee (TC) of the International Organisation for Standardisation (ISO), which develops and maintain standard on Health Informatics. TC 215 works on the standardisation of Health Information and Communications Technology (ICT). The aim of most of its standards is to allow for compatibility and interoperability between independent systems.

Table A.1 Security and Privacy Standards of the ISO/TC 215 - Health informatics

ISO CODE	GENERAL DESCRIPTION
ISO 17090-1:2008	PKI - Part 1: Digital certificate services
ISO 17090-2:2008	PKI - Part 2: Certificate profile
ISO 17090-3:2008	PKI - Part 3: Policy management of certification authority
ISO 22857:2004	Trans-border flows of personal health information
ISO 27799:2008	Information security management using ISO/IEC 27002
ISO/TS 22600-1:2006	Privilege management and access control - Part 1: Overview
ISO/TS 22600-2:2006	Privilege management and access control - Part 2: Formal models
ISO/TS 25238:2007	Classification of safety risks from health software
ISO/TR 21089:2004	Trusted end-to-end information flows
ISO/TR 27809:2007	Measures for ensuring patient safety of health software

Table A.2 ISO/IEEE Standards of the TC 215 - Health informatics

ISO/IEEE CODE	GENERAL DESCRIPTION
11073-10101:2004	PoC med. device comm. - 10101: Nomenclature
11073-10201:2004	PoC med. device comm. - 10201: Domain information model
11073-20101:2004	PoC med. device comm. - 20101: Application profiles - Base Std.
11073-30200:2004	PoC med. device comm. - 30200: Transport profile - Cable connected
11073-30300:2004	PoC med. device comm. - 30300: Transport profile - Infrared wireless
ISO 11073-90101:2008	PoC medical device comm. - 90101: Analytical instruments - PoC test
ISO/HL7 21731:2006	HL7 version 3 - Reference information model - Release 1
Abbreviations	
comm.	communication(s)
lab.	laboratory
PoC	Point-of-Care
std.	standard

Table A.3 ISO Standards of the TC 215 - Health informatics

ISO CODE	GENERAL DESCRIPTION
17090-1:2008	PKI - Part 1: Digital certificate services
17090-2:2008	PKI - Part 2: Certificate profile
17090-3:2008	PKI - Part 3: Policy management of certification authority
17115:2007	Vocabulary for terminological systems
13606-1:2008	Electronic health record comm. - 1: Reference model
17432:2004	Messages and comm. - Web access to DICOM persistent objects
18104:2003	Integration of a reference terminology model for nursing
18232:2006	Messages and comm. - Length-limited globally unique string IDs
18812:2003	Clin. analyser interfaces to lab. information systems - Use profiles
20301:2006	Health cards - General characteristics
20302:2006	Health cards - Numbering system and reg. procedure for issuer IDs
21549-1:2004	Healthcard Data - Part 1: General structure
21549-2:2004	Healthcard Data - Part 2: Common objects
21549-3:2004	Healthcard Data - Part 3: Limited clinical data
21549-4:2006	Healthcard Data - Part 4: Extended clinical data
21549-5:2008	Healthcard Data - Part 5: Identification data
21549-6:2008	Healthcard Data - Part 6: Administrative data
21549-7:2007	Healthcard Data - Part 7: Medication data
22857:2004	Trans-border flows of personal health information
27799:2008	Information security management using ISO/IEC 27002
Abbreviations	
PKI	Public Key Infrastructure
Clin.	Clinical
comm.	communication(s)
lab.	laboratory

Table A.4 ISO/TS Standards of the TC 215 - Health informatics

ISO/TS CODE	GENERAL DESCRIPTION
11073-92001:2007	Medical waveform format - 92001: Encoding rules
12052:2006	DICOM including workflow and data management
16058:2004	Interoperability of tele-learning systems
17117:2002	Controlled health terminology - Structure and high-level indicators
17120:2004	Country identifier standards
18308:2004	Requirements for an electronic health record architecture
21091:2005	Directory services for security, communications and identification
21667:2004	Health indicators conceptual framework
22600-1:2006	Privilege management and access control - Part 1: Overview
22600-2:2006	Privilege management and access control - Part 2: Formal models
25238:2007	Classification of safety risks from health software

Table A.5 ISO/TR Standards of the TC 215 - Health informatics

ISO/TR CODE	GENERAL DESCRIPTION
16056-1:2004	Interop. of tele-health systems & networks -1: Intro. and definitions
16056-2:2004	Interop. of tele-health systems & networks - 2: Real-time systems
17119:2005	Health informatics - Health informatics profiling framework
18307:2001	Interop. and compatibility in messaging and comm. standards
20514:2005	EHR - Definition, scope and context
21089:2004	Trusted end-to-end information flows
21730:2007	Mobile wireless comm. & IT Use in healthcare facilities
22221:2006	Good principles and practices for a clin. data warehouse
22790:2007	Functional characteristics of prescriber support systems
27809:2007	Measures for ensuring patient safety of health software
Abbreviations	
Clin.	Clinical
comm.	communication(s)
Interop.	Inter-operation
EHR	Electronic Healthcare Record
Intro.	Introduction

Index

Accountability principle, 39
American Society for Testing and Materials (ASTM) Committee E31, 79
Anonymisation, 43
Archetype, 48
ARTEMIS project, 46
Australian privacy laws, 66
Awareness principle, 39

Canadian Health Infoway, 105
Care Record Service (CRS), 106
Certification Commission for Healthcare Information Technology (CCHIT), 109
Clinical decision-support system (CDSS), 114
Clinical Document Architecture (CDA), 73
Clinical E-science Framework, 45
Clinical Practice Guidelines (CPG), 115
Committee for European Normalisation (CEN) Technical Committee (TC) 251 Standardisation, 74
Compliance metrics, 49
Confidentiality, 33
Continuity of Care Record (CCR), 83

Directive 95/46/EC, 63

e-Healthcare Information Systems (e-HIS), 101
Electronic personal healthcare records (e-PHRs), 109
Electronic Protected Health Information (EPHI), 69
electronic-health record (EHR), 20
Enforcement Rule, 69
Equity principle, 39
Ethics principle, 39
European Convention on Human Rights (ECHR), 63
European GEMSS project, 47
Evidence-based medicine, 115

Freedom of Information (FOI) Act 2003, 65
French Personal Medical Record (PMR), 43

Genetic data, 60
Google Health, 5
Google Health e-PHR, 110

Health Insurance Portability and Accountability Act (HIPAA) 1996, 68
Health Level 7 (HL7), 72
Health Regulation, 65
HealthSpace, 107
HealthVault, 111
Hippocratic Oath, 2

Identity Federation Token (IDFT), 112
Indivo, 112
Information Commissioner, 65
Integration principle, 39
International Standards Organisation Technical Committee (ISO/TC) 215 Healthcare Informatics Standardisation, 78
Ireland Data Protection Act (DPA) 1988, 2003, 64

Japanese Personal Data Protection (PDP) Act, 67
Justices of Peace Act 1361, 66

Laws, 61

Managed care, 50

Microsoft e-PHR, 111
Multi-disciplinary principle, 39

New Zealand's Privacy Act 1993, 66

openEHR, 75
Organisation-centred HIS, 102

Person-centred HIS, 103
Personal Information Protection and Electronic Documents Act (PIPEDA) 2000, 71
Privacy, 21, 33, 38, 60
Privacy Commissioner (PC), 66
Privacy Rule, 68
Process-centred HIS, 103
Proportionality principle, 39
Protected Health Information (PHI), 68
Pseudonymisation, 44

Re-assessment principle, 39
RE-Identification of Data In Trails (REIDIT), 45
Resilience metrics, 49

Security metrics, 49
Security Rule, 69
Shared Care, 40
Standards, 61
Summary Care Record (SCR), 107

Timeliness principle, 39
Transactions and Code Sets Rule, 69
Trust, 41

UK Data Protection Act (DPA) 1998, 66
UK National Healthcare Service (NHS), 106
Unique Identifiers Rule, 69
Unique Personal Identifier (UPI), 42

Veterans Health Information Systems and Technology Architecture (VistA), 108

Windows Live ID, 111
WorldVistA EHR System, 108

Zero-knowledge protocol, 91